Uprooted
Americans

Uprooted

The Japanese Americans

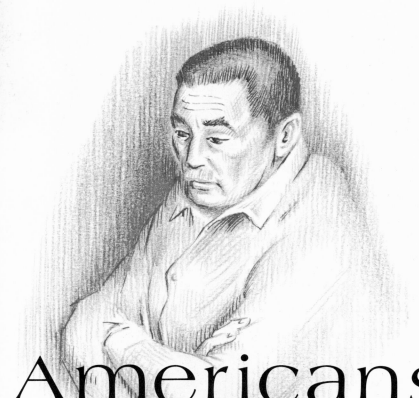

Americans

and the War Relocation Authority during World War II

DILLON S. MYER

THE UNIVERSITY OF ARIZONA PRESS

TUCSON   ARIZONA

About the author . . .

DILLON S. MYER was asked by President Franklin Delano Roosevelt, in June 1942, to become Director of the then three-month-old War Relocation Authority. Backgrounded by a Bachelor of Science degree in agriculture from Ohio State University, a Master of Education degree from Columbia University, and twenty-eight years of active and productive service in agricultural fields, Myer accepted the WRA directorship and went on to lead the WRA through tumultuous times to a successful conclusion four years later.

With the advent of the new deal in 1933, Myer supervised the Agricultural Adjustment Administration programs in Ohio during the first year of their existence. He later became Division Chief and eventually Assistant Chief of the Soil Conservation Service in Washington, D.C. Next he accepted the position of Assistant Administrator and Acting Administrator of the Agriculture Conservation Adjustment Administration, just six months prior to his four years with the WRA. Afterward his public service found him as Commissioner of the Federal Public Housing Administration, and later as President of the Institute of Inter-American Affairs. His last full-time governmental position was that of Commissioner of the Bureau of Indian Affairs.

After leaving government service in 1953, Myer served as Executive Director of the Group Health Association of Washington, D.C. In 1959 he accepted a United Nations assignment in Caracas, Venezuela. During the early 1960s he taught a seminar course in International Development at the University of Pittsburgh, and later served as consultant in a number of government agencies and with the Brookings Institution.

First printing 1971
Second printing 1972

THE UNIVERSITY OF ARIZONA PRESS

I. S. B. N.-0-8165-0402-4
L. C. No. 76-125169

To my wife,
JENNESS WIRT MYER,
who has provided
inspiration and support
for more than forty-five years

Contents

PART 4 — THE SUMMING UP

APPENDIXES

ILLUSTRATIONS

Foreword

AT THE TIME the War Relocation Authority was in its final stages of liquidation, the Japanese American Citizens League, representing not only its members but also the vast majority of all persons of Japanese ancestry in the United States, on May 22, 1946, held a testimonial banquet in honor of Dillon S. Myer, Director of the War Relocation Authority, at the Roosevelt Hotel in New York City, and presented him with a citation.*

That testimonial represented the affection and esteem in which Mr. Myer was held by the evacuees whose lives he had supervised through their great travail at the time the WRA was being terminated and as they were returning to their former homes on the West Coast and reestablishing themselves. More than two decades later, that testimonial has continued to represent the sentiments of those evacuees.

The unprecedented acceptance of Japanese Americans everywhere in the land in the 1960s is a living tribute to the correctness and vision of WRA policies and practices. Alien Japanese may now be admitted to the United States on the same basis as immigrants from other Old World countries, and persons of Japanese ancestry may now become naturalized American citizens.

---

*See Appendix O.

The more than 500 national, state, and local laws and ordinances that circumscribed and restricted the lives and opportunities of those of Japanese ancestry directly or indirectly in the pre-World War II era have all been nullified, voided, or rendered inoperative. For the first time since the birth of the nation, no laws appear on the federal statute books of the United States that discriminate against persons of Japanese ancestry.

The long-deserving Territory of Hawaii has become the fiftieth state in the Union. The new Japan that emerged out of the devastation of defeat and moved forward to the position of third leading industrial-trading country in the world, became an acknowledged ally of the United States, enjoying goodwill such as it had never before experienced. These remarkable achievements, among others, may be attributed at least in part to the WRA's humane and understanding administration of a difficult problem in a most troublesome time. Even more impressive as a testament to Dillon Myer is the dignity and the decency accorded to Americans who were suspect by their own government and who emerged to face, without bitterness or dispair, a promising future of limitless opportunities.

This tribute cannot begin to tell all that we who were unwanted and feared just a few years ago feel about Mr. Myer. As one who has probably lived closer to the experiences of those of Japanese ancestry in the United States from just before December 7, 1941, than almost any one else, first as the National Secretary of the Japanese American Citizens League on the West Coast prior to and during the Evacuation, and after service with the 442nd Regimental Combat Team, as the League's Washington representative, I have personal knowledge of what Dillon S. Myer has meant and means to those of Japanese ancestry in the United States.

MIKE M. MASAOKA

Washington Representative
Japanese American Citizens League

Preface

THE QUESTION MIGHT WELL BE RAISED as to why a book about Japanese Americans and the War Relocation Authority program during World War II is being written more than twenty years after the Japanese Americans were all resettled and after the WRA has become an agency of the past.

However, a number of factors show that the story continues to be of importance. The evacuation of more than 110,000 people from their homes, and their movement first into temporary Army Assembly Centers and later into WRA Relocation Centers, was an unprecedented action not widely understood. Both the action and the implications should be understood by the American public, if for no other reason than the hope of avoidance of similar action in the future.

These 110,000 people were moved en masse without charges or trial, the only criterion for removal being the fact of their having been born of Japanese parents. Fear of sabotage or espionage from among these people, and certain local pressures, together resulted in the uprooting of the whole Japanese American population from their homes in California, western Washington, Oregon, and Arizona, and their exclusion from these areas for nearly three years. Seventy thousand of these evacuees were American citizens, born on United States soil; the other 40,000, with few exceptions, had lived in the United States from 20 to 40 years, but were ineligible for citizenship under the laws of the United States.

The fear of sabotage or espionage proved to be wholly unfounded. In spite of the many rumors to the contrary, not one case of any act of espionage or sabotage by any Japanese American was ever reported, either on the mainland or in Hawaii.

At the time of the Japanese American uprooting, most people throughout the United States, except those along the West Coast, were so deeply involved in war work or news about the war that they paid little attention to the evacuation and the WRA program. In many cases the general public received information confused by scare headlines and trumped-up stories that helped to cover up the facts. The WRA centers were all too often referred to as concentration camps, which in the minds of many carried the implication that the centers were similar to Hitler's Dachau and other European prison camps. In truth, the relocation centers were just what the name implies; they were way-stations for persons willing to resettle in other parts of the United States, or they served as temporary homes for those persons who wished to remain until they could return to their permanent homes.

The WRA leave policy, which provided, along with other stipulations, that evacuees must have clearance to leave the centers, was decided upon for two reasons — first, to assure the American public that relocatees were not dangerous, in spite of the fact that they had been moved into camps guarded by the military, and, secondly, for the protection of the evacuees themselves in view of the stigma caused by the mass evacuation.

A review of developments over more than twenty years, in the light of WRA wartime policies, reveals that in spite of mistakes the results have generally been good. It was important to prove to the world that World War II was not a racial war but rather a war to maintain our democratic way of life and to leave the way open for other countries to develop the democratic concept. The proof was forthcoming because of the faith and loyalty of the overwhelming majority of the Nisei and the support of their Issei parents. These people provided a dramatic demonstration of loyalty through outstanding and unusually effective military service in both Europe and the Pacific. This wonderful record was compiled in spite of the bitterness and confusion of the early days of 1942 following the evacuation.

The results of the effort to correct what has sometimes been referred to as our worst wartime mistake have proved that a democracy such as ours can correct its mistakes, if there is a will to do so. I am delighted to say that the efforts of the loyal Nisei and the law-abiding Issei, when coupled with the work of WRA, of local re-settlement committees, and of people of good will generally, has been most fruitful. The "Yellow Peril" propaganda of more than forty years appears to be dead. Through the cooperation of American people of good will with the Japanese American population, the United States was able to prove to the world through loyalty, courage, sacrifice, and positive action that we can rise above the sordid hate and bitterness of racial antipathy and the discriminatory practices stemming therefrom.

I feel that the experience, actions, and results of the evacuation and relocation program has something important to contribute to the civil rights programs of today. The overcoming of bitterness, ignorance, and discrimination is going to need the solid cooperation of all folk of good will, regardless of race, to provide the positive planning and positive action so essential to progress. Somehow we must subdue the urge and efforts toward selfish personal power and must drive toward the democratic objective of the most good for the most people.

The Supreme Court did not act on the question of the constitutionality of the evacuation, ordered by the military in 1942, until December 18, 1944, after the War Department had announced plans for the revocation of the exclusion orders. By a division of 6 to 3 the court determined that the action was legal at the time it was taken, in view of the military judgment that it was a military necessity. Three dissenting opinions were expressed, one by Mr. Justice Jackson, who sounded a note of alarm that should never be forgotten by the people of the United States. In his dissenting opinion in the Korematsu case he said in part:

A military order, however unconstitutional, is not apt to last longer than the military emergency. Even during that period a succeeding commander may revoke it all. But once a judicial opinion rationalizes such an order to show that it conforms to the Constitution, or rather rationalizes the Constitution to show that the Constitution sanctions such an order, the court for all time has validated the principle of racial discrimination in criminal procedure and of transplanting American citizens. *The principle then lies about like a loaded weapon ready for the hand of any authority that can bring forward a plausible claim of an urgent need.*

Every repetition imbeds that principle more deeply in our law and thinking and expands it to new purposes. *(Korematsu* vs. *U.S.* [323 U.S. 214])
[Emphasis supplied by author]

This dramatic statement sounds a clear warning against any
repetition of this type of discriminatory action, even in terms of
military necessity.

Since we can't "unload the weapon," we must keep it on
"safety," even in times of war when hysteria is rife and emotions
are rampant.

I served as Director of the War Relocation Authority through
more than ninety percent of its active life as a wartime agency of
the United States government. In spite of our inexperience, lack of
precedents, and frustrations of the early months of the program, the
final results were most satisfying.

In this book I have tried to tell the WRA story as I remember
it, drawing on official documents and other sources where necessary
to supplement my recollections. It is my hope that the recounting
will help clear up misconceptions that have prevailed all too long,
that the experience will provide some helpful guides toward reaching and maintaining sound democratic objectives, and that the story
itself will prove to be as interesting to the reader as it was to one
who lived it.

D. S. M.

Acknowledgments

To Those Who Contributed
to the Success of This Book

WASHINGTON CONSULTANT and former executive officer of the Japanese American Citizens League, Mike Masaoka, with the use of effective argument backed by his usual enthusiasm, provided the final stimulus needed to compel me to start this book. Mike also read manuscript drafts, gave constructive criticism, and supplied many pertinent and important details.

William Hosokawa, Associate Editor of the *Denver Post,* read and reread the manuscript and made several constructive suggestions. Helen Pryor, long-time friend of the Myer family, also read and reread the manuscript, offering helpful suggestions as to organization and content.

M. M. Tozier, former Reports Officer of the War Relocation Authority, served as reader and constructive critic, but even more importantly he performed the task of editing my draft manuscript — for which I am most thankful and greatly indebted.

Philip Glick, former Solicitor and Assistant Director of the War Relocation Authority, served as reader and critic, and in addition supplied valuable and essential material regarding the key Supreme Court cases and legal action relating to the renunciants from Tule Lake.

Arthur Harris, former Superintendent-of Schools at the Poston center in Arizona, and later Associate Commissioner of the U.S. Office of Education, kindly provided detailed information regarding the pattern and problems of the educational program at the Poston center.

Miyeko Kosobayaski, Mary Toda, Gladys Shimasaki, and my daughter, Margaret McFaddin, all contributed to the typing of the manuscript at its various stages.

Dr. Edward H. Spicer, Professor of Anthropology, University of Arizona, read the completed manuscript and recommended publication by the University of Arizona Press.

To the University of Arizona Press, and to all these good people, my heartfelt thanks.

To Those Who Contributed
to the Success of the WRA

IN VIEW OF THE COMPLEXITY of the problems of the WRA, and the wonderful help received from many organizations, agencies, and individuals, I feel obliged to pay my respects to the many outstanding people who were there in time of need.

The Japanese American Citizens League kept in close touch with WRA throughout World War II, and since the war the League has been in the forefront of movements to eliminate discrimination and to aid generally in restitution of rights and property. The JACL has become a respected and influential organization, thanks to such people as Mike Masaoka and his good wife, Etsu, and the late Larry Tajiri and his wife, Guyo, who together edited the *Pacific Citizen* throughout the war and for some years afterward. George Inagaki and Touro (Joe) Kanagawa who were Washington liaison representatives during the war; Masao Satow, later to become executive director of JACL; Saburo Kido, wartime president of JACL; Dr. Thomas Yatabe; Hito Okada; the late Jimmie Sakamoto; and dozens of others have made their contribution not only to the Japanese American population but to all America.

The American Friends Service Committee, with its wonderful leaders and workers, included the late Clarence Pickett, executive officer of the committee during the war, who was a quiet but effective tower of strength, always available to give advice or to lend a hand. There were others, including Esther Rhodes who rendered tremendous service in the establishment and management of badly needed hostels for evacuees, and the late Anne Chloe Watson of San Francisco, executive secretary of the International Institute, and a real friend of the WRA.

Another great statesman, John Thomas from the Baptist Assembly, for a time chairman of the National Japanese American Student Relocation Council, was always helpful in time of need.

The Church of the Brethren was helpful in providing temporary hostels during the period of relocation of evacuees.

One of the many valuable contributions of Roswell Barnes and others associated with the Federal Council of Churches in America was the arrangement for the excellent service supplied by the late George Rundquist in the organization of community resettlement committees throughout the country. These committees, the bulwark and support for our relocation program, played a large part in putting the "Yellow Peril" propaganda to rest.

The late Galen Fisher, who served as a member of the West Coast Committee on American Principles and Fair Play throughout the war, was a staunch supporter in times of trouble, and his writings were helpful and informative. Monroe Deutsch, Vice President of the University of California, provided moral and intellectual leadership in the battle against racism.

Mrs. Ruth Kingman, executive officer of the Committee of American Principles and Fair Play, did yeoman service in organizing local committees and in providing ways and means for breaking down or offsetting efforts of the exclusionist groups up and down the West Coast. In addition, Ruth and her husband Harry were valued counselors of mine and of WRA generally throughout the war.

Roger Baldwin, executive officer of the American Civil Liberties Union, was helpful at all times and was a great source of comfort and support in times of trouble. Al Wirin of the Los Angeles ACLU was continuously busy in behalf of fairness and justice, and he and his legal staff made a great contribution. The late Alexander Meiklejohn, who served with the ACLU during the war, was in the forefront of the fighters for liberty and justice.

Esther Breimeir of the YWCA, in her quiet but effective manner, rendered great services to the evacuee population both within the relocation centers and throughout the country.

President John W. Nason of Swarthmore College deserves

tribute for service as chairman of the National Student Relocation Council for Nisei college students who were banned from the West Coast. With the help of Joseph Conard on the West Coast and President Robbins W. Barstow of the Hartford Theological Seminary in the East, Nason and his council helped to relocate some 250 college students from assembly and relocation centers into colleges and universities.

Thanks are extended to Reed Lewis of the American Council for Nationalities Service (formerly the Common Council for American Unity), who was always helpful in many ways, including his informative and timely publications.

My regards to Alan Barth of the *Washington Post,* who gave support to the cause of the evacuees by means of some fifteen excellent editorials throughout the four years.

The Washington office of the American Railway Association rendered a tremendous service by providing special trains on schedule to help move the more than 50,000 evacuees who wished to return to the West Coast during 1945.

General Joseph Stilwell, with his salty remarks about the "bar room commandos" and his aid in the honoring of a Medal of Honor winner, was especially helpful.

Assistant Secretary of War John J. McCloy, always sympathetic and helpful while serving as War Department liaison during the four years of WRA, rendered a great service when he carried the battle to open the way for the organization of the all-Japanese-American 442nd Combat Team and later the reinstitution of the Selective Service for the Nisei. It was he who cleared the way for conference with Colonel Oveta Culp Hobby of the Women's Army Corps, which led to the acceptance of Nisei volunteers in that arm of the service. These accomplishments were effectuated in spite of the persistent opposition of the commanding generals of both the Western Defense Command (General DeWitt) and the Eastern Defense Command (General Drum).

Among the contributions of the late Elmer Davis, director of the Office of War Information, was an insert in a draft of a letter which we in WRA had prepared to be signed by President Roosevelt and addressed to Secretary Stimson in connection with establishment of the 442nd Regimental Combat Team. The addition consisted of two sentences: "The principle on which this country was founded and by which it has always been governed is that Americanism is a matter of the mind and heart. Americanism is not, and never was, a matter of race or ancestry."

The late Harold Smith, who recommended Milton Eisenhower and later myself for the job of WRA Director, was a great comfort to me as director because of his willingness to listen to problems and to provide counsel.

Secretary Harold L. Ickes was a great and understanding superior during the last two years. He permitted us to make our own decisions and came to our support when needed.

Edward Ennis, who headed the Alien Division of the Department of Justice, was always understanding and helpful in our many problems during the war.

Ugo Carusi, Chief of the Immigration and Naturalization Service, and Willard Kelly of that service, were always cooperative and helpful in solving many problems relating to aliens throughout the war.

Philip Klutznick, as director of the Federal Public Housing Authority, went all out to help with the housing problems, temporary and otherwise, during the crucial final relocation period of 1945 and 1946 in California and the West Coast.

Governor Earl Warren of California helped to ease the way for evacuee returnees and for WRA during the hectic period of 1945 and 1946.

I also want to pay my respects to the late Earl Finch of Mississippi and in later years of Hawaii. Finch entertained Nisei soldiers, helped them arrange their furloughs, visited the wounded in hospitals, and helped their families during the resettlement period when the relocation centers were closed.

Last but not least, my respects and thanks are extended to the WRA staff members, those wonderful people who helped meet the incessant problems and pressures over a period of four years.

All these pressures — from within and without, governmental and private, from evacuees as well as from top levels within the Authority, and between headquarters and the field — had to be met with policies, procedures, and solutions. During all this, a wonderful esprit de corps was developed among the staff at all levels.

The Center Directors were the key staff members who had to deal with the problems both within the centers and with the outside public in their areas, and of course with the Washington office staff. As day-to-day buffers between the evacuees, the public, and Washington, they and their staff deserve much credit for a job well done.

The raison d'etre in the WRA was probably better understood by its employees than in most government agencies. The objectives of the program and the challenge of the job tended to attract and maintain high-quality personnel, which contributed to the good working relationships and excellent spirit. To all of those good people who helped to carry the load, my heartfelt thanks.

Hundreds of other people were helpful during this crucial period of World War II, and I am sincerely sorry that it is not possible to include the names of all who helped to get the job done.

D. S. M.

Chronology

1941

December 7 — Pearl Harbor was attacked by the Japanese.

December 15 — Statement was made by Secretary Knox of U. S. Navy alleging "effective fifth column work" in Hawaii.

1942

January 5 — John B. Hughes, in a radio broadcast, criticized the Department of Justice and urged evacuation of all Japanese. This kicked off the campaign for evacuation.

January 29 — U. S. Attorney General Francis Biddle issued the first of a series of orders establishing limited strategic areas along the Pacific Coast and requiring the removal of all enemy aliens from these areas.

January 30 — Colonel Karl Bendetsen, as the War Department's representative, appeared before the West Coast Congressional delegation and was reported as having stated that "military judgment on the West Coast on whether or not this evacuation of citizens and aliens should take place was positively in the affirmative."

February 10 (approx.) — Opinion was given to Attorney General Biddle by a team of lawyers (Cohen, Cox, and Rauh) upholding the legality of evacuation under the President's war powers.

February 12 — Walter Lippmann's syndicated column appeared. It was entitled "The Fifth Column on the Coast."

February 13 — West Coast Congressional delegation sent a letter to President Roosevelt recommending the "immediate evacuation of all persons of Japanese lineage . . . aliens and citizens alike" from the "entire strategic area" of California, Washington, and Oregon.

February 14 — Lt. Gen. John L. DeWitt, Commanding General of the Western Defense Command, sent a memorandum to Secretary of War Henry L. Stimson recommending the evacuation of "Japanese and other subversive persons" from the West Coast area.

February 19 — President Roosevelt signed Executive Order No. 9066 authorizing the Secretary of War or any military commander designated by the Secretary, to establish "military areas" and exclude therefrom "any or all persons."

February 20 — Secretary Stimson designated General DeWitt as a military commander empowered to carry out an evacuation within his command under the terms of Executive Order 9066.

February 21 — The Tolan Committee hearings were started in San Francisco and continued until March 12 on the West Coast.

February 23 — An enemy seaborne craft shelled Goleta, California, near Santa Barbara. A timely act from the standpoint of the exclusionists.

March 2 — General DeWitt issued Proclamation No. 1 designating the Western half of the three Pacific Coast states and the southern third of Arizona as a military area and stipulating that all persons of Japanese descent would eventually be removed therefrom.

March 11 — General DeWitt established the Wartime Civil Control Administration (WCCA), with Col. Karl R. Bendetsen as Director, to carry out the evacuation program.

March 18 — President Roosevelt signed Executive Order No. 9102 creating the War Relocation Authority to assist persons evacuated by the military under Executive Order No. 9066. Milton S. Eisenhower was named Director.

March 21 — President Roosevelt signed Public Law 503 (77th Congress) making it a federal offense to violate any order issued by a designated military commander under authority of Executive Order No. 9066.

March 22 — First large contingent of Japanese and Japanese Americans moved from Los Angeles to the Manzanar Assembly Center operated by the Army in the Owens Valley of California.

March 23 — General DeWitt issued Civilian Exclusion Order No. 1 ordering the evacuation of all people of Japanese descent from Bainbridge Island in Puget Sound, and their removal by March 30, to the Puyallup Army Assembly Center near Seattle.

March 27 — General DeWitt issued Proclamation No. 4 (effective March 29) forbidding further voluntary migration of Japanese and Japanese Americans from the West Coast military area.

April 7 — Representatives of the governments of the ten Western states met at Salt Lake City with Director Milton S. Eisenhower of WRA and Colonel Bendetsen of WCCA to discuss resettlement plans for the evacuated people. The majority of the conferees registered uncompromising protest against unrestricted migration or resettlement within the western states. (This meeting is referred to as the Governors' Conference).

May 8 — The first contingent of evacuees arrived at the Colorado River Relocation Center (Poston) near Parker, Arizona.

May 21 — Group of 15 evacuees left from the Portland Army Assembly Center for seasonal agricultural work in Malheur County, Oregon, under civilian restriction order of the Western Defense Command.

May 27 — First contingent of evacuees arrived at the Tule Lake Relocation Center in northern California.

May 29 — "National Student Relocation Council" was established, with John Nason as chairman.

June 1 — The Manzanar Army Assembly Center was transferred from WCCA to WRA and renamed Manzanar Relocation Center.

June 2 — General DeWitt issued Public Proclamation No. 6 forbidding further voluntary migration of people of Japanese descent from the eastern half of California and simultaneously announced that all such people would eventually be removed from this area directly to WRA centers.

June 17 — President Roosevelt appointed Dillon S. Myer to succeed Milton S. Eisenhower as director of WRA after Eisenhower's resignation to become Deputy Director of the Office of War Information.

July 20 — WRA adopted its first leave policy which launched the relocation program outside of centers. On this same date the Gila River Relocation Center in Arizona received its first contingent of evacuees from the Turlock Army Assembly Center in California.

August 7 — Western Defense Command announced the completion of evacuation of 110,000 from their homes in the military areas either to Army Assembly Centers or to WRA centers. The last of the residents of Japanese descent from eastern California were moved to relocation centers, even though most of them had already moved voluntarily from their homes near the West Coast to new homes farther inland.

August 10 — Minidoka Relocation Center near Twin Falls, Idaho, received the first contingent of evacuees from the Puyallup Army Assembly Center.

August 12 — Heart Mountain Relocation Center near Cody, Wyoming, received its first group of evacuees from the Pomona Army Assembly Center.

August 13 — WRA began an agency conference of key staff members in San Francisco to determine basic policies for the operation of relocation centers.

August 27 — The Granada Relocation Center near La Mar, Colorado, was opened with the arrival of a group of evacuees from the Merced Army Assembly Center.

September 11 — The Central Utah Relocation Center near Delta, Utah, received the first group of evacuees from the Tanforan Army Assembly Center.

September 18 — The Rohwer Relocation Center near McGhee, Arkansas, received its first group of evacuees from the Stockton Army Assembly Center.

September 26 — The WRA issued its revised and expanded basic leave regulations effective on October 1. These regulations laid the basis for an all-out resettlement program.

October 6 — The Jerome Relocation Center near Dermott, Arkansas, the last of the ten centers ready for business, received a group of evacuees from the Fresno Army Assembly Center.

November 3 — The transfer of evacuees from the Army Wartime Civil Control Administration to the WRA was completed with the arrival of the last group at the Jerome Center from Fresno.

November 14 — A community-wide strike and demonstration (The Poston Incident) was staged by the evacuees of Unit One of the Colorado River Center.

November 15 — Announcement was made of plans to eliminate the WRA regional offices as line offices, effective December 1.

November 23 — The Poston Incident was settled by an agreement between the administration and a committee of the residents.

December 6 — Some Manzanar residents staged a demonstration over the arrest of a resident. The military were called in and took over temporarily.

December 10 — A small group of troublemakers was moved from Manzanar to a Moab, Utah, abandoned CCC camp; aggressive pro-American Nisei were moved to a Death Valley CCC campsite to avoid more trouble at Manzanar.

1943

January 4 — WRA field offices were established in Chicago and Salt Lake City to facilitate relocation; soon thereafter, offices were opened in Cleveland, Minneapolis, Des Moines, New York, Denver, Kansas City, and Boston.

January 20 — Chairman Robert Reynolds of the Senate Committee on Military Affairs appointed a subcommittee under the chairmanship of Senator A. B. Chandler of Kentucky to investigate the WRA program and to consider a bill introduced by Senator Mon Wallgren to transfer the functions of WRA to the War Department.

January 28 — Secretary of War Henry L. Stimson announced plans to form a Japanese American Combat Team to be made up of volunteers from both the mainland and Hawaii.

February 8 — Army enlistment and leave clearance registration began at most of the relocation centers.

March 11 — WRA Director Dillon Myer wrote a letter to Secretary of War Stimson recommending an immediate relaxation of the West Coast Exclusion Orders against persons of Japanese descent. This recommendation was rejected in a reply dated May 10 in which segregation was strongly urged.

March 20 — Project directors were authorized to issue leave permits to persons wishing to relocate, in cases where leave clearance had been given by the Washington office.

April 8 — Senator Chandler wrote to Director Myer setting forth tentative recommendations of his subcommittee regarding the WRA program and urging that the "disloyal" evacuees be separated from the other residents of WRA centers.

May 6 — Mrs. Eleanor Roosevelt spent a full day at the Gila River Relocation Center.

May 12 — Two investigators from the staff of the House of Representatives Committee on Un-American Activities arrived unannounced at the Manzanar Relocation Center to begin a probe of the WRA program.

May 23 — Director and Mrs. Myer had lunch with President Roosevelt at the White House.

May 31 — Meeting of all project directors was held in Washington to discuss the situation in the various centers and the possibility of a segregation program. The directors were unanimous in favor of a segregation program.

June 3 — Chairman Martin Dies of the Committee on Un-American Activities announced the appointment of a three-man subcommittee, with John M. Costello of California as Chairman and Karl Mundt of South Dakota and Herman Eberharter of Pennsylvania as members, to investigate the WRA.

June 25 — Director Dillon Myer wrote to Assistant Secretary of War John J. McCloy regarding plans for a segragation program and the selection of Tule Lake as the segregation center.

July 6 — Director Myer appeared for the first time before the Costello Subcommittee to testify and to defend the administration of the WRA program.

August,

September, and

early October — More than 15,000 people were moved in and out of the Tule Lake Center.

October 11 — The last group of evacuees from other centers arrived at Tule Lake.

October 15 — A truck accident, which killed one evacuee, led to a farm strike at Tule Lake.

November 1 — A mass demonstration was staged at Tule Lake for the benefit of the National Director who was there on a visit.

November 4 — An outbreak of violence occurred at Tule Lake between WRA internal security staff and a group of dissident young evacuees. Troops were called in, and the center was transferred to military control.

November 8 — A so-called fact-finding committee of the California legislature began its investigation of the Tule Lake disturbance by holding hearings in the nearby village of Tule Lake.

November 16 — Director Dillon Myer met with the state commanders and state adjutants of the American Legion in Indianapolis.

November 24 — Director Myer testified before the Senate Committee on Military Affairs regarding the Tule Lake disturbance.

November 29 — The Costello Subcommittee began a series of hearings on the Tule Lake situation.

1944

January 14 — The control of the Tule Lake Center was transferred back to the WRA by the military.

January 20 — Secretary of War Stimson announced that in view of the record achieved by Japanese Americans in the Army, they would thereafter be recruited through the regular Selective Service procedures.

February 16 — President Roosevelt signed Executive Order 9423 transferring WRA to the Department of the Interior.

May — The 442nd Combat Team embarked for the Italian front.

June 8 — President Roosevelt announced a plan to bring approximately one thousand European refugees into the United States outside the regular immigration quotas and quarter them at an Emergency Refugee Shelter to be administered by WRA at Oswego, New York.

June 30 — The Jerome Relocation Center was closed and the five thousand remaining residents were transferred to other centers.

July 1 — President Roosevelt signed Public Law 405 (78th Congress) permitting United States citizens to renounce their citizenship on American soil in time of war under procedures approved by the Attorney General.

August 3 — European refugees arrived at New York en route to the Emergency Refugee Shelter at Oswego, New York.

December 17 — The War Department announced the revocation (effective on January 2, 1945) of the West Coast mass exclusion orders which had been in effect against people of Japanese descent since the spring of 1942.

December 18 — The WRA announced that all relocation centers would be closed before the end of 1945 and that the entire WRA program would be liquidated on June 30, 1946. On this same date the U.S. Supreme Court ruled in the Korematsu case that the West Coast evacuation was constitutional; the Court also ruled on the Endo case to the effect that WRA had no authority to detain a "concededly loyal" American citizen.

1945

January 8 — An attempt was made to burn and dynamite the packing shed of a returned evacuee in Placer County, California. This was the first of thirty West Coast incidents, over a period of five months from January to June.

January 10-20 — Field area offices were established at Los Angeles, San Francisco, and Seattle.

February 16 — An "all center" evacuee conference was held at Salt Lake City for the purpose of discussing and documenting the problems inherent in the liquidation of WRA centers.

April 30 — Director Myer, appearing before a House Appropriations Subcommittee, estimated that approximately 44,000 "relocatable" evacuees would be left in centers by June 30.

May 14 — Secretary of Interior Harold L. Ickes publicly denounced the incidents of West Coast terrorism and called for more vigorous local law enforcement.

June 20 — Director Dillon Myer and Assistant Director Robert Cozzens started on a trip of several days duration from Los Angeles up the big valley of California to visit returning evacuees, especially those who had been subjected to terrorism.

July 13 — WRA announced a schedule of closing dates for all centers, except Tule Lake, between October 15 and December 15.

July 16 — Captain George Grandstaff, a Caucasian officer with the 442nd Combat Team, began a speaking tour of the hot spots in California to plead for tolerance toward the returning evacuees.

August 1 — Director Myer issued Administrative Notice 289 calling for the scheduled relocation of remaining residents during the last six weeks of operation of each WRA center.

August 15 — VJ Day.

September 4 — The Western Defense Command issued Public Proclamation No. 24 revoking all individual exclusion orders and all further military restrictions against persons of Japanese descent.

December 1 — The last Relocation Center, except Tule Lake, was closed.

December 22 — President Truman announced that the refugees at Oswego should be considered for admission to the United States under regular immigration quotas.

1946

February 4 — Refugee Shelter at Fort Ontario, Oswego, New York, was closed.

February 23 — Last group of repatriates from Tule Lake to Japan sailed from Long Beach, California; 432 aboard ship at sailing time.

May 8 — The Director of WRA received "The Medal for Merit" as a result of the work of the agency during the war.

May 15 — The last of the WRA field offices were closed.

June 30 — The War Relocation Authority Program was officially terminated.

PART 1

Historical Background

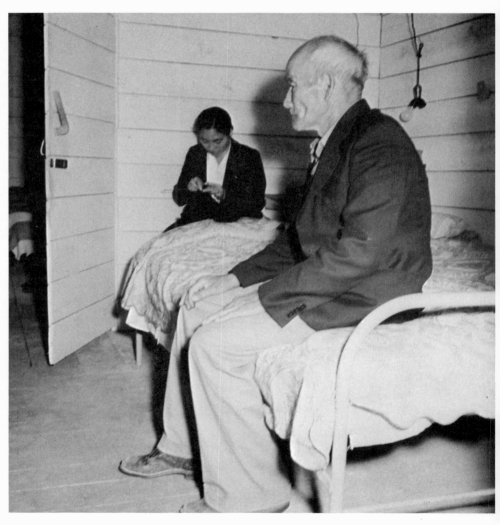

Elderly couple in an army assembly center, awaiting
transfer to a relocation center. (WRA photo)

CHAPTER 1

A Change in Command

ON SATURDAY, JUNE 13, 1942, Mrs. Myer and I were having a quiet and friendly party in our Falls Church, Virginia, home. Among those present were Milton Eisenhower and his wife, Helen.

Milton Eisenhower, later to become president of Johns Hopkins University, was an old friend with whom I had been closely associated in the Department of Agriculture for many years. Since March 18 he had been Director of the War Relocation Authority (WRA). On the evening of our party he was excited over having been asked to become the Deputy to Elmer Davis in the Office of War Information, a spot for which he was well qualified because of broad experience in government and in the information field. Milton asked if I would be willing to take on the directorship of WRA.

The following Monday evening we met to discuss the matter further. When, after about two hours of conversation, I asked Milton if he really thought that I should take the job, he replied, "Yes, if you can do the job and sleep at night." He said he had been unable to do so. I was sure that I could sleep, and so agreed to accept the position if he felt that I was the one to do it, although it was not something I would have chosen for myself.

Two days later, on the afternoon of June 17, I moved into the position of Director of the War Relocation Authority, with a letter of appointment already signed by President Roosevelt. The agency was then about three months old.

At that time the evacuation of all Japanese Americans living in the three West Coast states and in a portion of Arizona had been ordered and almost completed, except for a small number who were not moved until August 7. Most of the evacuees had been moved by the Army Western Defense Command into hurriedly improvised assembly centers at race tracks, or hastily constructed centers up and down the West Coast. Here they were to live until relocation centers could be constructed to receive them. The relocation centers were to be managed by the War Relocation Authority, a civilian agency established by Executive Order on March 18, 1942.

The first two relocation centers to be occupied were Manzanar in the Owens Valley of California and Poston on the Colorado Indian Reservation near Parker, Arizona. Both of these centers, originally constructed as army reception centers, were transferred to the WRA in early June. During the early months the Poston center was managed by the Bureau of Indian Affairs under contract with the WRA.

Gradually eight other centers were built, and the movement from the assembly centers to the new centers proceeded throughout the summer and fall of 1942. The last contingent arrived at the Jerome (Arkansas) center in November. Most of the evacuees moved into partially completed centers constructed by the army.

Prior to the evacuation order, the army had encouraged families to move out of the West Coast military areas. Approximately 8,000 evacuees moved voluntarily to the Mountain States toward the east. However, because many of the voluntary evacuees met with hostility and also because of other reasons, some of these people became residents of relocation centers.

The evacuation and the establishment of relocation centers were actions without precedent in American history. Consequently, with no guideposts, the WRA was faced with the immediate problem of establishing rules and policies for the guidance of both staff and evacuees. Fortunately, Milton Eisenhower had recruited an excellent group of key staff members and had established the organization pattern for the Washington office. A San Francisco regional office, badly needed in the early stages of setting up the western centers, had also been established.

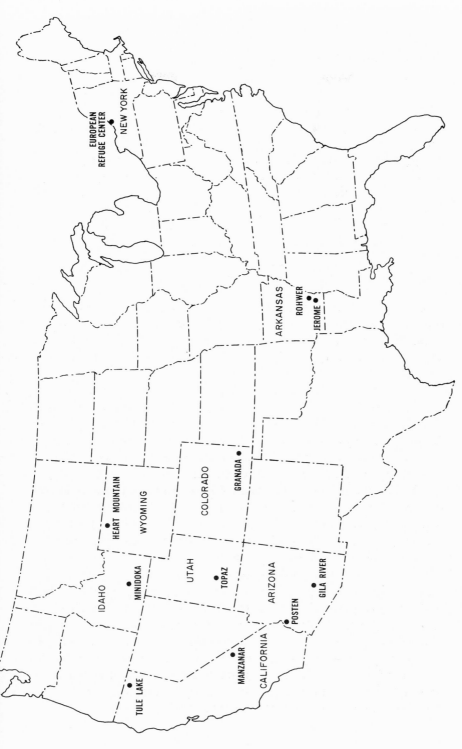

Sites of the ten relocation centers which housed Japanese Americans during World War II.

With the exception of two people, all the key staff members in Washington were old friends and associates of mine. They had been selected from the Department of Agriculture where both Milton Eisenhower and I had come to know them and to have confidence in their capabilities. The two unknown to me were Col. Erle Cress, who had been detailed from the army, and Thomas Holland, who headed the Employment Division. E. R. ("Si") Fryer, who headed the San Francisco regional office, had also been a friend and associate over the preceding several years. Lt. Cmdr. K. D. Ringle, a U.S. Naval District Intelligence Officer detailed to work with WRA during the first several weeks, had completed his detail by the time of my appointment.

At the first weekly staff meeting that I presided over, Tom Holland gave an articulate and impressive report about his recently completed trip to the centers then in operation and to some of the army assembly centers. Tom had been horrified by his experience. The main theme of his report was that the evacuees should be removed as soon as possible from the centers, because these centers were not normal places to live and were not good from any standpoint.

Almost immediately after this meeting I took some of the key staff members for a visit to the San Francisco regional office and to the unfinished Tule Lake and Poston centers, both of which were still receiving evacuees. This trip convinced me that Tom Holland was right and that something should be done about moving evacuees to locations outside of the centers as soon as possible.

In the meantime we were faced with many other problems demanding immediate attention — the need for additional staff, the necessity for formulation of policies, liaison with the military, public relations, and others.

Neither I nor most of my staff were well informed regarding the problems we faced. We lacked information about the evacuees and their history. We were generally uninformed regarding the anti-Oriental movements on the West Coast, and the pressures, rumors and fears that had led to the evacuation. It was imperative that we gain understanding and information as quickly as possible. Our historian, Miss Ruth McKee, Lt. Comdr. K. D. Ringle, and others brought together the invaluable information necessary to our understanding of how and why such a drastic move had come about.

CHAPTER 2

Before Pearl Harbor

COMPARED WITH OTHER ELEMENTS of United States population, the Japanese were latecomers. This circumstance was chiefly due to a strict policy of exclusion and inclusion adopted by Japan in 1638. The self-isolation of Japan was the result of a growing conviction over a period of years on the part of the early Tokugawa Shoguns that the political activities of foreign missionaries, especially the Jesuits, constituted a menace to the safety of the Empire. Accordingly the Japanese rulers forbade the construction of seaworthy vessels, destroyed the ones in existence, and retired from the world until Commodore Matthew C. Perry forced an opening of the country in 1854.

It was not, however, until 1884 that mass emigration of Japanese nationals was permitted by the Imperial Government. In that year the authorities finally yielded to the pleas of Hawaiian sugar planters for laborers.

Prior to 1860, when Japan sent her first ambassador to the United States, the only Japanese that Americans had seen had been a few castaways picked up in mid-ocean by western ships and brought to America, usually to California, until passage back to Japan could be arranged. The Americans viewed these castaways with friendly curiosity. In addition, because the United States was

becoming aware of the need for a fueling station in Japan, certain
politicians saw in the rescued seamen a potential wedge to open
Japan to trade. Thus, in the days before the establishment of diplomatic relations with Japan, the few Japanese who reached U.S.
shores were petted, exhibited, and made much of. Commodore
Perry's interpreter on the expedition to force the opening of Japan
owed his knowledge of the Japanese language to a castaway named
Senatro, a member of the expedition.

EARLY IMMIGRANTS

Aside from members of the embassies from Japan to the United
States during the 1860s, two small colonies of Japanese appeared
in California. One colony was composed of about a dozen farmers
who settled on land purchased at Gold Hill near Sacramento. A
Dutch adventurer who was a naturalized Japanese citizen and married to a Japanese woman had smuggled this little group of farmers
out of Japan to help him make a fortune out of a tea and silk
venture in the Sacramento valley. Fortune was against him, however, and after a year or so he returned to Japan, presumably to
get more plants and to raise more funds. He never came back. The
destitute Gold Hill farmers appealed to Charles W. Brooks, the
honorary consular agent in San Francisco, and through his efforts
found work in American families.

The other colony — the Alameda colony — was composed of
a small group of Japanese intellectuals and liberals. According to
a report in the *San Francisco Chronicle,* June 17, 1869, all them
were

. . . gentlemen of refinement and influence in their own country, from
which they were compelled to flee, because their travel in civilized countries had made them too liberal in their ideas to suit the Mikado. These
Japanese gentlemen, who spoke English and French, offered to work for
nothing for a year with any gentlemen who would teach them a useful
occupation, but could get none to accept their services. By the advice of
Mr. Van Reed they leased a farm in Alameda County, and hired a few
intelligent white men to instruct them.

After 1871, when the Emperor encouraged the youth of the
gentry to travel and study in the western world, a number of
Japanese students appeared on the American scene. The number
must have been limited, however, because the Japanese Consul in
San Francisco reported in 1884, just prior to the authorization of

general emigration by Japan, that there were only eighty Japanese in California.

During the first several years after 1884, when the Japanese were first free to emigrate, only a few resolute and daring individuals left Japan for the United States. For the most part those who came were youthful — mostly teen-aged boys or unmarried young men under 30 years of age. A few of the older ones left behind wives and children. These men came generally to San Francisco and arrived with very little money. Boarding-house keepers, who served also as employment agents, met them at the pier to recruit labor for the railroads and for agriculture.

The number of Japanese coming to the United States before 1890 was quite limited. In 1891 the annual number of arrivals exceeded 1,000 for the first time, and it was not until 1898 that the number exceeded 2,000.

During the first several years of the twentieth century, mass migration reached its peak. It dropped off sharply after 1908, when the Gentlemen's Agreement to curtail the migration of Japanese nationals to the United States and Hawaii became effective. Under terms of this unwritten agreement between the Theodore Roosevelt administration and the Japanese government, Japan agreed to issue passports only to nonlaborers, with the exception of those laborers who had established residence in the United States and wished to return with members of their immediate families.

In 1907 nearly 10,000 Japanese arrived on the mainland of the United States, and 21,000 went to Hawaii; during 1910 only 1,552 arrived in the United States and 1,239 in Hawaii. During the decade 1901 to 1910, inclusive, a total of 132,706 immigrated to the mainland shores and to the Hawaiian Islands; of these, nearly 55,000 came to the mainland. The total Japanese population in 1910 on the mainland was 72,157, of which only 4,502 were American citizens.

People of Japanese ancestry were not eligible to become United States citizens unless born here, because our first immigration law, passed in 1790, provided that only "free whites" could be naturalized. The number of persons of Japanese ancestry living in Hawaii in 1910 was 79,786, of which nearly 20,000 were United States citizens. These figures point up the fact that the Nisei or second generation from Hawaii as a group were older and more mature than those on the mainland at the time of World War II.

ANTI-JAPANESE FEELINGS IN CALIFORNIA

The Japanese immigrants were handicapped because the white settlers in California were notoriously hostile to Orientals. These early settlers, instigators of the Bear Flag Rebellion — during which California asserted independence, drove out its last Mexican governor, and in 1846 set up a republic under the Bear Flag — excluded the Mexicans and the Spanish, as well as Orientals and other dark-skinned people, from their definition of Americans.

The first anti-Oriental campaign, in the 1860s and 1870s, was directed against the Chinese, who had arrived in large numbers much earlier than had the Japanese. Pressures from the anti-Oriental groups resulted in the passage of the Chinese Exclusion Act in 1882; this act continued in force until 1943 as a result of several extensions and the 1924 Oriental Exclusion Act. It appears that from 1870 to 1920 the trade unions of San Francisco were the most active force against the Orientals. In his book, *Prejudice — Japanese Americans,* Carey McWilliams had this to say:

From 1870 to 1920 anti-Oriental agitation in California was fomented, directed, and financed by the powerful trade union movement that, from the earliest days, had centered in San Francisco. It is, indeed, remarkable that in a pioneer nonindustrial State a labor movement of such strength had developed that by 1879 it was able, through the Workingman's Party, to seize control of the State and enact a new, and in some respects quite radical, constitution. The secret of the success of this early movement lay in the fact that Irish immigrants constituted one-fourth of the large foreign-born element in the State. . . .

Most of the leaders of the anti-Oriental movement, in its early phases, were Irish and they were also the leaders of the San Francisco labor movement.[1]

As the Chinese labor force dwindled following the passage of the 1882 Chinese Exclusion Act, the Japanese immigrants were welcomed, even by the racists, as laborers in various fields but mainly within the growing agricultural industry in California, Washington, and Oregon. The California sugar-beet growers in particular had need of several thousand workers. The railroads were large users of Japanese labor. The hop fields of Northern California and Oregon attracted many young Japanese immigrants, because the Japanese ability and willingness to work long hours on a piece-work

---

[1]Carey McWilliams, *Prejudice* (Boston: Little, Brown, 1944), p. 20.

basis resulted in good pay. From the railroads, the sugar beet fields, and the hop farms, the Japanese found their way into seasonal work in fruit orchards, vineyards, berry farms, and vegetable farms.

These young immigrants were in great demand as laborers, but they were ambitious and they wanted to better themselves. As they learned the language and ways of America, they began to lease or purchase land or go into business so as to establish families and live a normal life. California and other West Coast farmers resented having their field laborers suddenly become competing farm operators. This resentment was economic rather than racist, but the racists saw in this transition from day laborer to operator another threat to white supremacy.

The anti-Japanese campaign began in a small way on May 7, 1900, in San Francisco, when a meeting called to consolidate pressure for the re-enactment of the Chinese Exclusion Act passed a resolution urging the adoption of a law to exclude all Japanese except members of the diplomatic staff. James Phelan, then mayor of San Francisco, later governor of California, and still later United States senator, played a prominent part in that meeting.

Between 1900 and 1910 the anti-Oriental campaign was stepped up, and the Japanese were the recipients of most of the attacks. The Japanese and Korean Exclusion League was organized in 1905. The Native Sons of the Golden West, which came into existence in 1875, became one of the most influential anti-Japanese groups about 1907. The Oriental Exclusion League held its first annual meeting in Seattle in 1908.

The Japanese victory over Russia in 1905 appeared to have stimulated the anti-Japanese crusade. In 1906 Mayor Schmitz of San Francisco and his political backer, Reuf, were in trouble with the law; needing something to divert the public interest, they pressured the school board into requiring that the Japanese school children be segregated. The children were then transferred to the school in Chinatown.

During this period the newspapers took up the cry against the Japanese, and in 1907 the Japanese from Hawaii, Canada, and Mexico were barred from entry into the United States. Then, in 1908, came the aforementioned Gentlemen's Agreement in which the Japanese government agreed to issue passports only to non-laborers, except for those persons already established in the United States.

The growing resentment against the Japanese was responsible for the passage, in 1913, of the California Alien Land Act, which made it illegal for aliens ineligible for citizenship to buy agricultural land or to lease such land for a period exceeding three years. It is important to re-emphasize here that the Japanese and Chinese were not eligible for American citizenship because of the previously cited 1790 law. This gave a convenient "handle" to the racists, and most of the discriminatory legislation passed by the states was based upon ineligibility to citizenship.

During World War I, 1914-1918, the campaign of the anti-Japanese group was muted somewhat because Japan was at least technically on the side of the United States in that conflict. Almost immediately after the close of the war, the anti-Japanese campaign was renewed with new vigor and new recruits. The American Legion in its first convention of 1919 passed a resolution recommending exclusion of the Japanese.

In the early 1920s the Joint Immigration Committee was formed, with V. S. McClatchy, publisher of the *Sacramento Bee,* as executive director, and with other members being the deputy adjutant of the California American Legion, the secretary-treasurer of the state Federation of Labor, the master of the California State Grange, the grand president of the Native Sons of the Golden West, a representative of the Associated Farmers, and the state attorney general. McClatchy had been active in the anti-Japanese crusade over many years and had retired from his business in 1919 to devote the balance of his life (until 1938) to anti-Japanese propaganda. With the membership of the Joint Immigration Committee behind him, he had powerful political support in behalf of the anti-Japanese campaign.

In July 1921 McClatchy prepared and filed with the United States Senate a brief stating the case of the racist groups for an exclusion act. The brief was presented to the Senate by Senator Hiram Johnson. In 1924 such an act was passed, denying admission to the United States of all immigrants ineligible for American citizenship, including Mongolians, Polynesians, and races indigenous to the Western Hemisphere — which, of course, meant American Indians.

This exclusion law remained in effect for all mentioned groups until 1940, when it was revised in regard to American Indians.

Then, in 1943, during World War II, when the United States was feeling friendly toward the Chinese, a quota was established for them. In 1946 a quota was established for East Indians and Filipinos. Naturalization privileges were provided by these acts. The Exclusion Act provisions affecting other Asiatics, including the Japanese, were finally repealed in 1952. These revisions also gave Japanese immigrants the right to become naturalized citizens, since the 1952 enactment eliminated race as a criterion for naturalization.

It is important to note that the major migration of Japanese took place during a period of less than 30 years between 1890 and 1920. The majority of the young men arrived between 1890 and 1910, and the "picture brides" joined them between 1905 and 1920, at which time the Japanese government agreed to withhold passports from prospective brides.

This period when the largest movement of immigrants took place coincided with the emergence of Japan as a major power in world affairs, as indicated by the Anglo-Japanese Alliance of 1902 and the Japanese victory over the Russians in 1905.

A developing fear of Japan was undoubtedly a factor in the anti-Japanese campaign that grew and flourished between the two world wars. Along with this, and probably more basically important, were the growing economic resentments resulting from the development of competition in agriculture, business, and the labor market.

In 1920 the anti-Japanese agitation became so violent that it affected other foreign-born groups. In some areas action against local Japanese took on the flavor of old-time vigilante antics. For example, in 1921 a band of white men rounded up 58 Japanese in the Turlock (California) area, put them on a train, and shipped them out. This type of violence died down with the passage of the 1924 Exclusion Act but was revived periodically between that time and 1942.

Many myths were manufactured and propagandized by the racists throughout the years after 1905. The population myth, which had two angles, was one of the most popular. One angle involved greatly exaggerated claims regarding the total population of Japanese in this country. This was aided and abetted by official sources in California who issued badly juggled statistics. The other angle was the charge that the birth rate of the Japanese was very high and that they "bred like rabbits." The public was told that for these reasons it would be only a matter of time until the Japanese population would be in the majority. This claim was finally squelched by the report of the Tolan Committee of the U.S. House of Representatives on May 28, 1942, which said:

Contrary to alarmist predictions about the reproductive tendencies of the American Japanese, their birth rate during the past decade has been insufficient to balance mortality and emigration. Since 1930 the Japanese population has decreased by 11,887 or 8.6 percent.[2]

Another popular myth stated that the Nisei owed their allegiance to Japan instead of the United States because of their dual citizenship. A crusade was carried on to amend the U.S. Constitution so that children born in the United States of parents ineligible for citizenship would themselves be ineligible to American citizenship. Fortunately, this campaign did not succeed, but it did result in generating suspicion regarding the loyalty of the Nisei. Later the Japanese language schools were charged with being subversive and anti-American, and with teaching emperor worship. The Nisei in uniform during World War II proved this charge to be untrue.

After Pearl Harbor, Lt. Gen. John G. DeWitt and his staff contributed other myths in justification of their recommendations for total evacuation. These myths and others continued to be bandied about so generally by the racists after Pearl Harbor that we in the War Relocation Authority prepared and distributed a pamphlet entitled *Myths and Facts* for the purpose of offsetting this type of propaganda.

---

[2]House, Select Committee Investigating National Defense Migration, *Problems of Evacuation of Enemy Aliens and Others From Prohibited Military Zones:* Hearings, Part 29, 1942.

CHAPTER 3

Pressures, Rumors, Fears, and Evacuation

IMMEDIATELY FOLLOWING THE ATTACK on Pearl Harbor, December 7, 1941, surprisingly little agitation occurred against the Japanese Americans. There were rumors of poisoned vegetables, which the *Los Angeles Times* reported as untrue, and one small California newspaper proposed evacuation. In general, a quiet period continued until after the turn of the year 1942, when the campaign of the racists picked up, reaching its peak about February 13.

During January and early February of 1942, various organizations urged action, ranging from surveillance by the army to complete evacuation or internment of all Japanese. These organizations included the California Department of the American Legion and many local posts; the Associated Farmers; the Grower-Shipper Vegetable Association; the Western Growers Protective Association; California Farm Bureau; Americanism Educational League; Kilsoo Haan, a Korean who claimed support from certain non-existent organizations; some labor unions; the Pacific League; and the Joint Immigration Committee.

In the meantime the Hearst publications and the *Los Angeles Times* kept up a drumfire of editorials, columns, and slanted news stories that pressured officials and caused the public generally to become fearful and emotional regarding the alleged dangers in their midst.

On December 15, Secretary of the Navy Frank Knox, on his return from a hurried trip to Hawaii, made a most unfortunate statement to reporters when he said "the most effective fifth column work of the entire war was done in Hawaii, with the possible exception of Norway." This was a loose statement because, as proved later, there was no fifth column activity on the part of the local population in Hawaii. The "fifth column" terminology did not properly describe what had happened in Hawaii; "espionage by paid consular agents" would have been accurate.

The statement by Secretary Knox regarding an "effective fifth column," when combined with the many false rumors regarding alleged happenings in Hawaii which gained credence in January, led to fears and served as fodder for the racist press and organizations. Among the actions of various groups and of members of the press during this period, perhaps the most effective in stirring up fears and in bringing pressures on officials were the resolutions adopted by local posts and state departments of the American Legion. These actions were reinforced by a resolution at the national level of the Legion on January 19 calling for evacuation and internment of "all enemy aliens and nationals."[1] This resolution was later interpreted to include all persons of Japanese descent.

LAUNCHING THE CAMPAIGN FOR EVACUATION

Morton Grodzins, in his excellent book, *Americans Betrayed,* describes how in early January 1942 the campaign for evacuation really got under way. He tells how radio commentator John B. Hughes and others, along with West Coast newspaper editorials, local law-enforcement officers, and Pacific Coast congressmen directed a campaign of criticism against the departments of both War and Justice. Demands were made for the mass evacuation of all Japanese — citizens and aliens alike.[2]

Growers' and shippers' groups pressured their individual congressmen, urging evacuation or internment or both. As a result of this pressure, Congressman John Z. Anderson introduced H. J. Resolution 305, 77th Congress, which by amendments to the U.S.

---

[1]House, Select Committee [Tolan] Investigating National Defense Migration, Hearings (1942), Part 30, p. 11430.
[2]Mortin Grodzins, *Americans Betrayed* (Chicago: Univ. of, 1942), pp. 253-54.

Constitution would have provided that persons borns of parents ineligible for citizenship should not become citizens by birth.

The Los Angeles Chamber of Commerce through its Washington representative, Thomas B. Drake, presented a Chamber resolution of January 30 to the West Coast congressional delegation, along with a draft resolution sponsored by Congressman John Costello, that called for army control over aliens and dual citizens and for mass evacuation of aliens and their families. The Joint Immigration Committee, which had been active and politically powerful for more than 20 years, met on February 1, 1942. The members urged evacuation and planned for further propaganda activity, which was their specialty. In early February the California State Personnel Board issued an order barring from civil service positions all citizens who were descendants of alien enemies. Although it covered all groups, this order was applied only against Japanese Americans. The order was issued in spite of Attorney General Earl Warren's formal dissent, in which he said in part:

A substantial portion of the population of California consists of naturalized citizens and citizens born of parents who migrated to this country from foreign lands. They have in the past and do now represent the highest standards of American citizenship. . . . [T]o question that loyalty or place them in a category different from other citizens is not only cruel in its effect upon them but is also disruptive of the national unity which is so essential in these times.[3]

This is Earl Warren at his best. In spite of this excellent statement, he had already publicly declared himself in favor of evacuation. He said:

I have come to the conclusion that the Japanese situation as it exists in this state today, may well be the Achilles heel of the entire civilian defense effort. Unless something is done it may bring about a repetition of Pearl Harbor.[4]

The attorney general took the position that political and civilian action was not feasible at this late date, that only the military could take the needed steps and that evacuation was the proper

---

[3]Attorney General's Opinion, No. 1 — N. S. 4083, February 7, 1943.
[4]Grodzins, p. 94.

move. This inconsistency on the part of Attorney General Warren was typical of the confusion evidenced in many places at that time.

In the meantime the *Los Angeles Times* and the Hearst press in particular were carrying on a day-by-day campaign. On January 29 and again on February 5, the *San Francisco Examiner,* a Hearst paper, published columns by Henry McLemore, a former sports writer who evidently was brought to the coast for this specific purpose. The following quote from one of his columns well illustrates the race baiting and irresponsible nature of the Hearst press attacks during this period. McLemore said:

> Everywhere that the Japanese have attacked to date, the Japanese population has risen to aid the attackers. Pearl Harbor, Manila. What is there to make the Government believe that the same wouldn't be true in California? Does it feel that the lovely California climate has changed them and that the thousands of Japanese who live in the boundaries of this state are all staunch and true Americans?
>
> I am for the immediate removal of every Japanese on the West Coast in a point deep in the interior. Herd 'em up, pack 'em off and give 'em the inside room in the Badlands. Let 'em be pinched, hurt, hungry and dead up against it.[5]

On January 15 Congressman Martin Dies, chairman of the Un-American Activities Committee, addressed the House of Representatives on the "fifth column" in America. Then on January 28 he declared that "a fear of displeasing foreign powers, and a maudlin attitude toward fifth columnists was largely responsible for the unparalleled tragedy at Pearl Harbor." He said further that a report of his committee would "disclose that if our committee had been permitted to reveal the facts last September the tragedy of Pearl Harbor might have been averted."[6]

The report referred to was not actually released until after authority had been given to the military for the evacuation. However, a committee spokesman, in summarizing what the report would contain, said that it would describe the activities of Japanese nationalistic organizations engaged in espionage and similar details. This report, called the "Yellow Report," after February 5 supplied material for scare stories for the racist press.

---

[5]WRA Report, *Wartime Exile,* pp. 108-109.
[6]Grodzins, pp. 84-85.

For example, the *Los Angeles Times* headlined the first disclosure of the Dies Committee findings: "Dies 'Yellow Paper' Reveals Jap Spying Attempts, Probably Successful, to Learn Los Angeles Aqueduct Secrets, Disclosed." This item was based on a request for information made by the Japanese consul twenty years before. Several days after the report was released, the *Times* devoted six full columns to its contents.

CONCERNS OF THE DEPARTMENT OF JUSTICE

Grodzins reports in some detail on the concerns of the Department of Justice at this time. While a representative of the War Department is reported to have stated that evacuation of citizens and aliens alike from the West Coast positively must take place, the Justice Department had indicated a belief that the steps already taken were appropriate to control enemy aliens. However, the political and public pressures against the War and Justice departments compelled officials to confer and to study the legal aspects of the problem.

According to Grodzins, Mr. Edward Ennis and Mr. James Rowe of the Justice Department, seeing no need for a mass removal of all Japanese Americans, studied legal means for restricting any dangerous elements. A report to the attorney general considered two possible approaches — first the theory that American-born Japanese who had returned to Japan for extended periods might be considered expatriated, and secondly that members of the Shinto cult would have sworn allegience to the Japanese state and thus would have expatriated themselves.

Grodzins also explains that legal doctrine existed for mass treatment of the Japanese Americans:

It should not be supposed that legal doctrine was lacking for the treatment of the citizen group en masse. In the obvious absence of clear-cut authority for such action, the wide range of undefined war power possessed by both the executive and legislature might be called into existence. This point was emphasized in an opinion given the Attorney-General by a team of government lawyers headed by Benjamin Cohen. (Cohen, Cox, and Rauh to Biddle; undated; probably near February 10, 1942).

The Constitution, they wrote, should not be interpreted in time of war to be either unworkable or nonexistent. Considered either as a matter of Constitutional law or wise statesmanship, the Japanese situation should be met by action "reasonably calculated to preserve the national safety." The President (the opinion continued) was justified in acting under his war powers without further legislation in view of the urgency of the situation. His authority to prohibit entry by the general public, citizens as well as aliens, into areas of special importance was clear. The legal power to prohibit entry into such areas by a particular class of persons rested upon the reasonableness of the classification. "So long as a classification of persons or citizens is reasonably related to a genuine war need and does not under the guise of national defense discriminate against any class of citizens for a purpose unrelated to the national defense, no constitutional guaranty is infringed."

It is significant that attorneys outside the Justice Department wrote this opinion. Lawyers of the Department were unwilling to produce such a document, partly because of their doubts as to the validity of such a constitutional doctrine but more importantly because of their conviction that mass movement of citizens was not necessary from the viewpoint of internal security. Every document extant demonstrates the Justice Department's unwillingness to ask for the evacuation of American citizens of Japanese ancestry.[7]

U.S. Attorney General Biddle, up to February 9, 1942, had authorized FBI raids, arrests of alien suspects, seizures of contraband, and the clearance of certain vital spots of enemy aliens. Except for these crucial spots in California, however, Biddle had opposed mass evacuation of both aliens and American-born citizens of alien parents; instead he had insisted that checks be made of individuals.

In the meantime Lt. Gen. John L. DeWitt, commanding officer of the army's Western Defense Command, had requested that the total Japanese population from Bainbridge Island, from parts of Washington, and from large areas of Oregon and Arizona be removed. On February 9, the attorney general's reply to the secretary of war in regard to General DeWitt's large-scale recommendations contained the following:

> Your recommendation of prohibited areas for Oregon and Washington include (s) the cities of Portland, Seattle, and Tacoma and therefore contemplate (s) a mass evacuation of many thousands. . . . No reasons were given for this mass evacuation. . . . I understand that Lieutenant General DeWitt has been requested to supply the War Department with further details and further material before any action is taken on these recommendations. I shall therefore await your further advice.

[7]Grodzins, pp. 254-60.

. . . The evacuation . . . from this area would, of course, present a problem of very great magnitude. The Department of Justice is not physically equipped to carry out any mass evacuation. It would mean that only the War Department has the equipment and personnel to manage the task. The proclamations directing the Department of Justice to apprehend, and where necessary, evacuate alien enemies, do not, of course, include American citizens of the Japanese race. If they have to be evacuated, I believe that this would have to be done as a military necessity in these particular areas. Such action therefore, should in my opinion, be taken by the War Department and not by the Department of Justice.[8]

The role of another Justice Department official, Mr. Thomas C. Clark, was sketched out by Grodzins. Mr. Clark was to act as coordinator of Justice and War department activities with Federal Security Agency activities. He was also "to act as spokesman for Justice Department views on the West Coast." It was expected that by giving reassurance that all was under control, and that additional action would be unnecessary, he would thereby reduce the popular demand for mass evacuation of the Japanese Americans. Instead, he "took no stand against the growing sentiment in favor of evacuation," but gave reassurance that all necessary steps would be taken and that he would abide by the decisions of the military authorities.[9]

THE FINAL PUSH

On February 11, Mayor Fletcher Bowron of Los Angeles, State Attorney General Warren, and Tom Clark of the U.S. Department of Justice met with General DeWitt. After the meeting Attorney General Warren announced that he felt that the problem was a "military one, not civil." Mayor Bowron said, "I feel that DeWitt is awake to the situation and doing all he can."

The mayor returned to Los Angeles in time to make a Lincoln's Birthday radio address in which he posed the question, "If Lincoln were alive today, what would he do . . . to defend the nation against the Japanese horde . . . the people born on American soil who have secret loyalty to the Japanese Emperor?"

Bowron answered the question as follows: "There isn't a shadow of a doubt but that Lincoln, the mild-mannered man whose memory we regard with almost saint-like reverence, would make

---

[8]Grodzins, pp. 260-61.
[9]Grodzins, pp. 242-43.

short work of rounding up the Japanese and putting them where they could do no harm." He said further: "The removal of all those of Japanese parentage must be effected before it is too late."

On February 12 Walter Lippmann, a nationally known and highly respected columnist, wrote a syndicated column entitled "The Fifth Column on the Coast"; in it he advocated setting aside the civil rights of citizens of Japanese ancestry. He put forth a specious argument that had been used by General DeWitt, Attorney General Warren, and others, which read like this:

Since the outbreak of the Japanese war there has been no important sabotage on the Pacific Coast. From what we know about Hawaii and the fifth column in Europe, this is not, as some have liked to think, a sign that there is nothing to be feared. *It is a sign that the blow is well organized and that it is held back until it can be struck with maximum effect.* [Emphasis supplied.]

When good men like Earl Warren and Walter Lippmann were convinced that such unrealistic thinking was valid, it is proof of the growing panic that had been fostered by the repetition of rumors, racist attacks, and fears of a possible Japanese attack. On February 13 the West Coast congressional delegation — under the goading of Leland Ford, John Costello, A. J. Elliott, and Jack Z. Anderson, all congressmen from California — passed a resolution demanding "immediate evacuation of all persons of Japanese lineage and all others, aliens and citizens alike, whose presence shall be deemed dangerous or inimical to the defense of the United States from all strategic areas."

On February 14 General DeWitt forwarded to the Secretary of War his recommendations on the subject of the "Evacuation of Japanese and other Subversive Persons from the Pacific Coast." After pointing out the probability of attacks on shipping, coastal cities, and vital installations in the coastal area; of air raids; and of sabotage of vital installations, De Witt set forth his convicitions about the nature of Japanese Americans. (See Appendix A. *Final Recommendations . . .* par. 1, b, (2).)

Following this statement DeWitt set forth in detail his formal recommendations, including a request for presidential direction and authority to designate military areas from which all Japanese and all alien enemies or suspected saboteurs of fifth columnists could be excluded. He set forth probable areas of exclusion and proposed "that the Secretary of War provide for the exclusion from such military areas, in his discretion, of the following classes of persons, viz: (a) Japanese aliens, (b) Japanese American citizens, (c) alien enemies other than Japanese aliens, (d) any and all other persons who are suspected, for any reason by the administering military authorities to be actual or potential saboteurs, espionage agents, fifth columnists or subversive persons." In addition, DeWitt provided details regarding proposed procedures. (See Appendix A. *Final Recommendations . . .*, par 2.)

After five more tumultous days, on February 19 the president signed Executive Order No. 9066, which authorized the secretary of war "and the military commanders whom he may from time to time designate . . . to prescribe military areas in such places and of such extent as he or the appropriate military commander may determine, from which any or all persons may be excluded." (See Appendix B.) It seems clear that the president had received a copy of the Cohen, Cox, Rauh memorandum to Attorney General Biddle.

On February 20 Secretary of War Stimson designated General DeWitt as military commander empowered to carry out an evacuation within his command under the terms of Executive Order No. 9066.

On February 21 Congressman John Tolan of Oakland, California, chairman of the House Select Committee on National Defense Migration, arrived in San Francisco to open hearings. These hearings continued until March 12. A few cool heads unsuccessfully tried to stem the tide. Mike Masaoka, national secretary of the Japanese American Citizens League, testified before this committee. Among other things, he said:

If in the judgment of military and Federal authorities, evacuation of Japanese residents from the West Coast is a primary step toward assuring the safety of this nation, we will have no hesitation in complying with the necessities implicit in that judgment. But if, on the other hand, such evacuation is primarily a measure whose surface urgency cloaks the desires of political or other pressure groups who want us to leave merely from motives of self-interest, we feel that we have every right to protest and to demand equitable judgment on our merits as American citizens.[10]

---

[10]WRA Report, *Wartime Exile*, p. 140.

The majority of people who appeared before the committee favored evacuation. Among those in opposition was Louis Goldblatt, secretary of the California State Industrial Union Council, an affiliate of the Congress of Industrial Organizations. Goldblatt presented a forceful statement that included the following:

We naturally go along and concur with all the recommendations that the Government deems necessary to safeguard this territory. We feel, however, that a good deal of this problem has gotten out of hand. Mr. Tolan, inasmuch as both the local and state authorities, instead of becoming bastions of defense of democracy and justice, joined the wolf pack when the cry came out "Let's get the yellow menace." As a matter of fact, we believe the present situation is a great victory for the yellow press and for the fifth column that is operating in this country, which is attempting to convert this war from a war against the Axis Powers into a war against the "yellow peril." We believe there is a large element of that particular factor in this present situation.

I am referring here particularly to the attack against the native-born Japanese, an attack which, as far as we can find out, was whipped up. There was a basis for it because there has always been a basis on the Pacific Coast for suspicion, racial suspicion, which has been well fostered, well bred, particularly by the Hearst newspapers over a period of 20 to 25 years.[11]

On Monday evening, February 23, 1942, an enemy seaborne craft shelled Goleta, California, near Santa Barbara. A memo from J. Edgar Hoover to Attorney General Biddle later confirmed the attack and reported that there was no evidence of ship-to-shore signaling.[12]

In the early hours of February 25, 1942, Los Angeles had a black-out, with anti-aircraft guns brought into use; it was claimed that five unidentified planes had been seen — either Japanese, civilian, or commercial. The War Department stated officially that the alarm was real; the Navy Department stated officially that it was a case of "jittery nerves."[13]

In any case these two incidents brought new demands for action from Congressman Alfred Elliott and others to move all of the Japanese into internment camps. These incidents came at the peak of the pressures and could not have been better timed from the standpoint of the exclusionists.

---

[11]WRA Report, pp. 140-42.
[12]WRA Report, pp. 144-45.
[13]WRA Report, p. 146.

On March 2, 1942, General DeWitt issued Public Proclamation No. 1 designating the western half of the three Pacific Coast states and the southern third of Arizona as a military area and stipulating that all persons of Japanese descent would eventually be removed therefrom. On March 11, General DeWitt established the Wartime Civil Control Administration, with Colonel Karl R. Bendetsen as director, to carry out the evacuation program.

On March 18, President Roosevelt signed Executive Order No. 9102, creating the War Relocation Authority to assist persons evacuated by the military under Executive Order 9066. (See Appendixes B & C.) Milton S. Eisenhower was named Director of the

With baggage stacked, persons of Japanese ancestry await a bus at Wartime Civil Control Administration station. (WRA photo)

WRA. Meanwhile the Congress had been busy, and on March 21 the president signed Public Law 503 (77th Congress), making it a federal offense to violate any order issued by a designated military commander under authority of Executive Order 9066.

On March 23 General DeWitt issued Civilian Exclusion Order No. 1, ordering evacuation of all people of Japanese descent from Bainbridge Island in Puget Sound. On March 27 he issued Public Proclamation No. 4, effective March 29, forbidding further voluntary migration of Japanese and Japanese Americans from the West Coast Military area. This was done on the recommendation of the director of WRA, because of the problems faced by the voluntary evacuees.

To complete the pattern, General DeWitt issued Public Proclamation No. 6, on June 2, forbidding further voluntary migration by people of Japanese descent from the eastern half of California, and simultaneously announcing that all such people would eventually be removed from this area to WRA centers. The removal took place on August 7. Earlier nearly 5,000 evacuees had moved out voluntarily from Military Area No. I into eastern California. When the voluntary evacuees were frozen in place by Public Proclamation No. 6 and then moved to relocation centers by the army, there was quite naturally much bitterness on the part of these persons who had tried to be cooperative and patriotic.

*   *   *

It is difficult for anyone who has not experienced the rampant emotions and the hysteria of a wartime period to believe that a situation such as that fomented on the West Coast could happen in these United States. But it did happen! Furthermore, many of us remember the same kind of hysteria during World War I that led to the harassment of many people of German ancestry, the renaming of German foods and towns and streets, and the banning of German music. The late H. V. Kaltenborn, who as a young man had suffered discrimination in his home state of Wisconsin, was constructive and sympathetic to the Japanese and the WRA in his wartime broadcasts.

PART 2

Life in the Relocation Centers

CHAPTER 4

Organizing the Relocation Centers

WHEN I BECAME DIRECTOR of the War Relocation Authority on June 17, 1942, the three-month-old agency was already engaged on a task without precedent in American history. Although I had little previous knowledge of Japanese American people, I soon learned that the complex program under way consisted of three important phases demanding immediate attention.

First and foremost was the problem of caring for roughly 110,000 people, ranging in age from newborn infants to persons of 65 years and older, who were being moved into ten relocation centers between May and November. Second was the longer-range, less immediately pressing, objective of getting these people out of the relocation centers and re-established in normal communities. Third was a problem not anticipated when the mass evacuation of Japanese Americans from the West Coast was decided upon in the earlier part of 1942. At that time it was expected that removal of the Japanese Americans from their homes to assembly centers and relocation centers would still the public outcry against them and permit a restoration of calmer perspectives. It had not, however, worked out that way. When I moved into the WRA director's chair in mid-June, the very elements of the West Coast press and public which had been most insistent in demanding complete evacuation, five and six months earlier, were still in full voice and engaged in persistent, vicious sniping at the evacuees and at WRA.

The first problem concerned the handling of the displaced people and their actions, reactions, and frustrations. More than 70,000 of the total 110,000 evacuees were American born and thus full-fledged citizens of the United States. During a six-month period most of these evacuees were moved first from their homes into army-managed assembly centers within the exclusion area of the three Pacific Coast states; then after a few weeks or months these people were moved a second time, into bare, dusty, unattractive, barracks-type dwellings in ten relocation centers scattered from California to Arkansas and from Idaho to Arizona. A few persons came from eastern California or from adjoining states without ever having been in assembly centers.

Two relocation centers were located in California — Man-

Arrivals from the Puyallup assembly center are being registered by fellow evacuee clerks on arrival at Minidoka, Idaho, relocation center.

Young evacuees carry their personal belongings into their newly constructed quarters in the Granada relocation center, Colorado. (WRA photo)

zanar in the Owens Valley and Tule Lake near the Oregon border. Two centers were in Arizona — Colorado River (more generally known by its post office name of Poston) near Parker, and Gila River (or Rivers) south of Phoenix. In Idaho, the Minidoka (or Hunt) center was near Twin Falls. Central Utah (or Topaz) was in desert country south of Salt Lake City. In Wyoming the Heart Mountain center was near Cody. The Granada (or Amache) center in Colorado was near Lamar. The two Arkansas centers — Jerome (or Denson) and Rohwer — were located in the eastern part of the state.

The period of moving in and getting settled ranged from May 1942 to March 1943. For the most part the dazed, confused, and frustrated evacuees arrived amidst the turmoil of partly completed centers that the army had constructed of wood and tar paper. The buildings were of the temporary barracks type constructed to house soldiers in dormitory style. No cooking or plumbing facilities existed in these barracks. In each block were a mess hall and a building that provided latrines, showers, and laundry facilities.

Quarters for evacuees of Japanese ancestry at Manzanar, California, relocation center. High Sierras are in the background.

Most centers were surrounded with woven-wire and barbed-wire fences, with watch towers for the army guards. These centers, located in out-of-the-way places, largely desert or wastelands, were desolate and forbidding — especially during the early months.

Here were ten abnormal cities having populations ranging from 7,000 to 20,000 each. The majority of the evacuees were between 10 and 30 years of age, with a large contingent of teenagers.

Within these centers we were faced with most or all of the problems of the small city and with some problems that were new and different. We were faced first with the problem of providing for each center a competent staff of people who not only had the necessary skills but were also tolerant and understanding in their dealings with the evacuees. In this latter respect we were not always successful in the early months, as some of the early staff members were not able to meet the problems and the emotional impact of the WRA

program adequately. Consequently we had some separations or resignations before the program was well under way.

In addition to housing problems, there were the problems of feeding the total population, employment and wages, community government, internal security, medical care, education, merchandising and community services, industry, agriculture, religious worship, and recreation.

FEEDING THE MULTITUDE

The problem of feeding thousands of people of varying ages and tastes in central block mess halls was immediate and difficult. In addition to the normal army mess hall requirements, we had the problems of baby bottles, baby foods, and invalid foods as well as the problem of providing the kind of foods to which the older Japanese were accustomed. Fortunately, the army authorities agreed to

Lunch time for Japanese evacuees at the Manzanar relocation center.

supply our purchased foods through their quartermaster corps, and they did an excellent job once we and they learned what our needs were.

A staff steward was placed in charge of mess operation at every center, but the cooking was done by a kitchen crew of evacuees. We adopted the policy early that as much food as possible would be provided through agricultural production on center lands. Vegetables were produced at all centers, and during the three or more years of the centers' existence the total yield was 110 million pounds with an estimated gross value of $3,650,000. All centers had hog farms of varying size, and all but one maintained some type of poultry project. The pork products produced were valued at $1,500,000 and the poultry products at $470,000.

Dairy herds were maintained only at Gila River, Arizona, and for a time at Granada, Colorado. Beef cattle herds at Central Utah,

Evacuee in her hobby garden. Vegetables were grown in 10-by-50-foot plots between rows of barracks. Below: Loading seed potatoes onto a feed rotary potato planter on the 500-acre farm at Tule Lake center, California.

Granada, Gila River, and Manzanar produced 3,500,000 pounds of beef valued at $750,000.

The WRA policy provided that the menus for all centers should be based on a ration cost of not more than 45 cents per person daily, that all wartime rationing regulations be strictly observed, and that food in the centers should not exceed in quality or quantity what the local civilian population could obtain in the market. In spite of these stringent policies, the race baiters found the supposedly over-generous feeding of the evacuees a favorite subject for fanciful rumors and fantastic claims.

INTERNAL SECURITY

Another problem demanding immediate decision was the matter of internal security inside the centers. The army had maintained a large force of about 40 or 50 or more security officers at each of the assembly centers, and some of the army staff were quite insistent that the WRA adopt the same policy. WRA policy provided that internal security was the responsibility of the project director; it authorized the appointment of a non-evacuee internal security officer at each of the centers, but it also provided for the organization of an internal security force to be recruited from the resident evacuee population. This force was responsible for the arrest of all offenders.

The WRA policy specifically prohibited the administration at any center from establishing an intelligence or investigative unit. If a project director felt that investigation of subversive activities was needed, he was instructed to call on the nearest office of the Federal Bureau of Investigation. This part of the policy led to some unhappy and at times chaotic situations in some of the centers, since, understandably, great antipathy toward the FBI existed among the evacuees. Informers were called "dogs." Furthermore, there were times when the FBI employees came into the centers without even notifying the project director, to question or occasionally to remove someone. This approach was most troublesome.

In December 1942, WRA asked the FBI to assign a competent person to study the law enforcement problem at the centers and to make recommendations. The study was made, and the FBI report was submitted in mid-March 1943. The report contained numerous recommendations covering almost every phase of project operations;

much of this we did not anticipate and considered gratuitous. However, on the more technical aspects of the organization and management of police work, the recommendations were helpful, and many were quickly incorporated in WRA security procedures.

The problem of internal security at the centers was simplified because we were dealing with a group of people who had achieved a high degree of intra-group discipline and had established a most noteworthy record of law-abiding behavior in the prewar period. On the other hand, difficulties grew out of the fact that these people had been suspected, scrutinized, questioned, and picked up for questioning to the point where they had almost developed a mass neurosis on the subject of investigations and "informers." Because of these fears, emotions, and the resulting contempt for recognized authority — especially among the adolescents and embittered young men — we had an unprecedented situation for a Japanese community. In some centers — especially the three or four that were initiated early in 1942 — gangs were formed to take care of informers and those too close to the administration. After a time this situation subsided in most of the centers, except at Tule Lake after segregation there of persons appearing to have pro-Japanese sympathies.

We in the WRA soon learned that the only solution to this type of situation lay in plans for removing the evacuees from the abnormal and highly charged atmosphere of the centers — where it was impossible to escape from such pressures — and restoring them to an environment where their ordinary law-abiding and cooperative impulses could reassert themselves. On the whole, the crime records in the centers were highly favorable when compared with crime rates in outside communities.

The centers had of course some gamblers, thieves, prostitutes, gangsters, and even a murder or two. However, these elements were no more typical in a relocation center community than in the average small city. In the WRA final report, entitled *A Story of Human Conservation,* Morrill Tozier, who did the major work of preparing this report, wrote:

The great majority of center residents were a psychologically bruised, badly puzzled and frequently apathetic group of people. But during their stay at the centers they continued their previous practices of religious worship, tried to achieve some semblance of order and dignity in their broken lives, and frequently showed an almost pathetic eagerness to hold their families together and to work back toward their prewar social and economic status. They bore little resemblance to the sly, ruthless, emperor-worshipping fanatics which some sensational newspaper and magazine writers, such as Ray Richards and James R. Young of the Hearst Enterprises, persisted in creating as the prototype of relocation center residents. But then, neither Mr. Richards nor Mr. Young ever bothered to visit a relocation center.[1]

The internal security policies underwent changes from time to time, as did some of our other policies, as experience indicated that revisions were needed.

In February 1943 we spelled out in considerable detail *(1)* the procedure to be followed in organizing an evacuee police force, *(2)* the rules to govern the making of arrests, and *(3)* the types of offenses that might be punished by disciplinary action of the project director. Thirty-five types of offenses were listed which were not felonies under state or federal law and which if not covered by ordinances of the community council would have to be dealt with by direct administrative action.

Any such cases covered by council ordinances came before the evacuee judicial commission for action or referral. Arrangements were made for jail space in nearby communities instead of maintaining a jail at each center. Employment of non-evacuee police in addition to the internal security officer was authorized; however, in all centers except the Tule Lake segregation center there were not more than two or three non-evacuee police. The procedure for arrests was framed in line with general nationwide policy and practice governing the issuance of warrants; WRA regulations stipulated that no resident could be arrested without a warrant from the project director unless caught in the act of committing a proscribed offense by a member of the internal security force.

COMMUNITY GOVERNMENT

From the beginning the WRA staff felt that the evacuees should participate in governing their own communities to the extent possible under the mandate given to WRA and to the extent that the people could be encouraged to accept responsibilities that could properly

---

[1]WRA Report, *A Story of Human Conservation*, p. 95.

be theirs. A division of opinion existed in the WRA only on the question as to whether we should await the development of an interest among the evacuees or whether we should proceed by laying down a framework of rules and letting the evacuees take it from there.

The general outlines of a policy were first set forth in an overall policy statement on May 29, 1942, and spelled out in more detail on June 5. This tentative policy provided for a temporary council consisting of one representative elected from each block, an executive committee, and a judicial committee. The elected officers were to be American citizens, and all residents 16 years of age and over were eligible to vote.

This policy, however, was not long in effect. On August 13-15 a general WRA policy conference was held in San Francisco, involving all Washington and regional key staff members and the project directors who had been appointed up to that time. The policy on evacuee self-government was one of those revised as a result of this session. The revised policy issued on August 24, 1942, provided that all residents 18 years (rather than 16 as previously) and over would have voting rights.

The question of whether the Issei should be eligible to hold elective office was debated at length, and the limitation providing that only U.S. citizens should serve was maintained, although Issei were made eligible for appointive positions. The councils to be elected were to have two main functions: *(1)* to serve as a two-way channel of communication between the resident community and the administration, and *(2)* to adopt and enforce ordinances and regulations in the interest of community welfare and security. Ordinances dealing with offenses were to include only those offenses not classified as felonies under the laws of the state, and each project director was given authority to veto any ordinance of the council which was in excess of its prescribed functions or in conflict with state or federal regulations.

By the end of 1942 eight of the ten centers had elected temporary councils, and seven had established commissions to draw up charters for community government.

At the Poston center the councils for each of the three camp units resigned under pressure from the community after the project meeting and general strike in Unit One in November 1942.

Manzanar was the only center that never elected a council but depended upon the elected block managers to serve the community. Because the block in each of the centers was the basic residential unit, block loyalties were important in center operations. Normally a block would include 12 residential barracks grouped around a common mess hall, a bath-and-laundry building, and a recreation barracks. A typical block consisted of about 250 people.

Early in 1943 the whole policy was reviewed again, and as a result the provision excluding Issei from eligibility to elective office was removed. This removed some of the evacuee objections to the earlier policy and gave new impetus to the community government movement.

In all centers except Manzanar, block managers were appointed generally by the project director. They had three major functions: *(1)* to assure that everday needs were met for such things as brooms, mops, soaps, and light bulbs, *(2)* to supervise the general maintenance of grounds and structures, and *(3)* to bring to the attention of the residents any official announcements and regulations issued by the administration. This last function overlapped somewhat the function of the council. Most of the block managers were highly respected Issei, and they were influential in center affairs. They were paid the going center wage of $16 per month.

EMPLOYMENT, COMPENSATION, AND INDUSTRY

The problems relating to employment, compensation, and center industry were most complex. On the one hand, a growing wartime manpower shortage ultimately became a key factor in our out-of-center relocation program. But following the meeting of governors of the western states at Salt Lake City on April 7, 1942, it was assumed that general outside relocation would not be possible for some time at least, since all of the governors except Governor Ralph Carr of Colorado were most vehement against relocation within their states.

It was clear that prolonged idleness would sharpen the frustration of the evacuees and probably bring public censure down upon them. It was also clear that the future of the evacuees was dependent in large part on their activities during the war emergency. The problem was complicated further by the fact that almost any industry planned for the centers would be opposed by manufacturers outside if it in any way competed with their wares.

Another problem involved the attempt to initiate a work corps, which was contemplated in the executive order establishing WRA. It was to be patterned in principle on the Civilian Conservation Corps. The theory was that those persons enrolled might be assigned to useful work such as land development, building irrigation structures, or large-scale food production. Others would engage within the centers in making products such as tents, camouflage nets, cartridge belts, and other items needed by the armed forces.

The first enrollment test for the work corps was tried at the Portland assembly center in May 1942 as a prerequisite to work in the beet fields of eastern Oregon. Only 15 men out of hundreds in the assembly center signed up. It was obvious that the evacuees did not like the work corps idea.

By the last of May the WRA had hit upon a formula that it hoped would be a stimulant to work performance, would not be costly, and would be acceptable to the public. The idea was that the operations at the centers would be partnership enterprises between the WRA and the work corps. WRA was to furnish the basic essentials for living and would try to develop an adequate number of work opportunities. The evacuee members of the corps would work toward three objectives: *(1)* to provide for the living requirements of the whole evacuee community to the fullest extent possible, *(2)* to develop land in the vicinity of the centers and improve its productive value, and *(3)* to produce a supply of agricultural and manufactured products surplus to the center needs for sale in the open market.

The policy further provided that a full accounting would be kept of maintenance costs on the one hand and the income from the sale of products surplus to the center needs on the other, and appraisals would be made of the increases in capital values of land and structures. At the end of each financial year, in case the balance sheets showed a profit, this profit was to be paid to the members of the work corps in the form of increased cash advances.

The cash advances, so called, were established at $12 a month for unskilled labor, $16 per month for the more responsible clerical and community service jobs, and $19 per month for highly skilled and professional employees. Those residents eligible for the work corps who did not join were to be charged $20 per month to cover the cost of food, shelter, medical care, and education for themselves and each of their dependents. In mid-June, just previous to the change in directors, these charges were eliminated for all except those engaged in private employment at prevailing wages.

An earlier approach to a wage scale brought a real burst of fire from the Hearst newspapers when on March 23 they charged that evacuees at Manzanar — at that time still under army control — were being paid from $50 to $94 per month, while American privates in the armed forces were receiving $21 per month. Although the director explained that deductions for room and board would bring the pay in line with army pay, there were still skeptics.

Because of complicated accounting, differences in productive capacity at the various centers, and the prospect of objection from private operators on the outside, the partnership enterprise idea was dropped for good before the policy conference in mid-August.

The policy statement that was issued following the mid-August conference provided (1) that the $12, $16, and $19 per month which had earlier been considered to be advances become the basic wage rates for work actually performed at the centers; (2) that in addition a cash allowance of $2.00 to $3.75 a month to cover the cost of clothing would be provided for each employed evacuee and each dependent; (3) that all evacuees assigned to jobs at the centers should be automatically enrolled in the work corps; (4) that unemployment compensation would be provided at rates from $1.50 to $4.75 per month for unemployed evacuees out of work through no fault of their own, and for each of their dependents; and (5) that evacuees working on privately sponsored projects at prevailing wages should receive only the standard center pay rates, while the balance paid in wages by the employer would be deposited in a trust fund to be administered for the benefit of the whole community.

The basic framework of this policy statement was maintained throughout the operation of the centers, except for the provision about prevailing wages, which was eliminated after contracts were completed. Provision 3, obviously a face saver, was almost the last dying gasp of the limping work corps idea.

Certain changes in industrial policy were made within a few months. The decision to encourage relocation outside the centers led to the curtailment of the industrial enterprises in October 1942. On December 15 the work corps idea was quietly terminated. The policy statement on center industries which was finally issued on

January 26, 1943, provided that all "industries, except those operated privately under previous commitments, would be operated as WRA projects." It also prohibited the establishment of evacuee-sponsored production enterprises and specified that all industrial workers (except those in the net factories) would be paid at standard WRA rates; it emphasized that preference should be given to those enterprises that offered the greatest opportunity for vocational training.

Two camouflage-net enterprises at the Arizona centers, the only private-enterprise projects initiated, were discontinued in May 1943 at the completion of the contracts. The camouflage-net factory at Manzanar was supervised by the Army Corps of Engineers and proved to be most troublesome. It was discontinued in early December 1942, after the Manzanar disturbance. A silk screen poster shop at the Granada center and a model warship factory at the Gila River center both made important contributions to the training program of the Navy Department.

During the summer and fall of 1942, plans were developed for a number of industrial enterprises, including a proposed tent factory at Tule Lake and a lens-grinding plant and a pottery establishment at Heart Mountain; but none of these actually got under way.

The bulk of enterprises established at the centers were of the internal-consumption type to meet the needs of the center residents or of community management. Among these were garment factories at Manzanar, Heart Mountain, and Minidoka; cabinet shops at Tule Lake, Manzanar, and Heart Mountain; sawmills at Heart Mountain and Jerome; a mattress factory at Manzanar; a bakery at Tule Lake; and carpentry and furniture repair shops and food processing plants for Japanese-type foods at all centers. The agricultural enterprises already have been described.

As a result of the policy established in August 1942, which emphasized an obligation to provide jobs for all able-bodied adult evacuees who expressed a desire to work, we were faced with some glaring abuses within a very few months. Over-staffing and the creation of boondoggling type jobs occurred at some centers, and the encouragement of slack work habits was found among many evacuees. While these abuses were building up, the resettlement program outside of the centers was moving very well, with work opportunities developing for evacuees in most sections of the country.

A prize-winning cabinet. A carpenter's plane was the first prize in a furniture-building contest in which all pieces of furniture were made from scrap lumber.

In view of these developments, we took steps in the spring of 1943 to tighten up the center employment procedures. Unemployment compensation was eliminated except for those who had been assigned to jobs but were unable to work because of illness. All centers were ordered to reduce their evacuee payrolls by 30 percent by July 1, 1943. Evacuee jobs were classified as essential or desirable, and other jobs were eliminated. Food and lodging were provided whether evacuees were employed or not.

Some of the center directors decided to make the cuts much sooner than the three months allowed for the operation, and in some cases too little consultation with the affected workers resulted in considerable opposition and protest by the evacuees. Nevertheless the revisions in policy and the tighter procedures had the desired effect.

This does not mean that all problems disappeared. There was the continuous problem of encouraging efficiency in a situation where little was to be gained by all-out effort. Of course many continued at top speed and took real pride in their work. Strikes or walkouts occurred on such jobs as unloading coal or handling garbage. On a couple of occasions the work stoppage was much more general and was center-wide. Work stoppages on jobs essential to the residents as a whole were easily cured by pressure from the community. Punitive measures were not resorted to by the WRA administration, since these were not prison camps. On the contrary, in the case of jobs essential to the welfare of the whole community, we depended on community pressure to get the work done.

In view of the stepping up of the relocation program, a paradox developed that affected the WRA program constantly. On the

Volunteers load trucks from the coal gondolas for delivery to barracks. Approximately four carloads of coal a day were required to provide heat for residents at Heart Mountain center in Wyoming. (WRA photo)

one hand we were at all times striving for the greatest possible efficiency, economy, and community service in the operation of the centers. On the other hand after October 1942 we were encouraging the most energetic, most skillful, and best adjusted evacuee workers to leave the centers and to take jobs in ordinary American communities. Whenever there was a conflict between these two objectives, relocation outside always had priority. This, of course, affected many important areas of service — such as hospital services, newspaper publication, and other areas of skilled occupations — but we managed to carry on in spite of these shortages.

BUSINESS ENTERPRISES AND SERVICES

Provision was needed in the centers for such services as shoe repair, cleaning and pressing, watch repair, and the host of others that residents take for granted in a normal city. Three possible plans were considered: (1) WRA management of shops and services, (2) granting of concessions to private operators, or (3) management by the residents on a consumer cooperative basis. The third plan was favored by most of the staff, and in early May Congressman Jerry Voorhis of California wrote to Director Eisenhower recommending the cooperative approach.

The May 29 policy statement provided that residents of the centers should be encouraged by the local officials to organize their own consumer enterprises to be operated on the cooperative non-profit plan. It stated that WRA would provide instructions and guidance and would consider applications for loans from any center cooperatives appropriately organized and managed.

The policy statement that emerged from the policy conference on August 25 not only authorized the establishment of consumer cooperatives but expressly prohibited the establishment of any other type of consumer services. The statement provided for the organization of one community-wide association in each center, and it set up definite standards of organization, membership participation, merchandising, pricing, and dividend distribution. It provided further that the accounts of each association should be regularly audited, and it specified the requirements to be met before loans would be granted. Temporary enterprises were authorized which were to be managed directly by the center administration to meet the needs until an evacuee-managed association could be established.

Manzanar was the only center that established an evacuee-managed association before the end of 1942. In the meantime the volume of business handled by the temporary enterprises mounted to levels much higher than we had expected.

On December 22, 1942, a revised policy statement was issued which provided that each enterprise association would reimburse WRA for salaries and allowances paid to all employees of the temporary enterprises retroactively from the time of their establishment and also that the associations should pay rent for the WRA building space and equipment.

Many of the evacuees protested this policy on the grounds that the temporary enterprises were none of their business and that it was not fair to ask them to assume the obligations for salaries over a period of months previous to their establishment. There was no serious objection to paying rent, but they did contend that the rents proposed were too high. After review, in late February 1943, WRA lowered the rates to be charged. There were difficulties in getting associations organized in two or three centers, but in spite of this, by July 1, 1943, all ten centers had evacuee enterprises under way.

All centers except Heart Mountain followed the procedures recommended for consumer cooperatives. Because of disputes among the evacuees and protest over the original rental rates proposed, Heart Mountain residents refused to organize a cooperative enterprise association. Instead a trust association was formed in January 1943 as an interim device to manage the enterprises until a cooperative association could be established. This trust association continued in effect throughout the life of the center. The main difference in this arrangement was that the community had a less active part in the formulation of management policies. Patronage dividends or refunds however were provided at all ten centers.

These ten cooperative associations operated a total of 270 different enterprises or services, an average of 27 in each center, ranging from a single-employee watch-repair shop or shoe-repair shop to moderate-sized department stores stocking a wide variety of goods with many employees.

All told, these ten enterprises did a gross business of $21,890,-167 and paid out $2,298,820 in refunds or patronage dividends. They provided employment and training for more than 7,000 center residents.

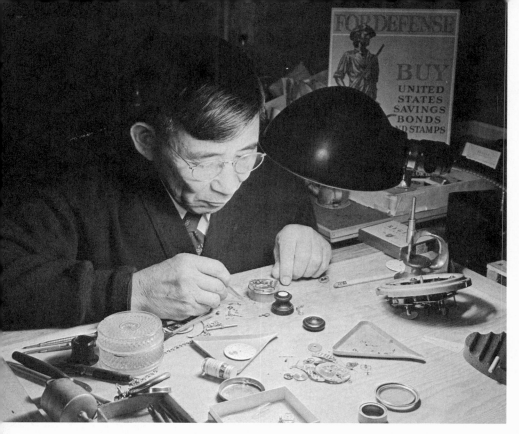

Former Seattle watchmaker serves as head watchmaker at
Minidoka, Idaho, relocation center. (WRA photo)

No loans were made, because the residents were able to acquire
their initial stocks of merchandise on credit. Generally speaking,
these associations were ably managed and proved to be a highly
profitable venture for all concerned.

EDUCATION

Schools through the high school level were established in all
centers. Teacher qualifications, curriculum content, and methods
of instruction were developed in close consultation with state educational authorities and in line with the recognized standards of the
state within which each center was located. As a result, all of the
schools except at Tule Lake were accredited by the state authorities.
This enabled the pupils to transfer to outside schools generally without loss of credit. More than 30,000 students were enrolled in the
school systems during early months of center operation, and more
than 7,000 were graduated from the center high schools.

Unfortunately school buildings and equipment were not provided for in the original construction of the barracks and other
facilities by the army engineers. This was most unfortunate, because,
during the first year or more, classes were held in barrack-type recreation halls without partitions in most cases; and desks or tables and
chairs were not always available at the beginning. At the Poston
(Arizona) center, which consisted of three units and was the largest
of the ten centers, schools were opened in October 1942 with no
tables, chairs, books, paper, or blackboards. The teachers and pupils
made tables, and blackboards were improvised from hard lumber
painted black.

Teacher recruitment and training were very real problems. The
appointed teachers from the outside were recruited at Poston from

Two young Nisei evacuee woodworkers construct benches for the
grade and high schools at Heart Mountain center. (WRA photo)

Clay toys command concentrated attention of nursery school children at Heart Mountain center. (WRA photo)

Indian schools, from the ranks of returning missionaries who had been in Japan, and from any other source available. In spite of the problems, nearly a hundred teachers were recruited from the outside, and more than 100 evacuees with two years or more of college were pressed into service as assistant teachers. Because of the teacher shortage, these "assistants" were called upon to assume a full teaching load in many cases.

The whole month of September 1942 was devoted to teacher training for both the appointed and the evacuee staff. Extension courses for teachers were pursued throughout the year, and in 1943 a summer session of four to six weeks was devoted to teacher training.

The curriculum at Poston followed the California standard studies for the most part, because of the expectation that most of the students would return to that state. The only vocational subjects were agriculture and automobile mechanics. The latter was helpful and probably essential to the maintenance of the trucks and cars which were required for center operations.

At Poston there were 5,200 students at the beginning, and the number in the third year was reduced to about 3,600.

Four- and five-year-olds were enrolled in nursery schools and kindergarten, under the supervision of Mary Lind, a trained teacher who did an excellent job with all evacuee teachers.

Instrumental music was taught only in Unit 3 at Poston.

Achievement testing was carried out the first year and again the third year, using the Stanford tests.

The acceleration from the first to the third year was tremendous. In the beginning English comprehension and mathematical reasoning ranked low, but the ranking of the pupils in the third year tests showed that they were above their grade level in nearly every subject in which the tests were given.

Extra-curricular activities included student council, class officers, high school annuals, and athletics — which included touch football, basketball, and baseball.

There was an active P.T.A. whose officers were mostly Issei or Nisei fluent in both Japanese and English.

At Poston the school buildings at Units 1 and 2 were built of sun-dried adobe bricks. The whole operation of preparing the adobe and building the schools was the work of evacuees. This was unique, and in one respect at least it avoided a very real problem — namely that of securing wartime priorities for construction materials. Poston, like other centers, continued to hold classes in barracks through the first year, and through the first two years for the high school.

Laboratory equipment was generally scarce or improvised until the third year. The biology teachers utilized the natural phenomena around the centers, such as irrigation ditches, streams, and other areas which provided specimens. Some of the best teaching was provided by evacuee college students or graduates in the fields of science and mathematics.

In addition to the regular curriculum, much time was devoted to discussion with students about relocation — what to wear, how to act, and how to meet the other problems to be faced.

The problems and procedures varied somewhat in the various centers, but all centers had some common problems such as teacher recruitment, training, and supervision, as well as the need to utilize temporary and inadequate quarters and equipment during the early months. In spite of all of these frustrations, however, the schools did an amazingly good job under very difficult conditions — thanks to the interest generally shown among the students and their parents, and the dedication of the teachers, including the evacuees who served full time as assistant teachers and who were paid at the project rate of $19 per month.

When WRA closed up shop in June 1946, the school records were turned over to the Office of Education. For four or five years, until the early 1950's, the full-time service of one person was required to meet requests for transcripts and other information.

The Office of Education provided two trained staff members on detail to assist WRA, and they were most helpful. Dr. Kelly Ade handled most of the contacts with the state and local authorities required from the national level. Mr. Nelson Viles was invaluable to us in the field of school administrative matters, such as budget preparation, the securing of equipment, and related matters.

MISCELLANEOUS SERVICES

Medical care was provided in center hospitals for all residents. These hospitals had a capacity of 200 beds, on the average. They were well equipped for the most part, but there was a severe short-

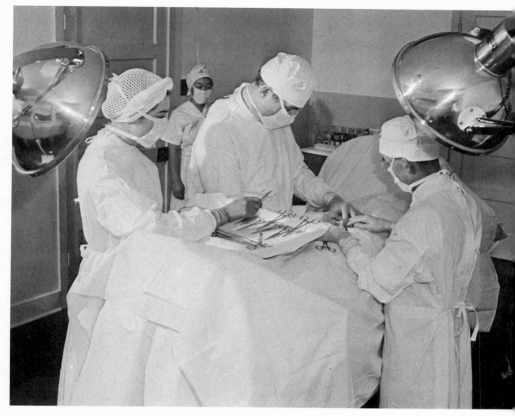

Physicians perform an emergency appendectomy in one of the two hospitals at Granada relocation center. (WRA photo)

age of qualified nursing personnel. The hospitals were planned after the army "theater of operations" type, and the long corridors did not add to the efficiency.

When I as director visited the individual centers, I made it a practice to visit each ward, each operating room, and all other cubicles, and it seemed to me that I walked ten miles during each visit. The hospitals were generally under the supervision of a non-evacuee doctor but staffed otherwise by evacuee doctors. At two or three of the centers the whole medical staff were evacuees. The health record on the whole was quite comparable with that of normal communities of similar size. Influenza epidemics occurred at two centers in the winter of 1943-44.

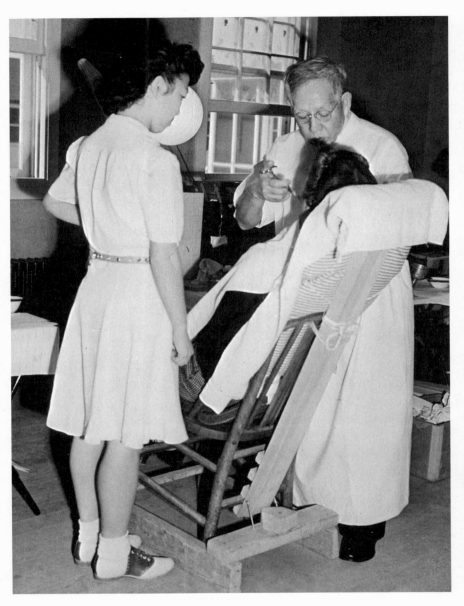

Despite makeshift equipment and temporary arrangements, a former Los Angeles dentist continues to perform the duties of his profession at Granada relocation center. (WRA photo)

A rather high incidence of peptic ulcers was found at most of the centers, which was not surprising when we consider the tensions and frustrations that most of the residents experienced during the early months. Undoubtedly many of the residents received better medical care during this period than ever before. There were reasons! The professional care was excellent; it was free; and the center residents had time to go to the doctor or the clinic when ill.

The welfare services, provided for residents without adequate means of support as well as for orphans and the handicapped, were similar to those furnished by the normal city.

A special children's village was maintained at the Manzanar center for orphans who were evacuated from orphanages on the West Coast. Of the 100 orphans who had been residents of the village, 84 were placed in private homes, 14 were returned to institutions, and two graduated at age 18.

Evacuee children enjoy a summer afternoon in the mountain creek flowing through the desert on the border of the Manzanar, California, relocation center.

A practice game is played between members of the Chick-a-dee softball team, which was kept intact when the players were evacuated from their Los Angeles homes to the Manzanar relocation center.

In view of the inflammable nature of the center buildings, the lack of experienced firemen among the residents, and a shortage of equipment, the centers maintained a remarkable record of efficiency. Heart Mountain won first place in a Wyoming statewide competition in 1944. Granada won second place in Colorado in a similar contest in fire-fighting skills. Except for one or two experienced supervisors, the departments were manned by evacuees who not only proved themselves effective firemen under trying conditions but also received excellent training.

COMMUNITY ACTIVITIES

Athletics, community theaters, flower-arrangement classes, adult English classes, and other organized leisure-time activities were embraced by the residents of the centers. The YMCA, YWCA, Boy Scouts, Girl Scouts, and Campfire Girls were all most helpful in advising in regard to these programs. Baseball led all other activities in interest, with some of the centers having as many as 100 teams.

Many of the older men enjoyed playing goh, a Japanese game similar to checkers.

All centers had community newspapers, published both in English and Japanese. These publications were supervised by the center information officer, but the editors and staffs were all evacuees. At three of the centers — Manzanar, Minidoka, and Heart Mountain — the newspapers were printed and managed by the community enterprise associations. At the other centers the pages were mimeographed. There was a minimum of supervision and almost no censorship.

Staff of the *Manzanar Free Press* at work. This mimeographed newspaper, published twice weekly, was printed mostly in English, with but one page translated into Japanese.

The policy regarding provision for religious worship was simple and satisfactory. A building was provided for services, and the residents were free to worship as they pleased. Schedules were established for the various services in order to avoid conflicts.

In spite of the strong pressures from various religious groups to establish separate churches, all such requests were refused, and the policy was maintained throughout. A large portion of the Issei evacuees were Buddhists and were served by their Buddhist priests. The same opportunities for worship were provided for both the Buddhists and the Christians.

Relatives and friends bid a final sad farewell to one of their midst.

CHAPTER 5

Dissatisfactions, Problems, and Crises

AS AN AID TO THE PROJECT DIRECTORS and to the national office, the reports on the reactions and crosscurrents within the center communities were prepared, for the most part, by community analysts principally trained as social anthropologists. One analyst was assigned to each center for the purpose of studying the social structure, reporting trends, and identifying the evacuees' most significant reactions.

GENERAL DISSATISFACTIONS

When the first four centers — Manzanar, Poston, Tule Lake, and Gila River — began their efforts at community living, the policies of the WRA were tentative and incomplete. This fact undoubtedly had a bearing on the later crises and turmoil in these centers. At the time of moving in, the centers were bare, dusty, dirty, unfinished, and isolated. As a result, life there has been described as having begun with a feeling of desolation in the midst of isolation.

A pattern of apathy and discouragement appeared, particularly among the younger men and women. A sizeable number of the young men, American citizens, felt rejected by their government, and they were bitter about this rejection.

In those early days, in general, a division existed between the

evacuees and the Caucasian members of the center staff. Dissatisfaction was quite general in regard to crowded and unpartitioned
housing in the barracks, difference in furniture supplied to staff, and
the fact that positions held by evacuees were almost all subordinate
ones. The evacuees were upset by the lack of freedom, the army's
search of packages and goods arriving (for contraband), the wage
scale, and the slowness in getting the pay into the hands of evacuee
employees.

The residents of the centers comprised three main groups. The
Issei, who were the elders, had been born in Japan and made up the
alien contingent; most of them had come to the United States during
the first decade of the century. The Nisei, the second generation,
were American-born and citizens of the United States. The Kibei
also were American-born second generation but had had much of
their education in Japan and in many cases were more Japanese than
were the Issei. This division of culture led to wide differences in
points of view, especially between the Nisei and the Kibei.

The center residents were easy prey for the rumormongers.
Anxieties increased, especially after the first two or three months
during which most of the occupants were busy trying to make the
block livable. The lack of freedom led to uncertainties, in a setting
where rumors were easily believed to be fact. There were worries
about possible food shortages, about deaths, and about rumored
mismanagement in the hospitals. There were speculations and worries about draft status, concern as to whether the residents were
prisoners of war, wondering as to who would benefit from the land
development by evacuees, uneasiness about the possibility of deportation, and concern as to what was next in view of past treatment and
the continuing demands of outside pressure groups.

The crowded living quarters and the communal life with common mess halls, latrines, and laundries led to loss of family controls.
Family differences grew in part out of the fact that the husband was
no longer the breadwinner. Much voluntary sorting and moving
took place as new barracks became available. Such matters as the
use of space for playgrounds versus fish ponds or vegetable gardens,
the decorating of mess halls, and the plantings around the barracks
were subject to joint decision. Many crosscurrents existed, and from
the standpoint of smoothly operating communities it was unfortunate

that most of the pre-evacuation leaders of the Japanese communities had been placed in internment camps as precautionary moves by the Department of Justice. As a result it was necessary that new leaders emerge, and this was sometimes a painful process.

During the first two to four months, especially in the first three centers, gangs began to form and beatings became one of the center problems. At the same time, in the face of increased outside hostility, 10,000 evacuees left these centers for outside farm labor in the beet and cotton fields. This outward movement, while good in itself, drained off some of the most constructively aggressive and active pro-American young men, thus making it easier for the disgruntled and the hoodlums to attempt their power plays.

The strongly pro-American Japanese American Citizens League, which had been in existence for more than ten years and which remained intact in spite of evacuation, held a meeting of local chapter leaders in the fall of 1942 in Salt Lake City. All but seven of the 50 local chapters were located in the evacuated area — many in the centers themselves. The chapter leaders passed a resolution endorsing the restoration of the right of Nisei to be drafted and to serve in the armed forces; they also passed a resolution in support of the War Relocation Authority. Following this action, when the leaders returned to their centers some were badly beaten by gangs.

The wide variety of anxieties, crosscurrents, and hatreds born out of bitterness led to crises in two of the centers in November and early December of 1942.

THE POSTON INCIDENT

About November 12, I visited the Poston Center near Parker, Arizona. During my visit I made a speech announcing the WRA policy of all-out relocation outside of the centers and the abandonment of plans to establish further industry at the centers, except for those industries that would serve the communities.

Then I learned that John Collier, Commissioner of the Bureau of Indian Affairs, whose agency was operating this particular center under contract with WRA, only a few weeks before had made a speech with which my statement was in direct conflict. Collier had discussed the importance of the stability of the community and the opportunity for a large program of irrigation and land development.

He had indicated that for the next forty years the evacuees might be using lands so developed.

How much these conflicting statements had to do with subsequent events was impossible to determine, but it was probably at least one straw among the sheaf of conflicts and anxieties that led to the general strike at Poston I, the largest of the three communities at this center.

On November 14, one of the councilmen, a Kibei who was suspected of being an informer, was beaten. The FBI was invited to assist in finding the culprits. As a result of the FBI visit on November 16, two arrests were made. Two young men — both popular, and one a judo expert — were incarcerated for two days in a project jail. Rumors were rife that the young men were going to be removed from the center. Crowds gathered around the jail, and demands were made for the release of the men.

In the meantime a strike ensued at Poston I in regard to all work except in those areas that were essential to daily living. The community council and the block managers resigned. An emergency committee came into being, consisting largely of Issei, many of whom had resented the fact that Issei could not serve on the elected community council. There were many gatherings and speeches. Pictures of "dogs" appeared, representing the antipathy to informers.

The project director Wade Head and his deputy Ralph Gelvin had accompanied me to Salt Lake City where we were having a meeting of key staff members from the western centers. In the absence of the two top men, Mr. John Evans was acting director. In spite of hysterical demands of part of the staff and the recommendation of the FBI agent that the military be called in, fortunately Evans refused to do so. Thank God! Instead, negotiations between the key staff and the emergency evacuee committee were initiated and proceeded throughout most of the week.

Agreement was finally reached. The two prisoners were released. One was discharged for lack of evidence, and the other was released with the understanding that he would be tried by the evacuee judicial commission. This flare-up was a result of emotional tensions that had built up over the weeks of residence and the wish of many among the evacuees to strike back at those they considered their oppressors.

THE MANZANAR INCIDENT

Within two weeks after the Poston strike, I was called out of bed after midnight on December 6 by Ralph Merritt, the new project director at Manzanar, who had been on the job about one week. He reported that they had found it desirable to call in the military as a result of a disturbance and that one evacuee had been killed and ten others wounded.

Manzanar had been used as an assembly center by the army in the beginning of the evacuation, and it was turned over to WRA for operation as a relocation center on June 1, 1942. The population was mainly from the Los Angeles area; and evacuees from Terminal Island, one of the first areas to be evacuated, were among the residents. Mr. Roy Nash, the first project director, had resigned during the summer, and temporary acting directors were assigned from the San Francisco office until Ralph Merritt was appointed in November.

Tension in this center had been increasing from the beginning. Among the residents were a sizable group of Japanese American Citizens League leaders who were active in support of the administration and in urging the right to serve in the armed forces of the United States. On the other hand, a large group of Kibei and some tough young men had organized a kitchen workers' union.

In October the center residents voted against the organization of a community council under WRA procedures for community government. Instead they elected their block managers. This group served throughout the life of the center.

Gang activity and pressures increased, and in early August a so-called Kibei meeting, with an attendance of 600 or more, was held at the center. The meeting evidently was stimulated by the issuance of our first leave policy on July 20, which prohibited leave from the centers for Kibei.

One of the leading dissidents in this meeting was Hawaiian-born Joe Kurihari, who had served in the U.S. armed forces in France during World War I. He had been an active leader among the Japanese Americans and an active force for Americanization previous to the evacuation. Soon after he came to Manzanar he became strongly anti-American and an active agitator for resistance to the administration. He turned his back on America because he thought America had turned its back on him.

Another pro-American patriot and World War I veteran, Tokutaro Nishimoto Slocum (better known as "Toki"), also attended the meeting and openly boasted of being an FBI informant. After this declaration Toki found it necessary to hustle out of the meeting for his own protection. The meeting became so boisterous that staff members intervened and asked for adjournment. This meeting was the forerunner of other events to follow during the next three months.

The immediate situation leading up to the December 6 affair was similar in pattern to the start of the Poston incident. A Japanese American Citizens League leader, suspected of being an informer, was beaten by a group of six masked men. A popular evacuee who was a leader of the kitchen workers' union was arrested as a suspect and taken to a nearby community jail at Lone Pine.

At a mass meeting held in the open spaces of the center the new project director moved among the crowd and finally negotiated with a committee of five who were presumably the leaders. After a short meeting the project director thought he had an agreement that the crowd would immediately be dispersed. In return he promised that the prisoner would be brought back to the center within two hours to stand trial by the center administration.

In announcing the results of the meeting, Joe Kurihari, the dissident veteran, allegedly distorted the facts rather badly. He is supposed to have told the crowd that a victory had been won over the administration and that they should reassemble at another point later in the day. When this later assembly took place, the project director, who felt that he had been double-crossed, immediately called in the military. They attempted to disperse the crowd with tear gas, and as the people and the soldiers faced each other with tensions at their peak, an irresponsible evacuee youth started a parked car, headed it toward one of the army machine guns and jumped out. In the confusion that followed, shots were fired into the crowd; a boy of 17, an innocent bystander, was killed instantly, and ten others were wounded. One of the wounded, a young man of 21, died in the hospital a few days later. The week following this incident, the community was subdued and sullen.

Immediately following the demonstration, on December 6, after the crowd had dispersed, the administration took steps to remove from the center some of the extremists on both sides of the evacuee conflict. A group of 65 outspoken patriots and pro-administration evacuees were removed to an abandoned CCC camp in Death Valley to protect them from physical violence. At the same time 16 of the alleged troublemakers were removed to jails in nearby towns and later were removed to an abandoned CCC camp at Moab, Utah.

More formal arrangements were made later for a so-called isolation center at Leupp, Arizona, on the grounds of an inactive Indian boarding school. The group from Moab was moved to Leupp in April 1943. In February 1943 we issued a confidential policy statement to all project directors to open the way for removal of incorrigible troublemakers from relocation centers after the submission of full documentation and approval by the National Director. Any Issei so labeled were sent to Justice Department internment camps, but others were sent to Leupp. There was turmoil at Manzanar for some time, but the incident cleared the air and opened the way for communication between staff and evacuees.

A REVIEW OF THE PROBLEMS

The period from the time of the Poston strike in mid-November through the month of December 1942 was the most difficult period for me as national director and for the staff in general. In spite of the fact that I had assured Milton Eisenhower in June 1942 that I would be able to sleep at night, I had many sleepless nights during this crucial period. Rumors were rife that blow-ups were planned at other centers; the outside pressure groups were insistent on total internment and asked that the army take over the centers. After several days of worry and indecision about what should be done next, I arrived at the office one morning after a sleepless night and told my deputy, Elmer Rowalt, to bring a pocketful of cigars and to come to my office where I was going to try to talk my way through the maze. We spent the whole forenoon together. Elmer was a patient listener, and I reviewed the problems, the rumors, and our policies.

One of the crucial questions was whether we had made a mistake in not taking the advice of the Wartime Civil Control Administration division of the Army's Western Defense Command to provide a large staff of internal security officers at each center.

The only important changes following this meeting were removal of the ban against Issei service on community councils, an authorization for adding two or three additional non-evacuee police to the center staffs, plus a more detailed policy statement for the organization of an evacuee police force, rules governing the making of arrests, and a listing of types of offenses that might be punished by disciplinary action of the project director. In the meantime we requested the FBI to detail an agent to visit all centers and review our internal security policies.

The later centers, which received the major portion of their population after WRA policies had been thoroughly established in August of 1942, had much less confusion and difficulty.

CHAPTER 6

Sorting, Leave Clearance, and Segregation

FROM THE TIME THAT WRA relocation centers were established, certain pressure groups were asking for all-out internment; others were insisting on segregation of the pro-Japanese and potentially disloyal from the rest of the evacuees.

By the time of our August 1942 policy conference we had come to the realization that such segregation would not be a simple process. In view of the complexities, we decided to postpone action on segregation since we were occupied with pressing problems of center management, outside public relations, and plans for our out-of-center relocation program. Consequently, the first step that we decided on in the sorting process was to establish a leave-clearance procedure for those who wished to relocate outside of the centers.

In July 1942 we received the first applications for relocating. In the early stages of our planning we called upon the Office of Naval Intelligence for reports on individual evacuees. This intelligence unit had been active in contacts with and studies of the Japanese residents over the years and was considered to be the best-informed agency in this area.

By early fall we had completed arrangements with the Federal Bureau of Investigation to make a record check of all applicants for leave clearance, whose names we would submit, and to provide us with a summary of any derogatory information on record. The FBI had access to the records of the other U.S. intelligence agencies. This service was continued throughout our leave-clearance program.

RECOMMENDATIONS REGARDING SEGREGATION

Lieutenant Commander Ringle, of Naval Intelligence, who had been detailed to the WRA, in late May or early June submitted a series of memoranda on "The Japanese Question in the United States." In addition to giving some "General Opinions" and "Backgrounds" he made recommendations regarding "Procedure for Segregation" and gave some brief "Conclusions." In these memoranda, he said in part:

Within the last eight or ten years the entire "Japanese question" in the United States has reversed itself. The alien menace is no longer paramount, and it is becoming of less importance almost daily, as the original alien immigrants grow older and die, and as more and more of the American-born children reach maturity. The primary present and future problem is that of dealing with the American-born United States citizens of Japanese ancestry, of whom it is considered that at least 75 percent are loyal to the United States. The ratio of these American citizens of Japanese ancestry to alien-born Japanese in the United States is at present three to one, and rapidly increasing.[1]

Of the Japanese-born alien residents, the large majority are at least passively loyal to the United States. That is, they would knowingly do nothing whatever to the injury of the United States, but at the same time would not do anything to the injury of Japan. Most of the remainder would not engage in active sabotage or insurrection, but might well do surreptitious observation work for Japanese interests if given a convenient opportunity.

However, there are among the Japanese, both alien and citizen, certain individuals, either deliberately placed by the Japanese Government or actuated by a fanatical loyalty to that country, who would act as saboteurs or agents. This number is estimated to be less than three percent of the total, or about 3,500 in the entire United States.

Of the persons mentioned above, the most dangerous are either already in custodial detention or are members of such organizations as the Black Dragon Society, the Kaigun Kyokai (Navy League), or the Heimush Kai (Military Service Men's League), or affiliated groups who have not yet been apprehended. The membership of these groups is already fairly well known to the Navy Intelligence and the Federal

---

[1]This was somewhat overstated. The actual ratio among those evacuated was about seven Nisei to four Issei.

Bureau of Investigation and should immediately be placed in custodial detention, irrespective of whether they are alien or citizen.

As a basic policy tending toward the permanent solution of this problem, the American citizens of Japanese ancestry should be officially encouraged in their efforts toward loyalty and acceptance as bona fide citizens. They [should] be accorded a place in the national war effort through such agencies as the Red Cross, USO, civilian defense, and even such activities as ship and aircraft building or other defense production, even though subject to greater investigative checks as to background and loyalty, etc., than caucasian Americans.

. . . The most potentially dangerous elements of all are those American citizens of Japanese ancestry who have spent a number of the formative years of their lives, from the age of 13 to the age of 20 in Japan and have returned to the United States to claim their legal American citizenship within the last few years. These people are essentially and inherently Japanese and may have been deliberately sent back to the United States by the Japanese Government to act as agents. In spite of their legal citizenship and the protection afforded them by the Bill of Rights, they should be looked upon as enemy aliens and many of them placed in custodial detention.

Under the heading "Procedure for Segregation" Lieutenant Commander Ringle's major suggestions were as follows:

Publish openly and genuinely the fact that any person desiring to announce himself as a loyal citizen of Japan may do so without fear of prejudice, irrespective of whether or not he holds American citizenship. Solemnly assure such people upon the word of the Government of the United States that they will be accorded the legal status of internees; that if they so desire and opportunity presents, they will be exchanged during the period of hostilities for American citizens held by the Japanese Government. Further assure them in writing, if desirable, that as soon as possible after the conclusion of hostilities they will, unless sooner exchanged, be repatriated to Japan by the United States Government. I believe it will be found that there are a number of people, both alien and citizen, who, if given assurance that such an admission will not result in bodily harm, will frankly state their desire to be considered Japanese nationals.

By a process of registration within assembly and relocation centers, determine the identity of parents, spouses and dependents, of all American citizens of Japanese ancestry who have spent three years or more in Japan since the age of 13. If it seems desirable or necessary, these lists may be checked against the records of the Federal investigative services including the records kept by the Bureau of Immigration and Naturalization. This second category will include those citizens of Japanese ancestry who, in all probability, may be considered as potentially dangerous. Parents or guardians of such persons are included for the reason that it was these parents or guardians who sent the children to Japan to be so educated and so indoctrinated that they are to all intentions and purposes citizens of Japan.

Commander Ringle further recommended that review boards be established at each center and that families not be divided except at their own wish, that the classification of the male in the family be the primary deciding factor for the rest of the family, and that children below 17 years take the classification of the parent.

He also suggested that these people be separated from the remainder of the evacuees, pending final removal to internee centers, if facilities would allow such separation.

His concluding paragraphs read as follows:

As a summary to the foregoing, there are two points which the writer believes should never be forgotten. The first is a racial one. Because these people have Oriental faces, it is natural to look for and probably stress the *differences* between them and caucasian Americans. This I believe is wrong; the points of *similarity* should be stressed. If this point of view is taken, I believe the intelligent observer will be amazed at how little different basically these people are from their American contemporaries.

The second point is the importance of the present time, the present few years, in dealing with them. As has been pointed out, the line between the generations is more clearly marked and defined than between any other groups. The Issei, the parents, average over 50 years of age, the Nisei in their early twenties. Therefore, within the present decade, the decade from 1940-1950, there will inevitably take place a complete and sharp shifting of leadership and power — political, economic, cultural, religious, and social — from the older alien generation to the younger American born and reared generation. Whether the younger and succeeding generations are truly American in thought, word, deed and sentiment will depend on the way in which they are treated now, and on how they are helped to meet the test of this war. In other words, I believe that whether or not we have a "Japanese problem" in the United States for the next hundred and fifty years will be decided by the attitude of the United States as a whole to the Japanese Americans before 1950.

Never were wiser or truer words spoken.

During the fall of 1942 General DeWitt submitted a number of varied recommendations to the War Department for a segregation program to be carried out in WRA centers. It is not clear why his proposals were not carried out in the army's own assembly centers. We criticized the categorical nature of his recommendations —

for example, the segregation of all Kibei. His proposals were rejected, and the general then sent forward a more comprehensive segregation plan, which was transmitted to us on December 30, 1942.

The new proposal was shocking, and a far cry from the recommendations of Lieutenant Commander Ringle. It called for the segregation of *(1)* all persons who had requested repatriation or expatriation to Japan, *(2)* all aliens paroled to WRA centers from detention stations or internment camps, *(3)* all evacuees with "evaluated" police records at the assembly or relocation centers, *(4)* all persons "listed and evaluated by the intelligence service as potentially dangerous," and *(5)* all immediate family members of persons in the first four categories who might wish to join them.

The most shocking portion of the proposal was the recommendation that on a designated day, and without any previous notice whatever, the segregants were to be picked up and transferred as quickly as possible to two of the three units of the Poston, Arizona, center; the persons in these two units would be moved out to other centers simultaneously. A director of segregation was to be appointed jointly by the Secretary of War and the Director of WRA. He was to have virtually unlimited control over WRA center operations until the program had been completed. The plan provided for "suitable security measures in order to insure against *probable* rioting and consequent bloodshed." The plan provided that on the designated day *(1)* each center would be placed under complete military control; *(2)* all incoming and outgoing communication at the projects except for messages essential to the segregation operation would be stopped; *(3)* all leaves, furloughs, and visiting privileges would be suspended, and project activities such as agricultural activities carried on beyond the center limits proper would be called to a halt.

Needless to say, the WRA rejected this brazen and cold-blooded proposal.

REGISTRATION AND RESULTS

In response to the insistence of WRA, the JACL, and the Hawaiian contingent of army officers, Secretary Stimson on January 28, 1943, announced plans for organization of a volunteer Japanese American unit later known as the 442nd Combat Team. At the same time it was announced that there would be a registration of all male Nisei of draft age at all centers with a questionnaire to be filled out during a recruitment drive.

A so-called joint board was to be established to evaluate the responses to the questionnaires to determine eligibility for work in war plants. In the hope of expediting our leave-clearance operation, WRA proposed that the registration and questionnaires be presented to all persons, both male and female, over 17 years of age. The forms used were labeled "Application for Leave Clearance," which proved to be disturbing to many Issei and others who did not want to leave the centers.

A bad mistake was made in the loyalty question, which read: "Will you swear unqualified allegiance to the United States of America and forswear any form of allegiance or obedience to the Japanese Emperor, or any other foreign government, power or organization?" This question, which had been planned for Nisei in the early stages, was entirely unfair to the Issei once they were included in the registration, because the Issei had never been allowed to acquire American citizenship. Thus they were being asked to forswear allegiance to the only country where they had citizenship status.

After this egregious oversight was noted, the question was changed four days later to read: "Will you swear to abide by the laws of the United States and to take no action which would in any way interfere with the war effort of the United States?" This change proved to be acceptable to most Issei, but much confusion had already been produced.

With the advent of the confusion of registration, the stepped-up relocation drive, and the increased activity of hostile groups such as the American Legion and the West Coast newspapers, tensions increased in most centers and conflict became rife again. Meetings were held with speeches pro and con regarding registration and volunteering for the armed forces. Crises occurred in the blocks and within families.

At Tule Lake the whole community was upset and disorganized. Gangs emerged again and resistance spread. The community council and planning board resigned. There was a feeling of further loss of self-determination. A suspicion arose that residents were to be forced out of the center and into the hostile environment of wartime America. Many felt that they had been thoroughly examined and tested previously and they now wanted to live in peace. There were objections to a segregated army unit and questions regarding the possible reinstitution of the draft. One of the evacuees called it "a great chess game in which the government made all of the moves."

At the Heart Mountain center in Wyoming a group of protesting Nisei formed a "citizens' congress"; at a meeting on February 11, after the registration had started, one speaker expressed the point of view of many Nisei as follows:

The minds of many of us are still shrouded in doubt and confusion as to the true motives of our government when they invite our voluntary enlistment at the present time. It has not been explained why some American citizens, who patriotically volunteered, at the beginning of the war, were rejected by the Army. Furthermore, our government has permitted damaging propaganda to continue against us. Also, she has failed to reinstate us in the eyes of the American public. We are placed on the spot, and our course of action is in the balance scale of justice; for our government's honest interpretation of our stand will mean absolute vindication and admission of the wrong committed. On the other hand, if interpreted otherwise by misrepresentations and misunderstandings, it will amount to renewed condemnation of this group.

Although we have yellow skins, we too are Americans. We have an American upbringing, therefore we believe in fair play. Our firm conviction is that we would be useless Americans if we did not assert our constitutional rights now; for, unless our status as citizens is cleared and we are really fighting for the perpetuation of democracy, especially when our fathers, mothers, and families are in concentration camps, even though they are not charged with any crime.

We believe that our nation's good faith is to be found in whether it moves to restore full privileges at the earliest opportunity.

Similar speeches were being made at other centers.

At Tule Lake approximately 3,000 refused to register. Requests for repatriation to Japan increased during this period.

Altogether there were about 7,600 "no" answers or qualified answers to the loyalty question, but these negative answers meant many things. Overall 11 percent of those eligible to register and about 25 percent of the males of military age answered "no" or gave a qualified answer. Thirteen percent of the young women said "no" or qualified their answers. Only six percent of the older Issei men and women did so.

Shortly after the completion of the registration period at Tule

Lake, where we had rebellion and protest against the filling out of questionnaires and non-cooperation in the program in general, I visited the center. Project Director Harvey Coverly then arranged for a meeting of all the center residents who wished to attend. The meeting was called for 8 P.M. and we played to a packed house. The atmosphere was tense and grim. I sensed a feeling among the residents of "What are we going to have to contend with next?"

My speech and responses to questions were translated into Japanese by the Reverend Dai Kitagawa. I took the opportunity to discuss our policies in some detail — particularly the WRA position in regard to relocation to the outside, army enlistment and service by the Nisei, and its importance to everyone, especially the evacuees. The speech itself lasted an hour or more, which of course included translation. The meeting then continued until well after 11 P.M., with question after question from an audience who for the first three hours or so were intensely serious.

At about 11 P.M. an old bachelor Issei farm worker, way in the back of the room, rose to say that he couldn't buy whiskey or beer at the center, that he wanted some badly, and was wondering why couldn't he get it. The audience roared. That question broke the tension, and it was all downhill for the rest of the way. The residents became friendly in general, and they objected en masse to critical comments or snide questions from their associates. When the meeting broke up, many of them came up to shake my hand. This was for me a memorable occasion.

Harvey Coverly, who served as acting project director at Manzanar for several weeks previous to taking over the job as director at Tule Lake, did a good job both at Manzanar and Tule Lake. He was in no way responsible for the snafu during the registration period at Tule Lake, and when he left the center on July 1 to join the armed forces, it was because he had been committed for quite some time to report to the army when called.

Ray Best — who had served as director of the Isolation Center at Moab, Utah, and also at Leupp, Arizona — on July 1 took over the tough job as director of the Tule Lake center, which was destined to be the segregation center. He carried on with honor in one of the toughest jobs in WRA until the center was closed.

The Poston and Manzanar demonstrations, coupled with the confusion of the registration period, especially at Tule Lake, brought further outbursts from some of the West Coast newspapers and from the anti-Oriental organizations, including the California American Legion, in early 1943. Senator Mon Wallgren of the state of Washington introduced a bill in the Senate to turn the centers over to the army. A series of hearings were held by a subcommittee of the Senate Committee on Military Affairs, headed by Senator A. B. Chandler of Kentucky. This committee in its report urged segregation of the pro-Japanese and the disloyal.

Assistant Secretary of War John McCloy appeared before the Senate Committee at one of its hearings and strongly recommended segregation. At about the same time, May 1943, we received a letter from Secretary Stimson saying that "The War Relocation Authority should take immediate steps to screen out from the centers and segregate in close confinement all individuals appearing to have pro-Japanese sympathies. This would include the already substantial number of individuals who have applied for repatriation, as well as the troublemakers."

The Japanese American Citizens League favored segregation, and many of the WRA staff felt strongly that segregation should be accomplished, but neither group favored the procedures recommended by General DeWitt. There were many arguments against a general move of the type recommended. Most of the people in the centers had moved twice already; the residents were settling down in most of the centers after the turmoil resulting from the registration program; and no centers were available of the size required to receive all of the potential segregants. On this latter point we had explored the possibility of securing an army cantonment or of getting a new center built, but the War Department said no quarters were available, and priorities for materials excluded the building of another center. As a consequence, any move of the scale proposed required moving people out of one center and simultaneously moving others in. Such a large movement would be costly, and the confusion would probably lead to other crises.

In view of these and other problems, I was hopeful that the desired results could be accomplished by *(1)* the establishment of the isolation center at Leupp, Arizona, for the troublemakers; *(2)* the cooperation of the Department of Justice in taking aliens who we felt should be interned; and *(3)* gradual out-of-center relocation for qualified persons.

ESTABLISHING THE SEGREGATION CENTER

On May 31, 1943, we had called all project directors to Washington, D.C., for a meeting to review the situation in general and specifically to discuss the problems in the various centers. After a thorough discussion the directors were unanimous in their recommendation that we proceed with a mass segregation program. Because I did not feel that I could ignore their unanimous judgment, I capitulated, although reluctantly. After careful consideration Tule Lake was selected as the segregation center because it was a large center and because its population included a large number of potential segregants.

We proceeded immediately to the formulation of policy which would apply to the segregation center and also the pattern of the segregation itself. It was decided that there would be no elective community self-government and no relocation program at the Tule Lake segregation center.

Those to be segregated included all who had applied for repatriation to Japan and who had not withdrawn their application by July 1, 1943, and all those who had answered "no" to the loyalty question during the registration. In view of the many hidden meanings to the "no" answer, people in this group were given the opportunity to have special hearings and to reconsider and explain their original answers. Some received clearance under the procedure. The third group included all those who were denied leave clearance due to some accumulation of adverse evidence in their records. The fourth group included the family members of segregants who chose to remain with the family.

Evacuees chose to join the segregated group for various reasons. Some of the segregants were defiant individuals who said "no" to the loyalty question mainly because they had developed persecution complexes; others wished to have security in a center for the duration of the war and did not want to be disturbed by pressure to relocate; and then there were those with family loyalties, Nisei who decided to stay with parents who had requested repatriation. For the repatriates, it was a step toward Japan and possible security; some Japanese patriots wanted to live in an environment of Japanese culture; and lastly, there were those who hoped to avoid the draft by going to Tule Lake.

The actual segregation movements were thoroughly planned in

detail. The War Department provided the trains and supplied the guards. In 33 train trips, 15,000 people moved in and out. Seventy-one evacuees from the Leupp Isolation Center in Arizona were removed to Tule Lake, and the Leupp Center was closed.

Everything went fairly smoothly, except at Tule Lake. Of the many people already there who were not classified as segregants, all who were willing were moved to other centers. About 4,000 non-segregants at Tule Lake chose to stay — some because they preferred not to leave California, or did not want to move again, or resented being pushed around. In view of this, 1,800 segregants were held at Manzanar until additional housing could be built at Tule Lake during the fall and winter of 1943 and 1944; they were moved in the early spring of 1944.

Because of the comparatively smooth operation of the segregation movements, and because everyone was so busy getting everything in order again, there was a tendency in WRA to assume that the segregation center and the other centers would be more harmonious communities after the separation had been completed. This was true of nine centers, but not of Tule Lake.

A number of the Washington staff members were sent to Tule Lake in the early fall to study the problems of administration there and to make recommendations. Due to the overwhelming job of receiving and accommodating the thousands of incoming residents, the staff became involved in the tremendous physical job and were unable to handle the more analytical tasks before the blow-up came.

THE TULE LAKE INCIDENT

On October 15, at about the time the last contingents from the other centers were arriving at Tule Lake, an accident occurred that touched off a serious conflict between a sizable group of evacuees and the administration. A truck that was being used to transport a crew of agricultural workers to the project farm overturned. Several of the workers were injured, and one died a few days later.

This incident gave rise to a power play by some of the dissident leaders who made a major issue out of the incident. They objected to producing food for other centers because, as they put it, they were Japanese and should not be called upon to produce food for those who had not agreed with their decision for a Japanese way of life. They pressured the agricultural workers into a full-scale farm strike. Since thousands of pounds of potatoes and barley were to be harvested, which the other centers needed, we arranged to recruit workers from the other centers to complete the harvest. The volunteers came in late October and were quartered in temporary accommodations out at the farm.

On October 26 a committee purporting to represent the community presented a series of demands to Raymond Best, the project director. They insisted that agricultural production at the center be for Tule Lake alone. They proposed a resegregation to separate the group that preferred the Japanese way of life and the group who were fencesitters or who wanted simply to avoid relocation. They also asked that once the resegregation was complete that they, the Japanese-Oriental group, be allowed to establish a community self-government and a cooperative community. Their other demands included the request for certain physical improvements and the discharge of certain project staff members.

The project director agreed that agricultural production for the future would be limited to Tule Lake needs but that the present year's harvest must be completed and distributed as planned. He denied the other demands and indicated that the committee was not properly representative and that the selection of an advisory committee would await the arrival of all incoming residents.

On the evening of October 31, I was in San Francisco to address the San Francisco Press Club as the guest of *New York Times* correspondent Lawrence Davies. At this meeting everything was serene, and I was met by a polite and friendly crowd. Although it appeared that peace with most of the West Coast press might finally have come to pass, this was not to be immediately true.

The following day I went to Tule Lake for a brief tour of consultation and inspection with the staff. Shortly after lunch, about 4,000 residents, summoned by unauthorized announcements at the mess hall, gathered outside the administration building where I was in conference with the project director and Robert Cozzens of our San Francisco office.

Earlier, the director had come to the mess hall while I was having lunch to tell me that he had had word of the announcements. Before returning to his office we got into his car and toured the project to see what was happening. Whole families with little children being led by the hand were gathering. The director said to me, "We had scheduled a meeting with the evacuees for you tomorrow, but I guess the boys have decided to have it today." When we returned to the administrative area, it was evident that the family groups were being herded in closely by some men obviously assigned to the task.

Some of the committee who had met with the project director a few days earlier appeared and asked for a conference with us. We agreed. The demands made by the committee were basically the same as the ones made a few days earlier, but in addition the committee now asked for dismissal of the project director and several members of his staff.

After hearing the rather unrestrained demands, I told them that I would not negotiate on the basis of demands but that the center staff would be prepared to entertain recommendations or requests from a properly constituted representative group of residents. I added that I doubted whether the present group could qualify as representative.

While this meeting was going on, some toughs visited the hospital, fell into an argument with the chief medical officer, and beat him rather badly. Obviously, from the attitude of the committee, this was not a part of their plan but rather a chance for some roughnecks to settle a grudge.

When the meeting was over, both the chairman of the committee and I addressed the gathering. He and another committeeman spoke in Japanese, and I spoke in English. I summarized for them the results of the conference inside, and the gathering adjourned.

In the meantime I had learned that the reports officer, or information officer, at the center had resigned and was not on duty.

Although the telephone system at the center was not reliable, Cozzens and I tried to reach Lawrence Davies, my host of the previous evening, as well as Cozzens' office, to report. We were unsuccessful. Our policy had always called for full cooperation with the press, but a combination of poor communication facilities and our inability to check all of the stories immediately made it impossible to satisfy the press in this instance.

In the meantime, outside tradesmen who had been in the center on business and some hysterical employees had left the center and given out wildly imaginative stories. This, of course, was real grist for the Hearst newspapers, and they went the limit. Thus our budding peace with the San Francisco press blew up over night.

After two days at Tule Lake I proceeded on my scheduled trip, with stops at Portland and Seattle. On the evening of November 4, two days after I had left the center, violence erupted at Tule Lake. A well-organized group of young men moved into the administration area with clubs in an attempt to prevent the removal of food from the warehouses for the volunteer workers from other centers who were billeted at the farm. There was a clash with the internal security force, and one staff member was injured. Then the rioters moved toward the project director's house with mayhem obviously in mind. At this time the military guard outside the center was called in to take over.

Upon taking command, the officer in charge refused access to newsmen and refused to provide any interviews or communication with reporters. The center remained under army control until January 14, 1944.

Appendix G contains the formal report of the Tule Lake incident.

CHAPTER 7

The Results of Segregation

DURING THE EARLY PART OF 1943, about 7,000 of the more restless and active residents of the centers, mostly Nisei, had relocated out of center. By late 1943, after completion of the segregation movements, in which a large number of persons were transferred to Tule Lake as the segregation center, those residents remaining in the other nine centers were interested in settling down and maintaining peaceful communities.

Routine work assignments were carried out with little trouble on the farms and in the centers. The recreation programs became more popular. Baseball took the lead, but goh (Japanese checkers), cards, wood carving, flower-arrangement classes, sewing classes, singing, poetry, English classes, reading, and theater all filled an important place in the lives of the residents.

The extreme elements had been eliminated by segregation and relocation. About the only reason for tension on the part of the remaining residents was a concern regarding administration moves that might be interpreted as WRA pressure for relocation. The reduction in size of the evacuee staff in the centers was one of the moves so interpreted.

There was increasing recognition, however, on the part of the Issei, that the War Relocation Authority was being honest and on

Starting with a bare barracks room, scrap materials, mail order lumber, and much ingenuity, ambitious Japanese Americans constructed this typically modern room. Furnishings provided by the government were: one cot, a mattress, and two blankets for each person; one stove and one light bulb for each apartment. All additional comforts were provided by the residents themselves. (WRA photo)

the level with them. My appearance on a March of Time radio program on June 24, 1943, evidently had a large group of listeners within the centers, and it helped to establish our position firmly in the minds of many Issei.

While the other nine centers were operating quietly and calmly in late 1943 and during 1944, Tule Lake was in turmoil and our public relations were at low ebb, especially on the West Coast. The resignation and inactivity of the reports officer at Tule Lake at the crucial period created a vacuum in news preparation and reporting. Our inability to reach friendly or neutral reporters in San Francisco, and the fact that the army contingent which took over on November 4 clamped down on all news, put us in a bad light in the eyes of the newspapermen, who of course did not understand our problems.

Added to this were the wild stories emanating from hysterical people who left the center from November 1 to 4, written by unprincipled reporters. These stories were so voluminous and complex that it took nearly ten days to check them all and to issue a press release in which we tried to put the record straight.

It was generally charged that I had been held prisoner for several hours on November 1. There were implications that the mass murder of WRA employees had been narrowly averted, charges that fires were about to be set, and many other equally unfounded charges. Ray Richards, the Hearst Press correspondent in Washington, filed one not untypical story in which he charged that the Tule Lake residents had run down the American flag and torn it to shreds. This was totally a figment of vicious imagination.

A former landscape gardener demonstrates his skill and ingenuity in creating from materials close at hand a desert garden alongside his barracks at the Manzanar, California, center.

THE HOUNDS LET LOOSE

Investigations were carried out by the California State Legislature; and the late Clair Engle, the then new congressman, representative of the Tule Lake area, joined in the clamor of the critics. The scalps of the project director and the national director were demanded. Twenty-two of the thirty-three West Coast congressmen petitioned the president during January 1944 to fire me from my job as director.

The *San Francisco Chronicle* up to this time had, on the whole, treated the WRA program objectively, but on November 5 the publication lashed out with an editorial in which the WRA top administrators were called "phonies" and "bad public servants" who were "examples of two-bit men pitchforked by bureaucracy into four-dollar jobs."

This editorial, in our minds, represented the low point of our relations with the public and the press.

We of course moved immediately to counteract the damage. As a first step we assigned Allan Markley of our Washington information staff to Tule Lake as reports officer with orders to go all out in making news available to the newspapers and other news sources by means of releases, urging visits to the center, making visits to editors in the area, and reporting to the press in detail immediately when anything unusual happened.

Later I took Markley to visit the *San Francisco Chronicle* and the editorial writer who had been so tough on us. During this meeting I explained our side of the story and assured them of full cooperation in securing any information they wished. I stated that I was sorry they felt as they did when they called us phonies and other names. The editorial writer listened and was still a bit adamant; however, he did say he would retract the "phony" charge but not the rest of it. We said we understood their feelings and let it go at that.

I then had lunch with Lawrence Davies of the *New York Times,* who had been my host at the press club on October 31. He was hurt and felt that he had been let down. After an hour and a half he accepted my explanations in good faith, and after a time we became good friends again.

The Hearst Press, the McClatchy papers, and the *Los Angeles Times* continued to beat the tom-toms of hate.

Rohwer relocation center, McGhee, Arkansas. (WRA photo)

On January 21, 1944, in Los Angeles, I addressed a luncheon meeting of the Town Hall on the topic "The Facts About the War Relocation Authority." The group who attended were either haters, antis, or at least skeptical. Among other things, I discussed our policies and problems at Poston, Manzanar, and Tule Lake. During the question-and-answer period a gentleman arose and rather belligerently said, "Mr. Myer, if the things that happened at Tule Lake had happened in Japan, what do you think the Japs would have done with the troublemakers?" I replied that they would have shot them, but that I thanked God we were living in a country that does not believe we should shoot people for what we think they are thinking. I received a hand on my reply, and the tensions eased.

An adult education class in pattern drafting at Granada relocation center in Colorado. (WRA photo)

A game of Japanese checkers, called goh, is played at the Manzanar center.

A MOVE TO COVER

Sometime during January or early February, Attorney General Francis Biddle sent a memorandum to the president recommending that WRA be placed within the Department of the Interior. On hearing of this proposal, I was opposed to the move. I visited Harold Smith, the budget director, to express my objections, and he told me I should see the attorney general. I felt that if any cabinet department was going to take us over, it should be the Department of Justice. The attorney general as usual was most gracious and told me he had written the memorandum because he felt that we needed someone to cover us in view of the storm that had arisen. It was evident that he did not want the responsibility. Harold Smith then referred me to James Byrnes, Director of War Mobilization. I presented my arguments to Byrnes, and he listened quietly. When I was finished, he said, "I think you should go to Interior." So that was that.

On February 16, 1944, President Roosevelt signed Executive Order 9423 transferring the WRA to the Department of the Interior. Although I had resisted the move, I have since been completely grateful for it. My opposition was based on a remembrance of the many battles between the departments of Interior and Agriculture previous to my leaving the Department of Agriculture to move to the WRA. Therefore, I was not sure that Secretary Harold Ickes and I would be able to work harmoniously together in regard to the WRA. As it turned out, we got along exceptionally well. Appendix H contains my report to Ickes after the WRA transfer to the Department of Interior.

RENUNCIATION OF CITIZENSHIP

During the fall and winter of 1943-1944 the 100th Battalion of Hawaiian National Guardsmen, an all Japanese American unit, went into action in Italy. In June the 442nd Regimental Combat Team went into the front lines. The wonderful record of these fighting units, coupled with the excellent reception of the relocatees across the country, helped to reestablish confidence in the Nisei and WRA. By the fall of 1944 it was no longer fashionable in most areas to bring irresponsible accusations against the Japanese American people.

In the meantime a serious development resulted from the segregation and the Tule Lake turmoil. This was the passage of a bill by the U.S. Congress known as Public Law 405 (78th Congress) which was signed by the president on July 1, 1944. This bill permitted United States citizens to renounce their citizenship voluntarily on American soil in time of war under procedures approved by the attorney general. We were very disappointed when we were informed that the attorney general had approved this bill. (See Appendix I.)

A short time before the committee hearing on the bill, former Congressman James P. McGranery (later himself attorney general under the Truman administration) had been appointed as assistant to the attorney general to serve as an aide in the field of congressional relations. It appears that Edward Ennis of the Justice Department Alien Division, who was quite well informed on evacuee problems, and Mr. McGranery both attended the committee hearing with the attorney general. We were told that at the time the question was asked as to whether the attorney general approved the bill, Edward Ennis' attention had been diverted briefly and he did not hear the question. At this critical moment Attorney General Biddle accepted the advice of Mr. McGranery, who recommended approval of the bill.

Mr. McGranery quite obviously thought that the approval was important to good congressional relations, but unfortunately he did not understand the complexity of the evacuee situation at that time and the damage to innocent people that might result from such a bill which was aimed at the Tule Lake segregants. For some reason, I as director of WRA was not called to testify on the bill. The hearing had been held in the early spring following the furore over the Tule Lake affair. The legislation lay dormant until late June, when it was brought up and quickly passed.

During the fall of 1944 a number of conferences were held between the Department of Justice and WRA to consider procedures for handling any renunciation applications. We in WRA repeatedly pointed out the abnormal character of the Tule Lake community. We knew that some of the Nisei had gone to Tule Lake in the hope of avoiding selective service. More importantly, we knew that many parents who planned to return to Japan would undoubtedly pressure young Nisei to request renunciation. Worst of all, we feared that the strong-armed pro-Japanese toughs would wield pressure to induce a large number of persons to renounce whether they wished to do so or not.

In the meantime the War Department was well along with plans to lift the exclusion order barring evacuees from return to the West Coast. We did our best to persuade the Department of Justice staff, and Assistant Attorney General Herbert Wechsler in particular, that this was the worst possible time to conduct renunciation hearings. However, Wechsler was adamant, and the Department of Justice sent a team of hearing officers to Tule Lake in December 1944 at about the same time that the War Department announced the lifting of the exclusion from the West Coast. The center was immediately thrown into a state of tension and turmoil.

Our worst fears were realized. Groups of noisy, defiant young residents took to gathering at the fence, which had been built between the resident area and the administrative area, and demanded the right to renounce immediately. The so-called Japanese patriotic societies seized the opportunity to increase their prestige and their membership. Early morning marching and demonstrations were stepped up. Rumors about impending government action were again rife, and these and other techniques were used as pressure on the young Nisei and Kibei to renounce their citizenship. The hearing officer made several speeches to the crowds that gathered, and, as pressure continued to develop, the Justice Department carried out a plan suggested by WRA to remove some renunciants and a few Issei to Justice Department internment camps. About 1,200 were removed from the center over a period of several months.

All told, over 5,700 requests for renunciation of citizenship were received. Over 95 percent were from Tule Lake. This was over and against the "300 to 1,000" that were mentioned by Attorney General Biddle at the hearings on Public Law 405 (78th Congress) that the proposed law was intended to deal with.

In the meantime the so-called re-segregation leaders at Tule Lake claimed that they had 10,000 names on a petition asking that the re-segregation proposal be carried out to separate the "fence-sitters" and pro-American from the pro-Japanese community. This was not feasible, and it was not done except in a limited manner by the relocation of those eligible and by removal of several hundred pro-Japanese to Justice Department internment camps.

The conflict and pressures continued at Tule Lake for several months. The strong-arm crew of the so-called Japanese patriotic societies continued to use violence where needed to gain their ends. In one instance they went the limit. The stockade which was established by the army for retention of troublemakers during the period of military control was maintained for several months; it was, of course, a rallying point for the dissidents.

The most stable element in the community was represented by the Business Enterprise group, along with a number of the block managers and elder statesmen among the Issei. The violence reached a peak in June 1944 when the general manager of the Business Enterprise Association was murdered. The atmosphere of terror increased, and this strengthened the patriotic societies, or Hoshidan. These pressures and conflcts continued well into 1945; but the Hoshidan group gradually lost power, and the dust began to settle at Tule Lake quite some time before final liquidation in March 1946.

CHAPTER 8

The Continuing Battle of the Racists

THROUGHOUT ITS FOUR-YEAR EXISTENCE, WRA was subject to continual attacks by certain segments of the press and certain organizations that devoted their efforts to besmirching the evacuees or finding fault with WRA policies and administration. But the variety and intensity of their attacks reached new highs from late 1942 to early 1944.

ADVERSE CRITICISMS

During September 1942 the American Legion at its convention in Kansas City passed a resolution — on the assumption that every evacuee was a potential saboteur — protesting the release of college students and harvest workers from the centers. The drafters of the resolution were obviously misinformed, since their text stated in part: "All Japanese both alien and native born were ordered confined to concentration camps for the duration of the war." The resolution also stated: "Resolved that those Japanese that escaped to states east of the Rockies be taken into custody and placed in these different camps or that they be placed under military control in their present location."

Never, of course, was there any policy of confinement for the duration, and those who had moved east of the Rockies did so at the suggestion of the military. The Legion resolution also asked that the control of the camps be turned over to the army.

Throughout late 1942 and 1943, stories about the quality, cost, and amounts of food provided to evacuees in the centers were popular with the newspapers that were propagandizing about waste, extravagance, and lax administration of the centers. Charges were rife that special privileges were being given the evacuees.

In January 1943 a correspondent of the Memphis *Commercial Appeal,* stationed at Little Rock, Arkansas, made a quick trip to the Jerome, Arkansas, center and subsequently wrote a series of stories of mismanagement, waste, and evacuee arrogance. These articles, based largely on interviews with crew members who had worked on the construction of the center, were published not only by the *Commercial Appeal* but by many other Scripps-Howard newspapers throughout the country. The series added fuel to the fire resulting from the Poston and Manzanar incidents.

Shortly after the appearance of this series, the publisher of the *Denver Post* assigned Jack Carberry, a sports writer, to prepare a series on the Heart Mountain center — apparently with instructions to make everything appear as black as possible. These articles appeared under streaming red headlines, one of which was "Food is Hoarded for Japs in the U.S. While Americans in Nippon are Tortured." This headline alone is enough to indicate the nature of the attack. Not only were the stories inaccurate in many respects but, even worse, the facts were presented in a manner well calculated to infuriate an already biased public. In one story, for example, it was pointed out that the center had $12,000 worth of baby food on hand with "only five babies in the hospital." The writer simply neglected to mention that there were dozens of well babies to be fed.

Our reports officer, John Baker, visited the publisher to protest the flagrant use of the *Post* to mislead and stir up hate. The publisher's response was that he regarded all of the people of Japanese descent as "enemies of the United States" and that he had every intention of guiding the editorial and reportorial policies of his paper in accordance with that fundamental thesis.

During the time the *Post*'s series of articles was being published, a local VFW (Veterans of Foreign Wars) post in a community close to our Granada center in southern Colorado passed a tough resolution regarding the WRA management of centers and "special privileges" for the evacuees. Congressman J. Edgar Chenoweth requested that I write to the commander of the VFW post and invite him and his associates to visit the Granada center for a tour of inspection and to check in detail on both policy and administration there.

The commander replied that he worked for the railroad and was absent when the resolution was passed. Furthermore he said that he had been a reader of the *Denver Post* for many years and had learned what to believe and what not to believe. He said he was not concerned about the administration of the Granada center, but if I was willing he would like to give my letter of invitation to the man who was responsible for the resolution. He added that he would urge this resolution drafter to visit the center, for he felt that this man needed the experience much more than he himself did. We of course urged the commander to send the other man.

The result was that the second man did go to the center and spent the day poking into warehouses, mess halls, and other areas. He asked many questions, and at the end of the day he came to the project director to say that he was fully satisfied that things were in good order and he would report back to his post accordingly. It was our policy to admit visitors generally if they had good reason for coming. Unfortunately all the critics did not accept our invitations as this man did.

SENATE SUBCOMMITTEE HEARINGS

In January 1943 a subcommittee of the Committee on Military Affairs of the U.S. Senate held hearings, presumably on S. 444, a bill to transfer the relocation centers to the War Department. This bill, introduced by Senator Mon C. Wallgren of Washington, had been proposed several months earlier by the American Legion. Senator Wallgren and Senator Rufus Holman of Oregon were most antagonistic to the evacuees and to WRA.

On January 28, the last day of the formal hearings, the Secretary of War announced plans for the organization of the all-Nisei 442nd Regimental Combat Team.

Senator A. B. Chandler, chairman of the subcommittee, visited Manzanar and other centers in March and issued a series of critical statements which made headlines; but the report of the committee, issued in May, was mild in comparison with the bluster during the hearings and earlier comments to the press. In summary, the committee felt that (*1*) the draft should apply to all Nisei the same as to

Dillon S. Myer with Eleanor Roosevelt leaving
the hospital at Gila relocation center.

other citizens; (2) all of the loyal, able-bodied Japanese should be
gotten out to work, at the earliest possible time, in areas where they
would be accepted and considered safe by the army; and (3) those
persons who answered "no" to the loyalty question during registration, and actual disloyal persons, should be placed in internment
camps.

At the time of issuance of the report, the first two findings were in full support of WRA policies and recommendations. As for the third, a few weeks later we moved to initiate the segregation program, including the transfer to Tule Lake of those who answered "no" to the loyalty question.

In connection with the Chandler subcommittee report, it is interesting to note that, at the suggestion of the president, Mrs. Eleanor Roosevelt arranged to visit the Gila River center in Arizona during late April or early May. I was on hand as guide and host to this most distinguished visitor. She did the full day's tour with her usual unflagging energy. After her visit, on our way back to Phoenix by car, I had an excellent opportunity to discuss our problems and to answer further questions. During this visit I told her that I would like very much to discuss our problems with the president. She said, "You should have that opportunity and I will arrange it." Within a few days Mrs. Myer and I received an invitation to the White House for luncheon on Mother's Day in May 1943.

The day of the luncheon was beautiful and warm. Mrs. Myer and I were seated at a small table on the White House lawn, with President Roosevelt and his daughter Anna. Mrs. Roosevelt, John Bottinger (Anna's husband), and Mr. and Mrs. Harry Hopkins were seated at another table some distance away. We spent a good hour and a half in friendly conversation and in the discussion of WRA problems. When I mentioned the hearings and the discussions with Senator Chandler and his subcommittee, the president said, "I think I can help you with that."

It seemed clear to us, after the temperate report of the committee, that we had had some help. Although I never learned for certain, I feel sure that the help received was transmitted through the late Senator Joe O'Mahoney of Wyoming, who was a member of the committee.

DIES SUBCOMMITTEE INVESTIGATIONS

In May 1943 we had no sooner finished with the Senate Military Affairs Subcommittee activities than two men who identified themselves as "investigators of the Dies committee" (the House Committee on Un-American Activities) appeared at the Manzanar center without previous warning or notice. It later developed that

Congressman Dies had appointed a three-man subcommittee to investigate WRA. The members were John Costello (chairman) of Los Angeles, California, Karl E. Mundt of South Dakota, and Herman P. Eberharter of Pennsylvania. The investigators visited a number of the western centers during May, and we asked that transcripts be provided covering the questions and answers so that we in Washington could know what was going on. I was greatly relieved when I read the transcripts, as they arrived one by one, to find that the project directors were thoroughly informed on policy and had met the questions with a frank, accurate, and honest discussion of the policies and the problems.

During May, at the same time that the two investigators were visiting the centers, Congressman J. Parnell Thomas of New Jersey, a member of the full committee but not of the subcommittee, made a trip to Los Angeles but did not visit any centers. Nevertheless he held a press conference at his hotel and accused WRA of pampering and overfeeding the evacuees and declared that the committee had evidence pointing to the existence of an organized division of the Japanese army on the West Coast before Pearl Harbor. He called for immediate termination of the "WRA policy of releasing disloyal Japs."

This visit by Representative Thomas was obviously intended to serve the purposes of the race-baiters, including those in the American Legion, and was planned as a forerunner to a series of hearings by the three-man subcommittee which started in Los Angeles on June 8 and continued for nine days.

During these hearings no WRA representatives were invited to testify, but the subcommittee spent much time questioning former employees of the Poston center who had been fired from their jobs. The hearings of course were open to the press. The last witness was a chap named Townshend who had been in charge of the motor pool at Poston until the strike in mid-November. At that time, after becoming hysterical because the army was not called in, he left the center without permission in a government car and was gone for a week. Upon his return he of course was fired after being questioned at length. As a witness before the Costello group he made many ridiculous statements, including claims of food cached in the desert by evacuees, presumably bent on escape and sabotage of the U.S.

war effort. He also declared that "over 1,000 Japanese soldiers and officers" were in the center, and he described the "poor simpleton, cowering Caucasian employees standing around like whipped children." All of these fantastic charges were given wide publicity across the country.

In the meantime Ray Richards of the Hearst press appeared on the Washington scene and about mid-May began spewing out a steady volume of daily stories based on "information" obtained from headquarters of the Dies committee. These stories and the statements and acts of Representative Thomas became so spectacular and erroneous that I felt it necessary to write to Representative Dies on June 2, 1943, as follows:

Hon. Martin Dies
Chairman, Special Committee to
   Investigate Un-American Activities
Washington, D.C.

Dear Mr. Dies:

I have noted in the press recently a number of statements by representatives of the Committee on Un-American Activities which have a direct bearing on the work of the War Relocation Authority, and have the effect of seriously interfering with the program which this agency has been instructed by the President and the Congress to carry out. The statements have been so misleading to the public, and so fraught with errors and half-truths, that I am impelled to record my comments for your information.

Several of the statements have dwelt upon the presence of organized and dangerous pro-Japanese elements in the West Coast population prior to the outbreak of war. No mention is made of the fact that the federal intelligence agencies apprehended several thousand suspects immediately after Pearl Harbor, and that those found guilty upon hearings have been incarcerated in internment camps. Instead the implication is strongly made that all such subversive individuals are to be found in the population of the relocation centers.

On May 29, Mr. Robert E. Stripling, identified as Chief Investigator of your Committee, was quoted in the press as saying that spies and saboteurs are being released from the relocation centers. The charges were not supported, but nevertheless they unquestionably would have the effect of arousing mistrust of all persons of Japanese ancestry who are seeking to relocate. Since the War Relocation Authority grants leave from its centers with the provision that an individual may be called back at any time for sufficient reason, I am only discharging my responsibilities when I request that I be supplied with the names of any persons released from relocation centers who are spies or saboteurs or who have been trained in saboteur schools. I suggest also that the names and evidence be made available immediately to the Federal Bureau of Investigation.

In a statement to the press on May 31, which I understand also was made by Mr. Stripling, it was charged that evacuees in relocation centers are provided with foods of kinds and quantities not available to the general public. Except for the amounts of food on hand at the Manzanar Relocation Center which presumably were accurately reported, the statement was erroneous and consequently misleading. The statement was made that "prime" beef was provided for the evacuees. The beef ordered for relocation centers is third grade. The Committee spokesman completely ignored the fact that rationing restrictions of the OPA are in force at relocation centers, that the actual cost of food is approximately 40 cents a day per person, and the WRA has deliberately refrained from purchasing certain kinds of food known to be scarce. These facts were made known to the committee's investigators who visited the Manzanar Relocation Center, and could have been quickly and readily confirmed by a telephone call to this office.

The Office of the President has just referred to me the telegram of May 19 from Representative J. Parnell Thomas, a member of your Committee, urging Presidential action in stopping further release of people of Japanese ancestry until Section II of your Committee's report on Axis activities can be issued, and the Committee's investigation of the relocation centers can be completed. In the absence of any supporting facts, we must regard Mr. Thomas' request as purely personal, and insufficient to warrant a change in the policies of this agency.

We have our own records on all persons above 17 years of age in the relocation centers, and we also have available to us information from the records of the federal investigative agencies. In the interest of national security we do not release any evacuee if his record indicates any reason why it would not be advisable for him to live outside a relocation center. On the other hand, the manpower situation plus the constitutional guarantees demand that loyal American citizens and law-abiding aliens be given every opportunity to contribute to the war effort by productive work in normal communities.

Investigators for your Committee have visited a number of relocation centers, and have received complete collaboration of the staff there. We in the national office will be glad to cooperate fully in providing facts which your committee may desire concerning the policies and procedures of this agency. To date no member or representative of the Committee has asked me for any information or has been in touch with any member of the Washington staff.

In the meantime, I hope it will be possible for representatives of your Committee to refrain from making public statements concerning the War Relocation Authority on the basis of incomplete information. Continuance of this practice of issuing irresponsible statements can only lead to the conclusion that the Committee has abandoned its assignment of fact-finding and in this instance is devoting itself to the oppression of a minority. Such a course can contribute only to national disunity and hinder the war effort.

Sincerely,
/s/ D. S. Myer
Director

After the hearings of the Dies subcommitttee in Los Angeles, with the widespread publicity given to the outrageous statements of Townshend and others, we insisted on an opportunity to appear before the subcommittee in an open hearing with the press present. We had spent much time documenting the dozens of charges and in preparing answers. So, when the Washington hearings started on July 6, we carried with us stacks upon stacks of mimeographed statements which we made available to the press as the questioning proceeded. We decided to open with a hard-hitting statement about the possible international effect of the committee's actions and the publicity of sensational statements, half-truths, and falsehoods. This statement follows:

Statement by Dillon S. Myer, Director of the War Relocation Authority, before the Costello Committee of the House Committee on Un-American Activities, July 6, 1943.

The manner in which the War Relocation Authority conducts its program is of concern to all the people in the United States, and it has a significance which goes far beyond the geographic boundaries of this country. Undoubtedly, the WRA program is being watched in Japan, where thousands of American soldiers and civilians are held as prisoners or internees; in China, India, Thailand, Burma, and many other countries whose collaboration we need if we are to defeat our enemies with a minimum loss of life.

The manner in which the problem is treated has a direct bearing on relations with our allies in winning the war, and on the position of this nation in establishing the terms of peace.

The grave international implications of this program demand that it be approached thoughtfully, soberly, and with maturity, and that public statements concerning it be made only after thorough understanding of the facts.

The program of the War Relocation Authority has been under investigation for the past eight weeks in such a manner as to achieve maximum publicity of sensational statements based on half-truths, exaggerations, and falsehoods; statements of witnesses have been released to the public without verification of their accuracy, thus giving nationwide currency to many distortions and downright untruths.

This practice has fostered a public feeling of mistrust, suspicion, and hatred that has had the effect of:

Providing the enemy with material which can be used to convince the peoples of the Orient that the United States is undemocratic and is fighting a racial war;

Undermining the unity of the American people;

Betraying the democratic objectives which this nation and its allies are fighting to preserve;

It may lead to further maltreatment of our citizens who are prisoners or who are interned.

One of the documents presented related to the Townshend testimony in Los Angeles; we said that he had lied or told half-truths 42 times during his testimony, and we verified each instance. This document was presented during a morning session of the hearing.

When the committee reopened the afternoon session, Representative Costello, the chairman, said, "Mr. Myer, we have reviewed your document on the Townshend testimony in which you say there were 42 lies or half-truths, but we find only 39." My response was, "Mr. Chairman, we will settle for 39."

The hearings continued for two days, and a report was issued on September 30, 1943. The report reviewed some of the charges that had appeared in the press during the course of the investigations and then concluded with three recommendations that seemed rather innocuous in view of the policies that were already in effect. The recommendations were:

1. That the War Relocation Authority expedite the segregation program (which was well under way);
2. That a board composed of representatives of the WRA and the various intelligence agencies of the federal government be constituted to investigate evacuees who apply for release and to pass finally upon their application;
3. That the WRA inaugurate a thoroughgoing program of Americanization for those Japanese who remain in the centers.

All of the members of the full committee approved these recommendations, except the late Representative Herman Eberharter (God bless his soul!). He submitted a minority report in which he said in part, "I cannot avoid the conclusion that the report of the majority is prejudiced and most of its statements are not proven." He then commented on the majority report point by point and agreed that a segregation program should be carried out, but he stated that he felt the WRA's preclearance investigation of evacuees and its efforts to foster Americanization at the relocation center were entirely adequate. He ended his report with this statement:

It is my conclusion that considering the magnitude of its job, the difficulty of the legal issues involved, and the complexity and delicacy of the problem of resettling a large group of people in the midst of a war, the War Relocation Authority has acted, by and large, efficiently and capably, and has carried out the spirit and intent of the President's Executive order under which it was established. I think it is better to let the War Relocation Authority carry on unhampered by unfair criticism.

Representative Eberharter's minority report came as a surprise, for he had given no inkling throughout the investigation that he felt as he did. After a year and a half of operation during which time we had taken it on the chin from many sources and had heard few kind words, his report was like manna from heaven to our overworked staff.

After the Tule Lake incident of November 1 to 3 of 1943, the Costello subcommittee held another series of hearings over a period of several days between November 29 and December 20, 1943, at which the committee staff and the majority of the subcommittee did their best again to prove laxness and ineptness on the part of WRA. Again, however, the final recommendations were comparatively mild. Once more Representative Eberharter came forth with a minority report defending WRA and calling for fair play.

CONGRESSIONAL CRITICS AND SUPPORTERS

Throughout the period of 1942, 1943, and early 1944 a number of California congressmen evidently felt that they must satisfy the demands of the West Coast exclusionist groups by making tough speeches on the floor of the House or by issuing statements to the press against the evacuees and the War Relocation Authority. Among those who continued to criticize or snipe were Congressmen Jack Z. Anderson, John Costello, Alfred Elliott, Clair Engle, Leland Ford, Bertram "Bud" Gearhardt, Carl Hinshaw, Leroy Johnston, John Phillips, Norris Poulson, Harry Shephard, and Richard Welch.

After this kind of harassment had continued for several weeks, Robert Gibson, a young WRA staff member from California who was employed in our Community Service Division, came into my office to express his concern and to ask permission to call on another member of the California delegation, Congressman Chet Holifield, whom he knew, with the object of telling the WRA side of the story. I readily agreed to his request. As a result, Congressman Holifield wrote a letter to me asking a series of questions which, of course, we answered quickly.

A few days after Holifield had received our reply, I was asked by Congressman Clarence Lea, chairman of the California delegation, to attend a meeting of the House of Representatives members from that state. I knew that Holifield had requested the meeting.

At the appointed time there were some tense moments as Chairman Lea addressed the delegation to report that Congressman Holifield was not present and that he himself was at a loss as to how to proceed. Fortunately Holifield arrived in the nick of time, and I stepped out into the aisle to shake his hand and to introduce myself.

At this meeting Holifield told the delegation that he had received from me much important information in reply to questions he had raised, and that he felt the whole delegation should have the opportunity to hear from me as Director of WRA. I then told the WRA story, and a hard-hitting questions-and-answer period followed.

After the meeting, Congressman Holifield and another delegation member, George Outland, suggested that we get together in Holifield's office. They were both ready and anxious to help. During this session Holifield made the valuable suggestion that I send a mimeographed newsletter regularly to each member of the West Coast delegation, every time there were important happenings or unfounded charges by the press or public. The newsletter would state the facts, so there would be no question about the delegates being properly informed. Holifield pointed out that responsible legislators, not otherwise informed, were free to quote the press and to repeat charges; but once it could be shown that the legislators had received the facts, they would "have their feet tied to the floor." The newsletter suggestion was adopted and utilized throughout the remainder of WRA's existence. It proved most helpful in keeping the record straight and avoiding repetition of irresponsible statements.

Thereafter Representative Holifield and Outland, as well as John Coffee of Washington state, continued to be most helpful throughout the WRA program in counseling, advising, and at times helping to carry the fight "on the side of the angels."

Norris Poulson of Los Angeles, a young Congressman during the 78th Congress (1942-1944), made probably the most vituperative speech among many directed against WRA, the evacuees, and me personally. He did not return to Congress for the 79th Session (1944-1946), but he returned in the 80th Congress and served for several years during the late 1940s and early 1950s, until elected Mayor of Los Angeles. Shortly after I took over the post of Commissioner of the Bureau of Indian Affairs in 1950, I happened to meet him in the lobby of the Capitol, and he said "Dillon, for some time I have been wanting to tell you that you were right and I was wrong during the war."

Some time later when the Interior Department appropriation was before the House, Representative George Bender of Ohio (my home state) made a slashing attack on the appropriation for the Bureau of Indian Affairs and upon me personally. Norris Poulson had the courage and honesty to rise to our defense. He said "You are wrong! I know Dillon Myer and I was critical of him during the war, but he was right and I was wrong."

After the first meeting with the California congressional delegation, there were others. These meetings were always tough and hard-hitting, and they served a useful purpose in providing a forum for the exchange of views and the opportunity to tell our side of the story.

MEETING THE AMERICAN LEGIONNAIRES

During the period of our operations, the late Homer Chaillaux from California, then executive officer of the Americanism Commission of the American Legion, was a real thorn in our side. He admitted to Clarence Pickett, who at that time was Executive Officer of the American Friends Service Committee, that the Legion's Americanism Commission had touched off the investigation by the Military Affairs Committee of the U. S. Senate under Senator Chandler. When that Committee failed to do the job that the Legion group hoped for, Chaillaux added, they got the Dies Committee to carry on an investigation.

Since Chaillaux had been the source of much of our trouble, we decided that we should have a hearing before key members of the American Legion if possible. We were surprised to discover that Frank Cross, a member of our information staff, not only was an active Legionnaire but for some years before World War II had served as executive officer of the Americanism Commission, the spot now held by Chaillaux. We learned further that Cross knew Jimmy O'Neal and others who were members of the commission. We assigned Cross the duty of visiting these friends, and Jimmy O'Neal of New England in particular, to explain our problem and to request help in getting a hearing.

The plan worked. O'Neal took the lead in insisting that we be invited to speak to the meeting of state commanders and state adjutants scheduled for Indianapolis, Indiana, on November 16, 1943, only two weeks after the Tule Lake affair. I was treated with courtesy and respect by everyone, except the two California officers who did their best to work me over during the free-swinging question period.

After the session ended, I left the meeting room and headed down a long hallway toward the men's room. Emerging from several other exits that opened from the meeting room into the hallway were numerous persons who rushed forth to compliment me on our position and the handling of the session. When, after about twenty minutes, I at last stepped through the door of the men's room, one of the Legionnaires spotted me and shouted, "By God, Mister, I was glad to hear you give it to those S.O.B.s!"

Needless to say, I felt well repaid for the trip and the effort.

OTHER DETRACTORS

Besides the American Legion, the California Joint Immigration Committee, the Hearst press, and the *Los Angeles Times,* lesser elements among the racists groups had to be faced from time to time. One of these was the Americanism Educational League, whose chairman was Jack Tenny. As a member of the California Legislature, Tenny headed the so-called Little Dies Committee in California. Executive director of the AEL was John R. Lechner, who was also chairman of the Americanism Commission of the 23rd District, American Legion Department of California. The District Legion Department backed Lechner for a time. It issued a booklet by Lechner called the "Inside Story of our Domestic Japanese Problem." We were told, however, that even the Legion tired of Lechner and failed to support him after a time.

In late 1942 one of our staff members, Theodore Waller, spent a short time making useful contacts in Seattle. While there he wrote to me urging that I invite Dave Beck, top man in the West Coast Teamsters Union, to come to see me when in Washington. Beck accepted my invitation and came to my office along with an associate. I explained to him our policy and program of relocation and asked for his cooperation in the program. He looked at me with his steely blue eyes and then said, "I believe that all of them should be relocated in the middle of the Pacific Ocean, and I will fight you to the last ditch in the program that you have presented." I was revolted that one of our labor unions had as a leader a cold and cruel person of this type. So I was not greatly surprised when we all learned a good many years later about Mr. Beck's unsavory activities.

The state of Arizona, where two of our centers were located, went all out to oppose the relocation of evacuees within the state. Members of the state legislature went so far as to enact a law which prevented the sale of merchandise to people of Japanese descent unless the would-be seller first published the intent to do so in the newspapers and filed documents to that effect with the governor. This bill was signed by the governor but was soon declared unconstitutional. The intent of the bill would have affected 600 local long-time residents of Japanese origin, had it been enforced. In addition, the growers of the Salt River Valley hired a press agent to carry on an anti-evacuee campaign for a period of time; the results of his work were of a very low order and served the purpose of stirring up real opposition in both Arizona and Nevada. This led to an interesting development.

In the early spring of 1943 the growers of early tomato and other plants in the Moapa Valley in Nevada were very short of labor and were fearful of heavy losses. They requested labor from our centers, but, since the governor of Nevada had been one of the most rabid ones in opposing the movement of Japanese into his state, we held up the movement because we had not had the required assurances in writing from the governor and the local authorities that they would provide protection and maintain law and order. Telegrams came in to WRA from a wide variety of organizations, including the American Legion Post, and from the governor of Nevada urging the release of labor to the valley.

H. Rex Lee, later to become governor of American Samoa, was in charge of the Salt Lake City area relocation office. In that capacity he visited the governor of Nevada to explain our policy. On that very day we had a telegram and a phone call from Senator Pat McCarran urging us to send in laborers. I then called Rex Lee's office in Salt Lake City and left word for him to contact me upon his return, regardless of how late. He phoned me that night to say that the Nevada governor had promised to send a letter that would meet our requirements. With Lee's assurance that he believed the governor would really send the letter I said, "Let the workers go!"

Some of the evacuees arrived in the Moapa Valley by truck before noon the very next day. Shortly thereafter Senator McCarran's office called to tell me that the senator wanted me to know that we had provided the most expeditious service he had ever experienced from any government agency. He of course did not know that the wheels were already turning when we had first heard from him, and I must confess I never took the trouble to enlighten him on that point.

There is a sequel to this story. The Arizona campaign had spilled over into Nevada, and some of the newspapers there started publishing scurrilous articles and editorials. Later in the spring, after the House of Representatives passed our appropriation bill without making any reductions in our request, we were surprised to get a call asking us to come up for a Senate appropriation committee hearing. This was quite unusual, in view of the fact that the Senate had received the bill from the House without any change in the requested amount. Such Senate hearings are held ordinarily to give the agencies of the executive branch an opportunity to testify in favor of "restorations" requested after the House has finished its cutting.

In this case it developed that Senator McCarran, a member of the committee, had asked for the hearing. He came to the hearing room with a handful of the scurrilous articles and editorials from back home, which he proceeded to read into the record one by one. After each reading, he would say: "This is what our editors think and I agree with them. But what do you think, Mr. Myer?" This went on for about 90 minutes, with equal time always being provided for me to reply. At the end the Senator said "Off the record," and then turned to the other members of the committee and said: "Gentlemen, this situation is pretty bad in my state, and it has gotten so bad that a constitutent wrote to me a few days ago and said if I didn't do something about it he would vote Republican the next time. Good day, gentlemen."

Before he was able to take his departure, I broke in with a statement and a question. "Senator McCarran," I said, "we sent some agricultural laborers to the Moapa Valley at your request sometime ago. Would you like us to remove them now?" He seemed ready for this and answered without hesitation, "By no means, Mr. Myer. You were most helpful, and the Japanese people are rendering a wonderful service in the Moapa Valley, and I want to thank you for sending them."

A few days later when a copy of the record of the hearings came to me for correction I noted that I had used the governor's name on two or three occasions. So I called the senator's office to inquire about the relations between the governor and the senator. The senator's administrative assistant said, "We just don't know, but why do you ask?" I replied that I could delete the reference or leave it, whichever was best. The assistant then asked, "Mr. Myer, do you have a copy of a wire from the governor urging the release of Japanese to the Moapa Valley?" When I answered in the affirmative, she said, "If you will send us a copy of the wire, we don't care what you do about the record." Thereafter there was a noticeable calming of the atmosphere in Nevada.

The first two years of our operation from March 1942 to March 1944 were the worst. With centers in turmoil and with three widely publicized incidents and the continued and intensive hounding by our detractors, we were kept busy. At the same time, however, we were learning our job by experience, and after the open hearings of the Dies committee in July 1943 we began to get some help. From that point on the good people of the country rolled up their sleeves and really went to work on our side.

Meanwhile the 100th Battalion and the 442nd Combat Team were beginning to win their laurels on the battlefield by early 1944, and on January 20 Secretary Stimson announced the reinstitution of selective service for the Nisei.

CHAPTER 9

The Emergency European Refugee Shelter

ON THE MORNING OF JUNE 10, 1944, the Director of the War Relocation Authority and the members of his staff were surprised to read in the newspapers that the agency had been given a new and somewhat different kind of responsibility. The president, the news stories of that day indicated, had decided to establish an emergency refugee shelter at Fort Ontario, Oswego, N. Y., for a group of approximately 1,000 war refugees to be brought in from Europe outside the regular immigration quotas. He had made WRA responsible for administration of this shelter. It was not until many weeks later that we learned the full background of events lying behind this unexpected expansion of our responsibilities.

In the early spring of 1944 the War Refugee Board felt that its rescue operations abroad were hampered by the fact that the United States had not yet made a concrete move in the direction of offering asylum to war refugees. The executive director of the board discussed the matter with the secretaries of State, Treasury, and War, who made up the board, and also with the president. As a result of the liberation of Rome, the executive director pointed out, displaced persons were streaming through the Allied lines in Italy and taxing supply lines seriously. When this situation was presented to the president, he decided to have approximately 1,000 refugees of assorted nationalities removed from the congested area and brought to the United States for war-duration shelter. The program was authorized in a cablegram which the president sent to Ambassador (at Large) Robert Murphy in Algiers on June 9; it was initiated almost immediately. The refugees to be given shelter were selected in Italy by a representative of the War Refugee Board, which sponsored the venture, and United States Army members of the Subcommission on Displaced Persons of the Allied Control Commission. The refugees embarked at Naples in mid-July on a troopship and arrived in the United States in early August.

THE REFUGEES

The refugees, at the time of arrival at Fort Ontario, were a decidedly bedraggled group. They were weary from the long journey, which included crowded quarters in an Army transport and an all-night ride by day coach to Oswego. But a deeper weariness, born of persecution, flight, internment, and war, showed on their faces. At Fort Ontario they found barracks, mess halls, a barbed wire fence — familiar reminders of life in other camps. In other respects, Fort Ontario in summer was an inviting spot. The refugees could relax as they viewed the lake front or strolled around the green parade ground.

At the gate, responsibility for the care of the refugees passed from the army to the War Relocation Authority. WRA was not happy at the prospect of running another camp. Out of its experience in the operation of relocation centers for Japanese American evacuees had come the conviction that detention in camps was an unnatural existence which should be avoided if any alternative was possible. The Authority had made last-minute attempts to alter the Oswego plan so that the refugees could be permitted, after a brief reception period, to live normal lives in outside communities. But President Roosevelt, in announcing the project, had stated that the refugees would remain at Fort Ontario "under appropriate security restrictions . . . for the duration of the war." As a consequence, both the War Refugee Board, which had the overall policy responsibility, and the Department of Justice, which held that these people were "not actually living within the United States," insisted upon a literal interpretation of the president's words even after the group had been screened for security by U.S. military intelligence officers.

So WRA set about the task of administering a shelter that

would give the residents the maximum of freedom consistent with the conditions governing their residence. Fortunately, the refugees' sense of isolation and confinement was lessened somewhat by the town's prevailing attitude of friendliness and solicitude of relatives, friends, and private agencies interested in their welfare. In fact, the amount of attention received, especially during the shelter's early days, was out of all proportion to the size and importance of the project as compared with the ten Japanese American relocation centers. Messages and packages came from all parts of the country as the newspapers and newsreels portrayed the gaunt and grimy company. Even the customs inspectors who examined the baggage chipped in and bought a complete outfit for a ragged 9-year-old boy. It was America's first close-up of a war refugee.

The 982 residents of Fort Ontario had in common their fund of refugee experience, but as individuals, and even as groups, they differed widely. In age, they ranged from a Spanish citizen of 80 who had been born in Salonika, Greece, to "International Harry" Maurer, delivered by an English army doctor to an Austrian mother in an American ambulance in Italy two days before the ship sailed.

The residents were predominantly Jewish, with small contingents of Roman Catholics, Greek Orthodox, and Protestants, but even the Jewish majority represented all shadings from extreme orthodoxy to reformed. The group was polyglot in the most literal sense. It contained persons of eighteen nationalities. WRA found that it had to use at least German, Serbo-Croatian, and Italian, in addition to English, to make itself understood by all the residents. Yugoslavs, Austrians, Poles, and Germans accounted for almost 90 percent of the group, while Czechs, Russians, Bulgarians, Turks, French, Hungarians, Rumanians, and other nationalities made up the remainder.

A substantial percentage of the Oswego refugees had a better than average education. For example, 713 of the 982 persons spoke one or more languages in addition to their native tongue. Many in the group had been successful business or professional people in their homelands. Whether by chance or design, the group that came to Fort Ontario included more persons with relatives in the United States and more who had applied for American visas in past years than a random selection would normally have produced. Over 50 families had "fireside" relatives in the United States, including spouses, parents, or children. The shelter population also included parents of more than a score of men in the American armed forces.

Many of the refugees had known extreme persecution — close to a hundred had been inmates of Dachau and Buchenwald. In the preceding five years most of them had personally experienced war and its deprivations — including the loss of immediate family members. All were anti-Nazis.

THE PROGRAM

Aside from its location in a zone where rigorous winter weather prevailed, the site of the Emergency Refugee Shelter was advantageous from a number of points of view. There were individuals in the town who were indifferent or even antagonistic toward the refugees, but they were a small minority. Most of the townspeople were friendly, and an advisory committee of town residents formed in the early days was consistently helpful to the shelter administration and to the refugee population.

By the opening of the fall term, arrangements had been made for almost 200 refugee children to attend Oswego's public and parochial schools. Because the town had lost population and teacher loads were down, there was room in the classes. Cooperating private agencies helped with books and supplies, and the shelter was close enough so that the younger children could all walk to school.

At first unfamiliarity with the English language made progress difficult for some of the children. But the majority made a surprisingly quick adjustment and were soon integrated into the various classes. It was a tremendously heartening experience both for the children and their parents.

WRA felt that its responsibility at Fort Ontario covered the essentials of everyday living — food, shelter, essential medical care, and grants to provide minimum clothing and incidentals. The Authority's policy was based on the belief that goods and services over and beyond these basic essentials should be provided from private sources.

At first a number of the private agencies vied with each other in offering educational, recreational, religious, and other services. Duplication of effort resulted until most of the agencies wisely decided to channel their efforts through a coordinating committee which established headquarters in Oswego. The committee's executive director consulted with the shelter director from time to time concerning offers of assistance made by private agencies.

The agencies sponsored and financed all educational, recreational, and religious activities. They provided supplies for publication of a weekly newspaper and arranged film programs several nights during the week. They furnished instruction and materials for English and vocational training classes, supported dramatic, musical, and arts and crafts activities, at times supplemented the government's clothing allowance and provided medical services which were valuable from a rehabilitative point of view. The agencies paid tuition and other costs for students attending the State Teachers' College, financed a nursery school, and reimbursed WRA to the extent of $9.50 a month per person for the employment of over fifty shelter residents in cultural and educational projects. Such personnel included the movie projectionist, librarian, music and art teachers, janitors of recreation and school buildings, the staff of a weekly newspaper, and community religious workers.

The refugees maintained their own households, and most of the able-bodied among them were employed in essential project duties at the rate of $18 per month. They completely staffed their own mess halls, provided a major portion of the services in the hospital, and assisted the appointed personnel in the offices, warehouses, and shops. Refugee hospital workers, for example, included five doctors, two dentists, a pharmacist, and various technicians.

The most difficult task was to recruit refugee workers for delivery of coal, removal of garbage, trash, and ashes, upkeep of the grounds, and similar arduous tasks. The quota of physically capable men was small and most of them were white-collar workers who had never before performed this type of labor. A rotation system was introduced in which each of the able-bodied persons was periodically excused from his regular job to do a weekly stint of the heavier chores, but the success of this plan was decidedly uneven throughout the project's life. An advisory council of shelter residents, elected on a basis of proportional nationality representation shortly after the group's arrival, tried for some weeks to create mutual understanding concerning these heavy-duty tasks between the shelter director and the population. The council resigned in December 1944 because of its inability to handle the work situation.

Under WRA policies the refugees were not permitted to work in private industry in or outside the shelter. The only exception was made in the fall of 1944 when an average of 50 refugees were recruited on an emergency basis over a period of several weeks to help save a local fruit crop. During this time they received prevailing wages.

THE FIRST YEAR

Generally speaking, the early fall of 1944 was a happy period at Fort Ontario. For the first time in years many of these people were enjoying good food; their wardrobes were replenished and a variety of other facilities were available to them. Many of them had visits from their American relatives and friends, and after the quarantine period they were permitted to go downtown to shop. Had Fort Ontario been a normal community, it would probably have settled into routine ways by Christmas, but it was by no means a normal community.

In many respects it did superficially resemble a town. Most of the adults worked; the children attended school; the people took part in social, recreational, and religious activities. In their store-bought clothes they were all but indistinguishable from the Oswego citizenry. Apart from the fact that they ate most of their meals in mess halls instead of at home, their daily habits resembled those of the average American family. But there was a subtle difference. One of the residents summed it up when he said that they possessed everything but the one thing they wanted most — freedom.

It is true that these people, before coming to the United States, had signed a statement indicating their understanding and acceptance of the conditions governing their residence at Fort Ontario and their return abroad at the war's end. Yet few of the residents were psychologically able to accept this as a commitment. They had always looked on the United States as the land of liberty and felt certain that they would be free agents on their arrival here or shortly thereafter.

As it became increasingly evident that this freedom was not to be, the people grew restive. Fort Ontario took on for them some of the characteristics of the internment camps and other places of detention in which they had been previously confined. They were grateful for the chance to come to the United States and appreciative of the arrangements made for their care, but they could not understand why, as anti-Nazis, they were subjected to restrictions more confining than they had experienced under the Allied occupation in

Italy. Even after they were security-checked by United States military intelligence, they needed a pass to go outside the shelter gate; they were not permitted to venture beyond the city's environs; and they could not accept private employment.

It was not just the fence that disturbed them; it was the indeterminate nature of their detention and the uncertainty of what lay beyond. Abroad, their very struggle for life had kept them going; now inaction strained some of them almost to the breaking point. They fretted ceaselessly. Minor events took on exaggerated meaning. Rumors were rampant. Nerves were rubbed raw.

After several futile attempts to effect a change in the detention policy which was being rigidly maintained by the War Refugee Board and Department of Justice, I sent a memorandum to the Secretary of the Interior, four months after the shelter opened, indicating that the shelter had already outlived its usefulness and that retrogression in the condition of the people might be expected beyond that point. Since acceptance of the shelter residents as ordinary quota immigrants seemed out of the question at that time, we pushed for a plan of "sponsored leave" under which private agencies, at their own expense, would undertake to resettle the shelter residents, assure their well-being in normal communities throughout the United States, pledge to the government that none would become a public charge, and agree to their return at any time and to any place designated by the government. WRA had been assured by a number of the private agencies that they would be willing to carry out such a program.

Secretary Ickes accepted the idea, finding it "intolerable that anti-Nazis should be kept under lock and key," but the War Refugee Board and the Department of Justice, to whom the proposal was subsequently made, were unwilling to permit any change in the leave regulations. WRA tried throughout the winter to obtain some relaxation which would permit residents to leave the shelter, if only for a temporary period, but such leave was permitted only in medical cases for which shelter hospital facilities were not adequate.

It was a bleak winter. A suicide and a death by accident depressed morale. The work situation was far from satisfactory. Heavy snows impeded the tasks at hand and made increasingly difficult the completion of chores essential to project maintenance and well-being.

In the spring, as the end of the war in Europe became increasingly imminent, the emphasis in the thinking of the shelter residents shifted to the second of the two original conditions mentioned by President Roosevelt — that the refugees "would be returned to their homelands" at the end of the war. The refugees, their relatives and friends, and numerous private organizations continued to campaign for the release, or at least parole, of the shelter residents. But a new concern was evident: that the second of the president's statements would be observed in the same literal sense as the first and that the refugees would be returned to their homelands. As reports came in from liberated portions of Europe, it became evident that such return would be involuntary on the part of most shelter residents. A survey of desires for future residence completed by WRA in April indicated that fewer than 14 percent were willing to return to their homelands and that the vast majority were hoping to remain in the United States.

By this time Brig. Gen. William O'Dwyer had succeeded John W. Pehle as executive director of the War Refugee Board. The board was going out of existence in a few months; the shelter was unfinished business; and the General was eager to dispose of it. He consulted with representatives of the agencies concerned — the State and Justice Departments, the War Relocation Authority, UNRRA, and the Intergovernmental Committee on Refugees. Meetings were held at which several possible solutions were discussed. Finally, it was decided that UNRRA and the Intergovernmental Committee would work with WRA on plans for those shelter residents who wished repatriation or emigration to other countries of their choice. This left the main issue unsettled, although hope was expressed that a solution would be found consistent with United Nations policy on displaced persons.

While these negotiations were proceeding, the shelter director despaired of any constructive solution and resigned his post in May in order to form a national committee which would work for the freedom of the shelter residents. A committee of 27 leading Oswego citizens also petitioned the president and Congress about this time, urging that the refugees be released and permitted to apply for admission to the United States under the immigration laws.

Early in June, President Truman transferred the overall policy responsibility for Fort Ontario from the moribund War Refugee

Board to the Department of the Interior. At this juncture Secretary Ickes strongly urged the president to approve a program of sponsored leave. The Department of Justice again objected, but this time proposed an alternate method by which, if certain conditions could be satisfied, the refugees might be brought within the scope of the immigration laws.

Meanwhile, the House Committee on Immigration and Naturalization, which had received many inquiries concerning the status of the refugees, decided to conduct its own investigation. A subcommittee, visiting Oswego in the latter part of June, took testimony from WRA officials, Oswego townspeople, and the refugees themselves. The committee members were impressed with the caliber of the refugee group, both in terms of their good behavior and their contributions to the cultural and educational life of the town. They inquired searchingly into the relationships and connections which the refugees still had in various parts of the world and were given substantial evidence indicating that most of the group no longer felt any meaningful ties with their homelands.

The House subcommittee reported back to the full committee on immigration, and the full committee issued a resolution on July 6 which asked the departments of State and Justice to ascertain whether it was "practicable" to return the refugees to their homelands. If so, they were to be returned at the first available opportunity. The committee also declared that "the continued expense of $600,000 per annum in maintaining the camp at Oswego is inadvisable, unwarranted, and should be discontinued." If the return of the refugees was not deemed practicable, the attorney general was requested to declare them illegally present in the country and to dispose of them in accordance with existing laws.

This focusing of attention on the shelter problem gave heart to the shelter population, who felt that their cause was being given some consideration, and that their detention would soon be at an end. The mood was lighter during the late spring and summer. An arts and crafts exhibit of the best work of shelter residents attracted such wide notice that a selection of the best objects was put on display at the Syracuse Art Museum. The theatrical and musical groups were active. The end of the school year found one-fifth of the forty refugee high school students on the honor roll; the other children in the junior high and elementary schools had done correspondingly well.

A few slight relaxations in the leave regulations were now made. Several children were placed in foster homes outside the shelter; refugees were permitted to visit next of kin in outside hospitals; and the boundary for passes was extended from the city limits of Oswego to a distance of 20 miles, enabling residents to visit nearby towns and state parks. At the same time, however, disquieting reports were coming in from liberated Europe, and the residents were becoming increasingly anxious about their future.

THE IMMIGRATION ISSUE

During this period a number of administrative regulations were put into effect at the shelter which improved the work situation, raised safety and sanitation standards, and brought about a substantial improvement in cooperative relationships with the private agencies. An executive committee of Fort Ontario residents also took office during this period and, for the first time since the resignation of the refugee advisory council over the work issue of December 1944, the shelter had a form of representative self-government. Following the resignation of the shelter director in May, the project was headed up for an interim period by members of the Washington staff on detail until a new shelter director was appointed in the latter part of July. The WRA chief engineer, who was named shelter director at that time, served until the project's end, seven months later.

Meanwhile, in Washington, Secretary Ickes, in a memorandum to the State and Justice departments on July 31, urged that those departments take steps to follow the course of action suggested by the attorney general and approved by the president to provide for the temporary admission, under appropriate immigration statutes, of those refugees whose return abroad was found to be impracticable. Another waiting period followed, but as a direct result of this correspondence, the State and Justice departments arranged for representatives to visit Oswego for the purpose of interviewing and classifying all shelter residents. The following categories were mentioned by Secretary of State Byrnes in a letter on August 23, to Secretary Ickes, in which the attorney general concurred:

1. In accordance with President Roosevelt's commitment to the

Congress, all of the refugees who can be returned to their homelands should be returned as soon as practicable, unless they desire to proceed to some other country.

2. Those refugees who do not wish to be returned to their home-lands, but who desire to proceed to some other country will be per-mitted to do so.

3. Those refugees who do not desire to leave the United States and who cannot, as a practical matter, be returned to their homelands, should be turned over to the Immigration and Naturalization Service by the War Relocation Authority and will be granted a temporary stay in the United States as nonimmigrants, the passport and nonimmigrant visa requirements being waived by me on an emergency basis. Any aliens in this group who are eligible for admission into the United States as immigrants will be permitted to proceed to Canada or some other country and obtain immigration visas from an American consular officer. Those who do not depart on or before the day their temporary stay expires will become subject to deportation proceedings, unless such stay is extended.

Secretary Byrnes stated that, in view of the House Resolution, the proposed action would not be taken "until the program is laid be-fore" the Senate and House committees on immigration. "If those committees do not disapprove," he continued, "the program will then be submitted to the President and if he approves will be placed in effect."

Before initiating the survey, the State and Justice departments invited the Interior Department (i.e. WRA) to participate, and in September four representatives from each of the three departments interviewed all shelter residents and classified them along the lines suggested by Secretary Byrnes. The shelter population at the time of the inquiry consisted of 918 persons. The review panel, consisting of one representative from each of the three departments, found that only 32 persons desired to return to their homelands. The State and Justice department representatives felt that it was practicable to classify an additional 695 persons as returnable to their countries of origin or former residence, despite their unwillingness to be repatriated.

The WRA refugee program officer, who headed the Interior Department group and served on the review panel, dissented on 90 percent of these cases. His position generally was that it was in-humane to force people to return abroad against their desires under prevailing conditions. He agreed, however, in most instances with the majority recommendation that 72 persons who were willing to leave the United States should be permitted to seek admission to the countries of their choice. There was a unanimous finding by all three departments that 119 persons should be classified as not practicable to return.

The difference of opinion between the State and Justice representatives on the one hand, and the Interior representative on the other, hinged on the meaning of the word "practicable." The State and Justice officials felt that it was "practicable" to return virtually all of the shelter residents except where there were close family ties in the United States or a clear showing that the individual's safety would be jeopardized by his repatriation — as, for example, in the case of returning White Russians to the Soviet Union. The refugee program officer, who had my full support on this question, felt that while it was probably physically possible to return the people, they should not be forced back against their will to countries where they feared continued religious or political persecution and where many of their immediate family members had been exterminated. In essence, WRA's position was that United States policy with respect to this tiny segment of the world's displaced population should be consistent with the policies of UNRRA, the Intergovernmental Committee on Refugees, and our own army in occupied zones of Europe. All of these agencies opposed involuntary repatriation.

The findings of the interdepartmental survey were forwarded to the three Cabinet officers in the latter part of October. Anticipating that there might be a delay in arriving at a decision, because of the broader policy questions involved, WRA on October 24 had recommended to Secretary Ickes that the department press for an interim policy of sponsored leave pending the final judgment of the government as to the practicability of the refugees' return. The secretary so recommended in a letter to the president, dated October 31.

Finally, a meeting was called for December 5, and representatives of the three departments met to consider a draft of a letter to Senator Russell and Congressman Dickstein which had been prepared for the signatures of the secretary of state, attorney general, and the secretary of the interior. This draft, which was written in the Justice Department, was intended to inform the chairmen of the two committees on immigration of the results of the survey made at Oswego and to urge upon them a settlement of the matter in line with the majority findings. The State Department representative concurred with the draft prepared by the Justice Department, but the Interior Department representative expressed belief that it would be unacceptable to his department. The issue again was over the meaning of the term "practicable." The Interior Department representative felt that the draft as prepared had no reference to United Nations or even United States policy on the handling of displaced persons. An alternate draft prepared in the Department of the Interior was forwarded to Attorney General Clark and Assistant Secretary of State Russell for their consideration in mid-December. However, neither draft was even sent to Senator Russell or Representative Dickstein.

Instead, after weeks of effort by the WRA and its supporters, the problem of the shelter was solved suddenly, unexpectedly, and finally. On December 22, 1945, President Truman, in a general statement on immigration to the United States, opened the way for residents of the shelter to apply for formal admission to the United States, by calling upon the secretary of state and the attorney general to adjust the immigration status of these people in strict accordance with existing laws and regulations. The president pointed out that a careful survey by the Department of State and the Immigration and Naturalization Service showed that most of the shelter residents would, upon application, be admissible under the immigration laws. He then declared, "It would be inhumane and wasteful to require these people to go all the way back to Europe merely for the purpose of applying there for immigration visas and returning to the United States." This was virtually the position which WRA had been taking all through the negotiations.

RESETTLEMENT AND LIQUIDATION

Plans for the resettlement of the shelter population and liquidation of the camp as soon as the opportunity arose had been drawn up well in advance of the president's announcement. Immediately after the announcement no time was lost in putting these plans into effect. Representatives of the State and Justice departments and of the United States Public Health Service assembled at the shelter on January 7, 1946, to begin the official immigration examination. On the same day the National Refugee Service, a private agency which had volunteered to accomplish the resettlement of the refugees and had been designated to do so by WRA, opened its Fort Ontario headquarters. Together with other cooperating private agencies, the National Refugee Service immediately began interviewing the shelter population and assisting them to make resettlement plans. One month later Fort Ontario was a ghost town.

The first party of slightly under 100 residents left by bus January 17 for Niagara Falls, Canada, where they received their immigration visas. The remainder of the shelter population departed between that date and February 5. The vast majority of the shelter residents desired to enter the United States and were able to meet the immigration and quota requirements.

Of the original 982 travel-weary refugees who had arrived at Fort Ontario in August 1944, 69 had voluntarily departed from the United States before the period of shelter liquidation. Sixty-six of these had been voluntarily repatriated to Yugoslavia and one each had gone to Czechoslovakia, Uruguay, and the Union of South Africa. During the 18-month period, 14 refugees had died and 23 babies were born at the shelter. This left 922 persons in residence at the shelter at the time when the final processing began.

Of the 922 residents, 765 journeyed to Niagara Falls and were admitted to the United States as permanent immigrants. A total of 134 received temporary permits to enter the United States. Of those temporarily admitted, the majority (88 persons) were awaiting permanent immigration in March, when quota numbers would be available for their entry. The remainder of the 134 consisted of 19 persons awaiting voluntary repatriation, 8 awaiting emigration to countries of their choice, and 19 found by the immigration officers to be inadmissible to the United States for reasons of health. The 23 children born in the shelter were adjudged United States citizens by birth.

After the long months of delay, the speed with which the final processing was carried on served as a bracing tonic. Had the immigration processing or resettlement planning been stretched out over a long period, it is possible that, desirous as they were of leaving, a number of the shelter residents might have become apprehensive about quitting the security of the shelter. As it turned out, time did not permit indecision.

Families having relatives or friends willing and able to bear responsibility for their future welfare were encouraged to resettle in the communities where their sponsors resided. Those whose ties were nonexistent or tenuous were aided in the selection of communities where they would be assisted by a cooperating agency in finding housing, employment, and other resources for social adjustment. Thus every member of the shelter population, whether admitted to the United States on a permanent or temporary basis, had a definite resettlement plan at the time of his departure, involving either family or agency sponsorship. The private agencies pledged the government that none would become a public charge.

While many of the refugees settled in the East, particularly in New York City where a number had close kinship ties, the shelter population actually spread to 70 communities in 21 states throughout the country. Accomplishing the resettlement of the entire group within the time allotted called for close coordination at every step between the WRA staff at the shelter and the private agencies who were developing the placement plans and taking over full responsibility at the shelter gate. It represented the high point of a unique collaboration between the government and the private agencies which had begun in the project's earliest days and had characterized its development throughout.

As the refugees left the shelter, the government officials, Oswego townspeople, and the private agency workers who had come to know them best believed that most of them had a high potential for successful adjustment in the United States. During their stay they had learned to speak English, in many cases quite fluently. Although they had only seen the main street of an upstate New York town of 20,000 population and had spent most of their time behind barbed wire, they had learned a surprising amount about American customs and habits and had acquired a sense of values which enabled them to face their future realistically. The remarkable record of the children had caused the Oswego superintendent of education to predict that they would get along without difficulty in any schools to which they transferred.

The last resident left Fort Ontario February 5, and after property questions and other liquidation matters had been satisfactorily settled, the historic post was turned back to the army on February 28, 1946. During the shelter's life WRA consistently tried to perform its stewardship in a humane and reasonable manner. As in the case of the relocation centers for Japanese Americans, however, the Authority's most acute sense of accomplishment came at the end when it could close the camp and release the residents to free lives in normal communities throughout the United States.

PART 3

The Relocation Program

CHAPTER 10

The Out-of-Center Relocation Program

IN THE EARLY DAYS of the WRA program, Milton Eisenhower had tentative plans for establishing as many as fifty centers or work camps for evacuees throughout the West by utilizing abandoned CCC camps and similar facilities. It was hoped that such a plan would serve two purposes: (1) provide an opportunity for evacuees to work on farms, and (2) lay the basis for resettlement with the camps operating as dispersion points from which evacuees could relocate to jobs in urban areas as well as on farms. In March 1942 pressures not only from Japanese people who had moved voluntarily and were stranded but also from local officials in the western states increased to such an extent that WRA officials recommended to General DeWitt that he prohibit further uncontrolled evacuation. On March 27 Public Proclamation No. 4 was issued requiring all Japanese to remain within Military Area No. I without change of residence, effective after midnight March 29. This action was subsequent to an order on March 24 establishing a curfew in Military Area No. I, effective between 8 P.M. and 6 A.M.

THE WESTERN GOVERNORS' CONFERENCE

Because of the confusion and misunderstanding regarding the evacuation and the status of evacuees, a meeting was called at Salt Lake City on April 7 to explain the situation to the officials of the western states. This meeting was attended by western governors or their representatives, attorneys general, state agriculture extension directors, state agricultural war board chairmen, and Farm Security Administration directors. The gathering is generally referred to as the Governors' Conference.

The federal contingent included Colonel Karl B. Bendetsen, assistant chief of staff in charge of civil affairs, Western Defense Command, and Fourth Army; Tom C. Clark, an official of the U.S. Department of Justice and chief of the civilian staff, Wartime Civil Control Administration; and Milton Eisenhower, director of WRA.

After the WRA director had explained the status of the evacuees and described the tentative plans for resettlement, the governors generally expressed such vehement opposition or laid down such stringent proposals for handling the evacuees that any attempts at resettlement in the near future appeared futile. The only one who took a constructive approach was the representative of Governor Carr of Colorado.

It was made clear by the agricultural representatives that farm labor was badly needed, especially in the sugar beet fields. Director Eisenhower stated at the close of the meeting that immediate requests for evacuee workers would have to be denied in view of the attitude expressed.

The chief result of this conference was the establishment of the type of relocation centers that came into being during the spring and summer. Furthermore, because Director Eisenhower came to the conclusion that large-scale relocation outside of centers would not be feasible for a considerable period, WRA established an industrial division on the assumption that there would be need for industries to be established within the centers as a means of providing employment for substantial numbers of evacuees from strictly urban areas.

SEASONAL LEAVE

Ironically, within a week after the ill-fated Salt Lake City conference, requests for farm workers began flowing into WRA's San Francisco regional office. The demands intensified throughout the rest of April and early May. In view of these insistent demands, the WRA officials realized that their position would be untenable if they had a sizable reserve of workers sitting idle in relocation centers. In mid-May four officials journeyed to the Portland assembly center with the idea of enlisting evacuees in the "work corps" which was provided for in Executive Order No. 9102. On arrival the officials soon discovered that the evacuees were emphatically not interested in joining a work corps. The result was a shelving of the work corps concept and a shift of focus to seasonal leave. The trip to Portland was not a total loss, however, for on May 20 a small group of evacuees from the assembly center journeyed to Nyssa, Oregon, to explore working and living conditions in Malheur county. They reported favorably upon their return to the center, and immediately additional workers were recruited. This was the beginning of seasonal leave.

In the meantime the Director of WRA and the head of the Wartime Civil Control Administration (WCCA) drew up a plan whereby evacuees could be released from army assembly centers for seasonal agricultural work. This agreement provided that the governors at the state level, and the sheriffs, prosecuting attorneys, commissioners, and judges at the county level, sign a pledge that labor was needed and that they would guarantee the safety of the workers. The agreement further provided that transportation to and from the centers would be furnished by the employers, that prevailing wages would be paid, that there would be no replacement of local labor, and finally that the U.S. Employment Service in the counties would provide housing, without cost to the evacuees, in the area of employment.

A number of counties in Idaho, Utah, and Montana made application for workers, and by the end of June 1,500 workers had been recruited in spite of the pressures by many officials to change the rules. There were few incidents, and these were minor. WRA threatened to withdraw workers on a number of occasions as a result of threats by local bullies, but in each such case employers saw to it that conditions were immediately improved. The evacuees were so well liked and established such a reputation for efficiency that labor pirating by prospective employers came into vogue in several areas. As a result labor contracts between employers and evacuee groups became necessary.

By September 1942 the demand for seasonal labor by farmers and sugar beet companies became so great that an additional employee to handle seasonal leave was added to the San Francisco office staff, making two at the regional level. Field inspectors' offices consisting of one man and a secretary were found necessary and were established in Boise and Idaho Falls in Idaho; Helena and Havre, Montana; Salt Lake City, Utah; and one each in Colorado and Wyoming. There were requests for tens of thousands of workers, and there was much criticism of both WRA and the evacuees because more could not be provided. This criticism arose in spite of the fact that 10,000 evacuees were on seasonal leave by mid-October.

A young Los Angeles Nisei from the Heart Mountain center, who volunteered for work in the beet fields of Montana, takes his first swipe at a beet top under the direction of a supervising farmer. (WRA photo)

STUDENT LEAVE

During the spring of 1942, even before the movement into assembly centers was completed, several organizations became concerned about the plight of Nisei students who had been forced to leave college as a result of the evacuation orders. It became apparent that organized assistance to these students was badly needed.

Director Eisenhower called upon Clarence Pickett, executive director of the American Friends Service Committee, to help establish an organization that could handle this assistance. Pickett's efforts resulted in the establishment of the National Student Relocation Council, at a meeting in Chicago on May 29, 1942. John Nason, President of Swarthmore College, was named chairman of the Council. A West Coast subcommittee, functioning under the leadership of Joseph Conrad, centered its efforts on finding students who were interested in transfer and on investigating their academic fitness and financial status.

An Eastern subcommittee, with President Robbins W. Barstow of Hartford (Connecticut) Theological Seminary as executive secretary, directed its efforts toward determining which colleges or universities outside of the evacuated area would accept students, and how many. WRA handled clearance of colleges with the War and Navy departments, and eventually 143 institutions of higher education were cleared for acceptance of evacuee students. Prior to September 30, 1942, 250 students from assembly and relocation centers were granted educational leaves under the WRA tentative leave policy.

GENERAL RELOCATION AND LEAVE POLICY

On June 17, 1942, when I took over as WRA Director, seasonal leave was already under way, and the plans for college leave were well started. But plans for a more general relocation program had been at least temporarily abandoned due to the all-out objections of the western governors at the Salt Lake City meeting and due to what appeared to be a solid front against relocation, except for seasonal agricultural labor.

Tom Holland, chief of the WRA employment division, had returned from a field trip during which he had visited the Portland Assembly Center and participated in the ill-starred attempt at recruitment for the work corps. At my very first staff meeting, his report of his visit to centers and his strong feelings about the horrors of maintaining such unnatural communities had impressed me very deeply.

On my first visit to two centers in late June and early July I found that I was continuously thinking of Tom Holland's report. Upon my return from this trip I reported to the staff that I agreed with the point of view which he had expressed, and I authorized immediate work on plans for a relocation program.

Morrill Tozier of our Information Staff was, at the time of this staff meeting, deeply skeptical about the feasibility of relocation in view of the widespread public hostility to everything Japanese. However, his mind was changed by my statement that I was fearful we would have something akin to Indian reservations to deal with if steps were not taken soon to move the Japanese Americans back into the mainstream of American life.

The first relocation policy statement, issued on July 20, 1942, was a cautious one. Leave was granted only to American-born Nisei who had never studied in Japan and to those in this category who had a definite offer of employment. For those still in assembly centers, army permits were required. Many of these requests were turned down by the army. Throughout the summer and fall, relocation was on a "retail basis," in the words of the chief of the employment division. Each application was processed individually both at the center and in Washington. Sometimes many weeks went by before the applicant was cleared for departure, and often job offers were cancelled because of the length of time required for clearance. Very few evacuees other than college students relocated as a result of this first and perhaps over-cautious leave policy.

Immediately after the issuance of the July 20 statement a staff committee was put to work to hammer out a more comprehensive policy. One possibility considered was an all-out program which would provide that any evacuee could leave a center at his or her own discretion. While this would have been ideal from a civil liberties standpoint, the lack of public understanding and the experience of the voluntary evacuees earlier made such a drastic policy seem wholly impractical.

We decided about mid-August to place the matter before the solicitor general of the United States. A set of carefully drafted regulations was prepared and submitted to the solicitor general in September. At the time of presentation we pointed out that we would prefer to open the gates of the centers without procedural restrictions if the Justice Department would sanction and support such free movements of the evacuees. In case the Justice Department was not willing to support such a policy, we were then prepared to publish the leave regulations as drafted. But we wanted the assurance from the department that the legal validity of the regulations would be approved and defended by the department in case of litigation. The solicitor general stated that throwing wide the center gates seemed unwise. He then approved the draft of the regulations and agreed to defend them in court if need be.

These regulations were published in the *Federal Register* on September 26 and became effective on October 1, 1942. They covered all types of leave.

1. *Short-term leave* was intended for the evacuees who found it necessary to leave the center for a short time for medical consultation, property arrangements or other personal business. This type of leave was granted by the project director after investigation.

2. *Work-group leave,* or *seasonal leave* (as it was more commonly known), was designed to provide for the widespread demand for agricultural labor. Here again the project director had authority to grant such leave, usually after a record check by the intelligence agencies.

3. *Indefinite leave* was granted at that time only by the national director after four specific requirements were met: *(a)* An applicant had to have a definite job offer or some other means of support; *(b)* there must be no evidence either in the applicant's record at the center or in the files of the intelligence agencies indicating that he might endanger the national security; *(c)* there had to be reasonable evidence that the applicant's presence would be acceptable where he planned to live; and *(d)* the applicant had to agree to keep WRA informed of any change in address. All of these provisions were felt to be essential in order to assure communities that the evacuees would not become public charges and that they were not dangerous. In addition the evacuees needed to be assured about the kind of reception they might expect, and the notice-of-change-of-address provision was included to enable WRA to better serve the evacuees.

By the time of the issuance of the October 1 regulations the key staff members were convinced that for several good reasons such a program was essential:

1. We recognized that loyalty could not flourish in an atmosphere of restriction and discriminatory segregation.

2. It was recognized that such a wide and enforced deviation from normal cultural and living patterns might very well have lasting and unfavorable effects upon individuals, particularly children and young people, who made up a large part of the population.

3. There was an obligation on the part of the War Relocation Authority both to the evacuees and to the people of the United States generally to restore all loyal citizens and law-abiding aliens to a normal useful American life with all possible speed.

4. Confinement in relocation centers fostered suspicion of evacuee loyalties and added to evacuee discouragements.

5. We did not want to be responsible for fostering a new set of reservations in the United States akin to Indian reservations.

In the meantime there was a growing realization that a tremendous demand for workers and an acceptance of the evacuees could be widespread if the public were properly informed and reassured.

In mid-November, about the time of the Poston incident, while we were in Salt Lake City for a conference of western WRA directors, we were implored by some local citizens to recruit workers for the local federal ordnance plant there. This appeared to me to be almost the ultimate in community acceptance, and it helped to make up my mind to go all-out in our relocation program.

We went on to San Francisco from Salt Lake City to visit the regional office and while there we made two important announcements: (1) that we were closing the regional offices as they then existed and were moving most of the functions to Washington and (2) that we were going to establish relocation field offices across the country to expedite the relocation process.

Tom Holland, our employment chief, was on a field trip in Wyoming, and I wired him to join us in San Francisco. Upon his arrival I told him of the decision to go all-out including the establishment of field relocation offices. I asked him for an estimate as to how soon we could staff six or eight key area offices across the country. He was reluctant to give an estimate but reviewed for me the names of three or four people who he felt were capable of heading up these key offices.

Seven district offices already were located in the west, established originally to administer the seasonal work program. They already were devoting some time to promoting indefinite leave among the seasonal workers.

AREA RELOCATION OFFICES

H. Rex Lee, who had been supervising the seasonal leave program from San Francisco, moved to Salt Lake City to establish the area relocation office there. The first midwestern field office was opened on January 4, 1943, in Chicago. Soon thereafter similar offices were opened in Cleveland, Minneapolis, Des Moines, Milwaukee, New York City, and numerous other cities. By June 30, the close of the fiscal year, 42 field offices were scattered from Spokane to Boston. Eight of these were area relocation offices, each headed by a relocation supervisor who was generally responsible for relocation work in a broad area. They supervised the district offices within their area, but at the same time they functioned as local relocation offices within the cities where they were located. These area offices were located in Chicago, Cleveland, Denver, Salt Lake City, Kansas City (Mo.), Little Rock (Ark.), New York, and Boston.

In the early months these offices were primarily concerned with creating favorable community acceptance and in finding suitable jobs for evacuees and in working closely with community resettlement committees. The officers gave talks to business, professional, social, civic, church and fraternal groups. They met with employers individually and in groups, enlisted the aid of unions, and spoke to employees in plants where the employment of Japanese was contemplated. They supplied news to the press and carried on a public relations job in general.

LOCAL RESETTLEMENT COMMITTEES

From the beginning of the relocation program in mid-summer of 1942, WRA realized that there would be a definite need for the assistance and support of citizens groups within the various localities in order to gain public acceptance and to assist evacuees in making adjustments in their new communities. The chief of the employment division wrote in his final report about this important matter as it related to his thoughts during the mid-summer and early fall of 1942.

It appeared to me quite possible that we could locate a small but effective group of people who were deeply interested in the problems growing out of the evacuation and were willing to give their support to doing something practical to solve them. It seemed fruitless to try to convince the whole population of the rightness and the necessity of a relocation program. It could be conceded that a majority of the people in any community would not understand the problem or sympathize with the way out that we were taking. . . . It appeared to me that the most practical way to relocate these people was to find a few sympathetic people in the community who were willing to put in their time and energy. In the larger places these people could most likely form a committee to coordinate their activities. As we saw the relocation machinery early in August 1942, it looked as if WRA would do a minimum in the way of field work. We would spend the most of our energy on locating interested people, advising on the organization of committees, providing educational material on evacuation and relocation, and supplying local sponsors with information about the occupational background of evacuees who wanted to relocate.

As a result of a trip to the midwest by the employment chief and the interest of many church people, local resettlement committees were formed in the fall of 1942 in Minneapolis, Madison (Wisconsin), Chicago, and Cleveland. These committees came into existence weeks before the establishment of field offices in the midwest.

As we moved into high gear in the fall of 1942, Roswell Barnes of the Federal Council of Churches of Christ in America, who had kept in close touch with the WRA program, convinced his executive board that the council should supply funds to hire a traveling representative to assist in the stimulation and organization of resettlement committees across the country. Mr. George Rundquist was assigned to this post, and he rendered yeoman service in getting these community committees established. While local church people usually took the lead, the committees generally took in civic leaders, representatives of local organizations such as the YMCA and YWCA, and other social-minded individuals and groups.

By the end of 1943, twenty-six local resettlement committees had been established across the country from Salt Lake City, Utah, to Washington, D. C.

The first job of these committees was to help create a favorable public sentiment toward the incoming evacuees. This was done by personal contact with key officials and leading citizens in the community. They sponsored meetings at which WRA officials might explain the nature and purpose of the program and they utilized a variety of public information devices. The second phase of their work, which was equally important, was to help the incoming evacuees in making adjustments to their new environment. In the early stages they helped in contacting potential employers, but it was not long before a surplus of jobs became available and such contacts became unnecessary. Other forms of community-adjustment assistance included the tough job of finding adequate housing, getting evacuee children in school, aiding breadwinners to become members of local labor unions, and helping evacuees generally in establishing church and other social contacts.

As the program broadened and more persons relocated, there was a need not only to assist evacuees in employment, housing, and public relations, but also to implement locally national agreements which had been worked out by WRA and to coordinate the efforts of other groups and agencies so that services of all types available in the normal community would be readily available to evacuees. As this need developed, a staff member of each WRA field office was designated to assist in the organization of community resources and to serve as the liaison with the resettlement committees. It was important to ease the transition of the evacuees from the isolated and socially artificial center environment to life in a normal community by meeting the resettlers with an understanding of their needs. It was also important to encourage relocated evacuees to assist their family members and friends to relocate.

Most of the people who relocated early were young and inexperienced and needed the reassurance and security of family support. By the fall of 1943 more parents of young evacuees left the centers to join their children, and the infusion of the older generation provided a more stable and better-integrated social situation in areas where resettlement had taken place.

The Cleveland resettlement committee, one of the first to be

organized in 1942, continued to be one of the most active under
the leadership of the late George Trundle, industrialist who gave
a great deal of time and effort to the fine work of the committee.
Some of the committees were quite active and in some cases performed functions which WRA would have normally regarded as
its own responsibility.

As we moved toward the job of helping evacuees to return
to the West Coast, community committees in California, Washington, and Oregon rendered yeoman service in giving badly needed
encouragement to timid evacuees and in helping to fight the battles
on the home front where there was opposition to the return.

One committee that covered a much wider territory than the
community committees was the Pacific Coast Committee on American Principles and Fair Play. It was organized in 1942. Galen
Fisher, vice-chairman of the Western Area Protestant Church Commission for Wartime Japanese Service, was a member. Its executive
officer was Mrs. Ruth Kingman of Berkeley, California. This organization helped to fight the battles of the Japanese Americans
most effectively throughout the war. Due to the active and effective
work of Ruth Kingman, local "fair play" committees were established under the leadership of the main committee all up and down
the West Coast.

In the last months of the resettlement program these committees not only continued to oppose the racists and to fight the battles
of the Japanese Americans, but they supplemented the efforts of
George Rundquist of the Federal Council of Churches of Christ
in America and WRA by helping to establish additional local resettlement committees throughout the West Coast area.

RELOCATION SPEEDED UP

By March 1943 the tempo of relocation had speeded up so
much that certain changes in the procedures had to be made. The
handling of applications for indefinite leave was decentralized to
the project director for granting clearance and to the field offices
for checking community attitudes. Also a system of financial aids
was established for those relocating without independent means.
Fifty dollars was provided for those without dependents, seventy-
five dollars if there was one dependent, and one hundred dollars

if there were two or more dependents. These grants were later revised so as to provide $25 per person regardless of family size, $3 per diem while in travel status, plus coach fare.

Once the center registration was complete and all of the dockets had been processed through the intelligence agencies for a name check, WRA authorized the project directors to grant indefinite leave to all except those who were to be listed as segregants and those who were to relocate in the area of the Army's Eastern Defense command.

The Japanese American Joint Board, established by the War Department on January 20, 1943, was composed of representatives of WRA, the Office of Naval Intelligence, Army Intelligence, and the Provost Marshal General's Office — one man from each agency. The theory behind the establishment of this board was that it would help in identifying pro-Japanese individuals and especially in determining eligibility of Japanese American citizens for work in war plants.

The board was to make recommendation to WRA on all evacuee citizens regarding the granting of indefinite leave. These recommendations were not binding on WRA, but we did make further investigations of our own in cases where the recommendation was negative.

General Hugh Drum, who headed the Eastern Defense Command, insisted that none of the evacuees be relocated within his command area, which included most of the industrialized northeastern part of the country. However, Assistant Secretary of War John J. McCloy overruled General Drum and insisted that the Joint Board clearance be accepted for relocation in the eastern area. So for some months this condition for relocation on the eastern seaboard was accepted by the WRA.

The review process by the board was so slow that many eligible evacuees lost the opportunity to accept desirable jobs. Consequently on December 14, 1943, after the Tule Lake movement of segregants was completed, WRA withdrew from this agreement to clear relocatees into the Eastern Defense Command with the Joint Board.

Early in 1944 the Joint Board was dissolved. The board returned to WRA about 1,000 dockets on which no action had been taken. The actions of the board were looked upon by the evacuees as one more case of discrimination, and for this reason it served as a deterrent to relocation instead of an aid as was intended.

By the end of 1943 over 77,000 record checks were completed by the FBI, and in early 1944 only about 2,000 cases remained for processing. The elaborate system of leave clearance was made necessary because of the stigma placed upon the Japanese Americans by the evacuation itself. Positive assurance to communities that careful checks had been made was necessary both to gain acceptance and to insure the safety and welfare of the evacuees.

By July 1943 the demands for manpower were so great that from the Chicago area alone we had 10,000 requests for evacuees which could not be filled. The demand increased as the evacuee relocatees demonstrated their efficiency as workers, and as general acceptance of them spread into dozens of communities across the country.

Because of the demand and the reluctance on the part of many evacuees to relocate, WRA conducted surveys at a number of centers to find out what the deterrent factors were. The principal deterrent proved to be a quite understandable uncertainty regarding public sentiment. Other factors were lack of funds, lack of information about conditions in the destination communities, fear of inability to support dependents, and worry about possible lack of living quarters.

It was clear that the pattern of institutionalization, which many of us in WRA had feared almost from the beginning, was already well established. We learned also that seasonal leave was competing with indefinite leave and was more attractive to many evacuees because they could leave families within the security of the centers and return to them at the end of the contracts.

In the early months some evacuees commuted to work from the centers to nearby farms. This became a problem because communities further away objected. We had to agree that the practice was unfair and based simply on the accidents of geography. So it was abandoned. Seasonal leave proved to be helpful to more permanent relocation as indicated by the fact that by December 1943, 3,900 persons had relocated within the Salt Lake City area and 3,000 in the Denver area, with these two areas accounting for almost 40 percent of the nationwide total.

By mid-1943 hostels were being operated by church groups in

Chicago, Cleveland, Cincinnati, and Des Moines. These facilities offered temporary living accommodations at reasonable prices, an important initial sense of security, and a base for seeking satisfactory employment. It was a highly desirable and helpful service.

During the summer and fall, "reports" or public information officers were employed at all area relocation offices to help supply information to evacuees in the centers. Newsletters and pamphlets sent to the centers from the field offices provided information about farming, community acceptance, welfare, small business opportunities, job offers, and evacuee experiences on the outside. A trial leave of four to six months was provided for, but it was not very helpful. Increasing emphasis was placed on evacuee participation in relocation planning in the centers. By the end of the year all centers had evacuee relocation planning commissions, and at two of the centers these commissions were joint evacuee and staff committees. The Issei were well represented on these committees and they took their work quite seriously.

In view of the large number of experienced farmers among the evacuees, a type of group relocation for agricultural enterprise was encouraged. However, because of lack of capital or unwillingness of evacuees to risk their capital in new fields, it was not very successful. The Seabrook Farms enterprise in southern New Jersey attracted about 2,000 evacuees for labor in their fields, and their plant operations and the Becker Farms in Michigan also attracted a sizeable group.

An interesting development occurred at the Rohwer center in Arkansas. Groups of center residents there were encouraged to investigate three or four sizeable plantations where the opportunities for relocation seemed excellent, but nothing further happened. We eventually learned that some of the most active leaders of this promotional activity were pre-evacuation businessmen intent on keeping their Japanese American former customers intact as a group until the businessmen had completed plans for their own relocation. In the interim these men were discouraging the relocation of their Japanese friends. After these leaders had finally decided on Chicago as the most likely spot for their own future — which was intended to include the future of their Japanese customers — they were quite helpful in rounding up a sizeable group of pre-evacuation clients or customers to accompany them to their new location.

During the summer of 1943 it was also found desirable to emphasize individual and family counseling if families were to be encouraged to relocate. Consequently a separate welfare counseling unit was established at each center with a view to breaking down the rationalization of reluctant families and to gathering information which would enable us to plan more realistically for future programs. This counseling proved most valuable from mid-1943 on, and especially at the time of center closings.

Also on the welfare front WRA worked out an agreement with the Social Security Board whereby aliens and others affected by restrictive governmental action could be served if in need, in all states except Colorado. Residence of one to three years was a requirement in most states before regular relief service could be provided. This agreement with the Social Security Board provided that people in need could have the essential services financed from WRA funds during emergencies, regardless of residence.

At about this same time an agreement was concluded with the National Housing Agency which was designed to assist in meeting one of the most critical relocation problems. Under this agreement many local housing units were encouraged to cooperate in finding housing for the evacuees.

In addition to other procedures to inform evacuees and encourage relocation, teams from the various field offices frequently visited the centers to meet with evacuees and provide information directly about opportunities and acceptance. A number of techniques were used, including motion pictures in some cases, to help evacuees visualize the destination communities and opportunities. Employers hoping to hire large numbers of evacuees began sending recruiters directly to centers to meet with evacuees. This proved quite successful in many cases, as for example with Seabrook Farms. Other successful mass recruiters included the International Harvester Company and the Stevens Hotel in Chicago. Railways, government agencies, and especially ordnance depots were good customers because they often had housing.

Until the last part of 1943 the employment divisions in the centers were responsible for the relocation phase in the centers, along with their responsibility for center employment. They were being asked to do the impossible, for they were having to build up a community with one hand while tearing it down with the other.

A Relocation Division was established in Washington separately from the Employment Division in the fall of 1943, and thereafter separate relocation units were established at the centers.

In the first half of 1944 ten district offices, mostly in the intermountain states, were closed and four new offices were opened. One of these was in Savannah and another in New Orleans. This move spread the service to all parts of the country except the West Coast, where the exclusion orders remained in effect until December 1944.

During 1944 about 10,000 people relocated the first six months and about 8,000 in the second half, making an annual total of 18,000 relocatees up through December.

With the recession of the exclusion orders affecting the West Coast, the relocation problems and pattern changed in many respects.

CHAPTER 11

Nisei in the Armed Forces

ON JUNE 17, 1942, the same day that I reported as Director of WRA, the War Department declared the Nisei unacceptable for service in the armed forces "except as may be authorized in special cases." More than two months earlier, on March 30, they had been exempted from the draft by being placed in a 4F classification. Soon thereafter, on September 14, a special classification of 4C (declarant and nondeclarant aliens) was provided, indicating that the Japanese Americans were not acceptable in the army. Many, though not all, of the 6,000 or more already in the armed forces were dismissed. Those still in the army at the time of the organization of the 442nd Combat Team served as the cadre for this unit during the training period.

Early in July of 1942 I began pressing Assistant Secretary John McCloy to do something about a revision of the army's policy so that Nisei could volunteer to serve and be drafted like other American boys. There were two very important reasons for our position. First, we felt that these boys, as American citizens, should have the same rights and responsibilities as other American citizens, including the responsibility of fighting for their country. Secondly, it was important to the future of the Nisei that they have the opportunity to prove their patriotism in a dramatic manner, in view of the race-baiting pressure groups and their ceaseless clamor that "a Jap is a Jap" regardless of citizenship or upbringing. At every opportunity we continued to press the case for inclusion of Nisei in the armed forces.

Our case was greatly strengthened in the early fall of 1942 when the leaders of the Japanese American Citizens League met at Salt Lake City and passed a resolution strongly favoring the right of Nisei to serve in the armed forces. This action required courage of a high order, and because of their stand some of these leaders were badly beaten on their return to their respective centers.

ARMY INTELLIGENCE RECRUITMENT

Early in 1942 the Army Intelligence Service began recruitment of Nisei for training in the Japanese language, looking to their assignment to military units in the Pacific area to serve as scouts and interpreters. John Aiso, later to become judge of the Los Angeles Superior Court, was brought into the army's San Francisco headquarters very early in the war to lay the groundwork for this training program. The school was soon thereafter established at Camp Savage, and later at Fort Snelling, near Minneapolis in Minnesota, under the leadership of Col. Kai Rasmussen. During September and October 1942 recruiting officers were sent out to all WRA centers to try to enlist volunteers from among the male citizens who already had a good working knowledge of the Japanese language and who could become expert with only a brief and intensive training period. It was ironical that most of those who could qualify were Kibei who had had a long or short period of education in Japan and who were considered by Commander Ringle and other experts to be generally the most disaffected element within the Japanese American population. By the end of 1942 the army intelligence authorities had already made a good start. They had recruited 167 American citizens for the language school.

During a visit to the Gila River center, while the recruiters were interviewing prospects there, I overheard a conversation in the men's washroom between two young Nisei. One of them asked the other, "Are you going to join the army?" The other boy replied: "Hell No! Nobody but a damned Kibei can get into this man's army." Upon my return to Washington I repeated this conversation to Assistant Secretary John McCloy to help prove our point that many Nisei wanted very badly to have the opportunity to demonstrate their loyalty. He was impressed and promised to redouble his efforts to secure a change in policy.

About this same time real support came from army officers stationed in Hawaii. Colonel Fielder, an intelligence officer assigned to Hawaii, came to Washington and spent several week in helping to convince high officials in the War Department that a change of policy was important and badly wanted by many Hawaiians of Japanese lineage.

The 100th Battalion, an all-Nisei National Guard unit from Hawaii, was moved to Camp McCoy in Wisconsin in the fall of 1942 for further training.

THE 442ND COMBAT TEAM

The combination of pressures plus the persistence of Assistant Secretary McCloy paid off with the announcement on January 28, 1943, of plans for the organization of the 442nd Combat Team, an all Japanese American volunteer unit consisting of about 6,000 men. While this was good news, I must confess I was not wholly overjoyed at the time. My first reaction was that a segregated unit was wrong in principle. My hopes had been for unsegregated drafting and enlistment. This, however, was one case where principle was undoubtedly less important than other considerations, because the record of the segregated combat team stood out like a beacon on a dark night.

Looking back on it today, I have no doubt that America's conscience would not have been so dramatically reawakened on the Japanese American question as it was during the latter part of the war if Nisei had merely been scattered through the armed forces.

About 1,200 Nisei volunteered from relocation centers, and a much larger number came from Hawaii where they had not been subjected to evacuation and center life. Mike Masaoka, executive director of the JACL, was the first to volunteer.

The 442nd Combat Team went into training at Camp Shelby, Mississippi, in April 1943. These volunteers made an excellent record during their months of intensive training.

Later the 100th Battalion was moved to Camp Shelby to complete its training.

THE ITALIAN FRONT

In August 1943 the 100th Battalion was transferred to the battle front in Italy, where the members immediately distinguished themselves and their unit. Within the first several months they had received over 1,000 Purple Hearts, 33 Silver Stars, 31 Bronze Stars, 9 Distinguished Service Crosses, and 3 Legion of Merit Badges. Even though the normal contingent was about 1,000 men, with replacements about 1,300 had served in the unit. In mid-1944 the

Infantry recruiting officer swears in a group of Nisei youth — loyal Japanese Americans — for service in the United States Army. All of these boys, from the Granada relocation center, had formerly held draft classification cards 4C. (WRA photo)

battalion received a Presidential Citation for "outstanding performance of duty in action on June 26 and 27, at Belvedere and Sassetta in Italy." Meanwhile the 442nd Combat Team continued training at Camp Shelby. On three different occasions in January and February it supplied replacements for the 100th Battalion that totaled 40 officers and 530 men.

In May 1944, when the unit was transferred to the Italian front, the 100th Battalion became the first battalion of the 442nd Combat Team. These Nisei fighting men continued to distinguish themselves in battles throughout the Italian campaign and on up through France. During the war nearly 9,000 Japanese Americans served with the unit. Of this number 113 were commissioned officers, and more than 1,600 were sergeants.

Battles were fought by the Nisei at Volturno River, Rapido River, Cassino, Anzio Beachhead, Hill 140, Belvedere, Luciana, Leghorn, Arno River, invasion of Southern France, Bruyeres, rescue of the Lost Battalion, Maritime Alps, La Spezia, Massa, Carrara, and Genoa. Casualties, finally, amounted to 314 percent of original strength of the unit.

Individual awards and decorations presented to the Nisei fighters included 1 Congressional Medal of Honor, 52 Distinguished Service Crosses, 1 Distinguished Service Medal, 28 Oak Leaf Clusters to the Silver Star, 360 Silver Stars, 22 Legions of Merit, 15 Soldier's Medals, approximately 1,200 Oak Leaf Clusters to the Bronze Star Medal, approximately 4,000 Bronze Stars, 12 French Croix de Guerre, 2 Palms to the French Croix de Guerre, 2 Italian Crosses for Military Merit, 2 Italian Medals for Military Valor, 7 Presidential Distinguished Unit Citations, 2 Meritorious Service Unit Plaques, and 1 Army Unit Commendation.

On July 15, 1946, the 442 Regimental Combat Team came to Washington, D. C., following their return from Europe. They paraded down Constitution Avenue to the Ellipse, where they received the Presidential Distinguished Unit Citation from President Truman. After reviewing the troops, President Harry S. Truman spoke as follows:

It is a very great pleasure to me today to be able to put the Seventh Regimental Citation on your banners.

You are to be congratulated on what you have done for this great country of ours. I think it was my predecessor who said that Americanism is not a matter of race or creed, it is a matter of the heart.

You fought for the free nations of the world along with the rest of us. I congratulate you on that, and I can't tell you how very much the United States of America thinks of what you have done.

You are now on your way home. You fought not only the enemy, but you fought prejudice and you have won. Keep up that fight, and we will continue to win — to make this great republic stand for just what the Constitution says it stands for: the welfare of all people all of the time.

Convalescent veterans of the 442nd Combat Team present a check to President Harry S. Truman for $4300 contributed by Nisei veterans for a memorial to their former commander-in-chief, Franklin Delano Roosevelt. Not in uniform are Earl Finch (left), President Truman and Harold Ickes (center), and Dillon S. Myer (right). (Press Association, Inc. photo)

General Jacob L. Devers, U.S. Army, Retired, in a speech delivered on June 2, 1963, at a Commemorative Service at the Arlington National Cemetery to mark the 20th anniversary of Japanese American military service in World War II, had this to say in part:

. . . During its 11 months of combat the 442nd suffered 9,480 casualties, including 600 killed in action. This was more than three times its original infantry strength. Nearly 9,500 Purple Hearts were awarded to its members, including oak leaf clusters, some men earning three of them.

. . . On numerous occasions it has been officially stated that the regiment was "the most decorated unit in American Military history for its size and length of service." It had more than justified its motto "Go for Broke."

THE PACIFIC FRONT

In the meantime the Nisei and Kibei language school graduates assigned to the Pacific area were rendering a most important service, as indicated by two reports the WRA received during the summer of 1944. The first one was a memorandum sent forward to me by Assistant Secretary McCloy on June 15, 1944, which is reproduced here in its entirety:

Subject: Nisei.

1. A report by Lt. Colonel Marcel G. Crombez, AGF Special Representative in CBI,* contains the following which will be of interest to you in connection with Nisei training.

a. The Nisei personnel which were attached to First Galahad (475th Infantry Regiment) have proven to be of great value to that organization. In every instance the men have been loyal and demonstrated great courage in carrying out their assignments.

b. They have proven their usefulness in the following manner:
   (1) Interpreting for U.S. officers Japanese commands which were clearly distinguishable in close combat in which this organization took part.
   (2) Translating, identifying, and selecting important Japanese documents for immediate dispatch to higher headquarters.
   (3) As interpreters accompanying patrols.

c. One incident is worthy of note. During the early stages of the campaign in the Mogaung Valley the Second Galahad Battalion, executing a flanking movement, was surrounded by Jap elements for a period of thirteen days. During the last day the Japanese attacked the Second

---

*The China-Burma-India theater.

Battalion's position sixteen times. Each time the battalion commander was able to anticipate the direction of the attack due to the fact that the Nisei attached to his staff were able to overhear the Jap officers' instructions which they were shouting to their subordinates. The visibility in the area averaged 20 to 30 yards, and the attacking force was but 20 to 70 yards away, and the commands could be clearly heard. Through the interpretation of their commands the Second Battalion Commander, Lt. Colonel George A. Magee, Jr., was able to shift his troops to block the main Jap effort and to concentrate his fire on the Japs as they endeavored to penetrate the battalion's lines. At the end of the day the interpreters told the battalion commander that the Jap officers were reprimanding the Jap soldiers for lack of courage, to which the soldiers were replying and offering as an excuse the numbers that had been killed or were missing.

/s/ W. H. Wood
Colonel, G. S. C.
Chief, Asiatic Theatre
Theatre Group, OPD

The other quote came from one of the Caucasian soldiers with Merrill's Marauders in the China-Burma-India theater. Speaking of the Japanese American boys, he wrote as follows:

Every Marauder knows these boys by name even if they don't know ours . . . . This is due to the courage and bravery shown by them. One of our platoons owe their lives to Sergeant Hank G. who translated Jap orders . . . foolishly yelled to the effect that they were attempting a flanking movement. Hank . . . we called him "Horizontal Hank" because he has been pinned down so many times by Jap machine gun fire . . . guided the machine gun fire on our side which killed every Jap on that side. The boys who fought alongside of Hank agree that they have never seen a more calm, cool, and collected man under fire . . . he was always so eager to be where he could be of the most use and effectiveness and that was most always the hot spot . . . . And yet while the other boys boast of the number of Japs they got he doesn't talk very much about the three he had to his account. He usually changes the subject by saying "Honorable ancestors much regret meeting Merrill's Marauders." I hope I haven't given the impression that I'm trying to glorify him. Many of the boys and myself especially, never knew a Japanese American or what one was like . . . . Now we know and the Marauders want you to know that they are backing the Nisei 100 per cent. It makes the boys and myself raging mad to read about movements against Japanese Americans by the 4-F'ers back home. We would dare them to say things like they have in front of us.

I am fortunate in that I count the Hank Gosho referred to above as one of my very good friends. Hank grew up in Seattle, Washington, where his father was an Issei pharmacist. Like many Issei who were leaders in the Japanese community, Hank's father was sent to a Justice Department internment camp for the most of the war, while his son was rendering such wonderful service in the United States and to his buddies in the Pacific.

Col. Sidney F. Mashbir, who commanded the Asiatic Theatre Intelligence Service, had this to say of the Japanese American contribution to victory in the Pacific.

Had it not been for the loyalty, fidelity, patriotism, and ability of these American Nisei, that part of the war in the Pacific which was dependent upon intelligence gleaned from captured documents and prisoners of war would have been a far more hazardous, long drawn out affair.

At a highly conservative estimate, thousands of American lives were preserved and millions of dollars in material were saved as a result of their contribution to the war effort.

Another outstanding Nisei soldier was Ben Kuroki who came from Nebraska and consequently was not an evacuee. He literally battled his way into the Air Force, served as a tail gunner on 29 flights over Hitler's Europe, and participated in the crucially important bombing raid over the Ploesti oil fields in Rumania. He later asked for service in the Pacific and was granted the opportunity. There he flew an additional 29 flights, making a total of 58 combat missions. While still in uniform, he was asked to speak before the Commonwealth Club in San Francisco. At the conclusion of his remarks he was given a ten-minute standing ovation.

SELECTIVE SERVICE REESTABLISHED

As a result of the excellent showing of the 100th Battalion and the 442nd Combat Team, Secretary of War Stimson announced on January 21, 1944, that the Nisei would be restored to normal selective service status and would henceforth be subject to the draft on the same basis as all other citizens. Later it became the policy of the War Department to classify as not acceptable for service Japanese American citizens who had requested expatriation to Japan prior to January 21, 1944. After that date there was a rather marked increase in requests for expatriation, especially at Tule Lake. In most of these cases it was clear that there was no real desire to return to Japan but rather a strong desire to avoid the draft. In view of the policy established by the War Department, and because there were evident attempts to avoid service by some persons, we urged that the draft be applied to all center residents who were eligible for service on January 21, 1944, including those at Tule Lake. This policy was approved, and in a limited number of cases draftees refused to serve and went to jail instead.

In a publication of the Selective Service System in 1953, there appeared the following statement:[1] "Once inducted, the restrictions on assignment which had heretofore applied to all persons of Japanese ancestry, were modified to permit allocation as individual replacements in the European and North African Theater without regard to specific units."

First priority, however, went to the recently organized Military Intelligence Service Language School at Camp Savage (later Fort Snelling), Minnesota. It had first call on any person of Japanese ancestry who was linguistically qualified in Japanese. So great was the need for registrants who could speak Japanese that in many cases the War Department issued waivers of certain physical defects as well as of age to procure the services of these men.

THE NISEI WAR RECORD

On March 28, 1945, the New York *Herald Tribune* reported that 17,600 Nisei had been inducted into the armed forces since November 1940. Some of this number were probably released when war with Japan was declared. More recent figures from Selective Service show that during the World War II period 25,000 Nisei were registered and more than 21,000 were inducted. Counting not only draftees but volunteers and pre-Pearl Harbor enlistees maintained in service after the outbreak of war, through 1967 a total of 33,300 Japanese Americans had served in the armed forces. More than half of this total served in World War II, and more than half of those served in the Pacific. In 1966 the American Legion magazine published an article about the Nisei service in the Pacific area and said 6,000 Nisei had served in that area. Up to the time of VJ Day 3,000 of them were serving in the Army Intelligence branch in the Pacific Theater.

---

[1]Selective Service System, *Special Groups,* Special Monograph No. 10, Vol. 1, 1953, pp. 124-25.

The outstanding record of the 100th Battalion and the 442nd Combat Team in the European Theater and the magnificent service provided by the Nisei soldiers assigned to combat intelligence work in the Pacific Theater proved to be of tremendous importance to the evacuees and to WRA during the final days of relocation in 1945. With the help of the War Department we were able to give wide publicity to the group exploits of the 442nd Combat Team, and from time to time an opportunity was provided for the dramatization of the heroic acts of individual Nisei.

Three cases will illustrate the importance of Nisei military service to the evacuees generally and to the job of breaking down the intense campaigns of the race baiters.

The first of these cases related to the campaign in the Hood River Valley of Oregon, where an energetic group of bigots went all out to keep the evacuees from returning to the area. These bigots were so extreme in their approach that some members of the local post of the American Legion took chisels and removed the names of sixteen Nisei from the public-square memorial bearing the names of servicemen. One of the boys whose name was removed had been killed in action in the Pacific Theater while crawling toward the Japanese lines to secure information for his command. Several of the merchants put up signs announcing "No Japanese trade wanted." Some weeks after the exclusion order was lifted, I visited Hood River among other hot spots on the West Coast. An economic boycott was in full swing.

A small group of Hood River citizens who believed in fair play and individual rights, headed by a storekeeper named Mrs. Max Moore, formed a Hood River citizens league which printed its own advertisements telling the evacuees that they could legally come back and that they would receive the protection afforded by law. It was this group that I was to meet on my visit to Hood River.

As we arrived in the town, and I stepped out of the car, a man came forward and said, "Mr. Myer, my name is Frye, a member of the American Legion here. We understand that there is to be a meeting with you and we wish to know whether a group of us might attend." I assured him that I had no objections.

At the meeting Mrs. Moore and her group sat on one side, and Mr. Frye with his group of about twenty men sat on the other. I proceeded to tell those assembled about our plans for completing the relocation and WRA program, and I indicated a need for Hood

River and other communities to assist the evacuees in getting settled again in their chosen homeland.

The moment that I had finished Mr. Frye sprang to his feet and said, "Mr. Myer, I would like to introduce these gentlemen who have accompanied me. All of them are fathers of boys in the service, and some of them have received news from the War Department that their sons have been killed in action fighting the Japs." He then said he would like to have "a vote by these gentlemen as to whether they want the Japs to return to Hood River."

I came to my feet quickly and proceeded to compliment the fathers of soldiers on the service of their sons. Then I told them that I felt sure there was no group who could better understand the feelings of the Issei fathers and mothers in relocation centers who had received the same type of telegrams announcing the loss of a son. After pressing my point briefly I said: "Now, gentlemen, I am ready for a vote." For a full minute you could have heard the proverbial pin drop, and there was no vote. This bit of drama helped greatly to put an end to the opposition. I have often wondered what would have happened if we had not had the backing of thousands of Nisei soldiers.

The second illustrative case concerned the final drive in WRA's campaign against West Coast discrimination, which was built around a group of American army officers who had served with the Nisei in combat. The impetus for this program came from Capt. George H. Grandstaff, a Californian and a staff officer with the 100th Infantry Battalion. He wrote to the War Department on June 15th, 1945, from his home in Arcadia, California, where he was on furlough, and asked for a speaking assignment in California. His letter read in part as follows:

As one of the few white officers who have served with the Japanese American 100th Battalion for some two and a half years, my main interest is to see that the splendid work they have done in combat is called to the attention of the people of the Pacific Coast in order that Japanese Americans who desire to return here may receive fair treatment.

Captain Grandstaff was assigned to WRA for 30 days; three of his fellow officers from the 442nd Combat Team served at our request for 30 to 60 days as speakers in areas of most pronounced anti-evacuee sentiment where they brought the first-hand story of Nisei heroism directly to the people. They delivered public speeches before civic organizations and other local groups and talked individually with key people such as local editors, mayors, chiefs of police, sheriffs and district attorneys. The last of the army speakers, Lieut. Col. Wallace Moore, had the additional advantage of having commanded a group of Nisei soldiers in combat intelligence work in the Pacific theater. Thus Colonel Moore was able to break down completely the myth — almost a last-ditch salvo of the racists — that the Nisei soldiers had not seen service against the Japanese enemy.

The third case, and a fitting climax to these activities, occurred on December 8, 1945, at the small town of Talbert near Santa Ana in southern California. In this town, some six months earlier, an evacuee girl by the name of Mary Masuda, recently returned from a relocation center, had been visited by a committee of local citizens who indicated that she might suffer if she returned.

As it happened, Miss Masuda was the sister of a Nisei soldier who had displayed extraordinary heroism on the field of battle in Italy and subsequently been killed. The War Department had determined that a posthumous Distinguished Service Cross (the second highest award in the United States Army) should be awarded to some member of the family. When WRA heard this news, it attempted immediately to have the award made to Mary Masuda, in Talbert, and by a well-known American officer.

These efforts were successful, and the award was made on December 8, 1945, by General Joseph Stilwell, who flew across the country from Washington especially for the occasion. The incident was extremely widely featured in the nation's press and was covered by several of the newsreels. It virtually eliminated all the really significant vestiges of anti-evacuee feeling on the Pacific Coast.

CHAPTER 12

The Battle Against the Exclusion Order

AFTER A YEAR OF WRA OPERATIONS we felt more deeply than ever that relocation centers were for many reasons not socially sound or healthy communities. We also felt strongly that there was little chance of any danger being done to the war effort by any of the evacuees. Furthermore we were convinced that much was to be gained in behalf of the war effort by bringing the evacuees out of centers and into normal communities where they could make a real contribution.

In March 1943, one year after the issuance of the Executive Order establishing the War Relocation Authority, I, as director, issued an anniversary statement in which among other things I said:

The uninitiated person is apt to regard the evacuees as a homogeneous group, when nothing could be further from the truth. They include the old and the young, alien and native-born people with Japanese and American backgrounds. Some are strongly American in their sympathies, others actively pro-Japanese, and still others in a middle ground. Some have determined to make the best of a bad situation and to do whatever is necessary to keep the community in operation; others are embittered and express their bitterness in a generally defiant attitude. There are roughneck elements in some of the centers, as in any city, in striking contrast to the gentility of the majority; there are well-to-do families, and others who are living better in a relocation center than they were able to live outside. A great many are university graduates, and others are virtually illiterate.

The difference in culture has brought about some significant rifts in sentiment between the aliens and their American-born children. In many instances there are schisms among the aliens and among the American citizens, some of them dating back to pre-war days, some of them developed in relocation centers. Out of these factional disputes have grown certain administrative problems, some of which have had public attention. As a rule the more serious have been over-simplified by the general public and have been called "pro-axis," when as a matter of fact most of the differences of opinion have found staunchly pro-American evacuees on both sides of the question. Many loyal Americans have chosen various means of expressing their protests over un-American treatment which they have received, and such protests are easily misinterpreted.

After many months of operating relocation centers, the War Relocation Authority is convinced that they are undesirable institutions and should be removed from the American scene as soon as possible. Life in a relocation center is an unnatural and un-American sort of life. Keep in mind that the evacuees were charged with nothing except having Japanese ancestors; yet the very fact of their confinement in relocation centers fosters suspicion of their loyalties and adds to their discouragement. It has added weight to the contention of the enemy that we are fighting a race war: that this nation preaches democracy and practices racial discrimination. Many of the evacuees are now living in Japanese communities for the first time, and the small group of pro-Japanese which entered the relocation centers has gained converts.

. . . There are approximately 40,000 young people below the age of 20 years in the relocation centers. It is not the American way to have children growing up behind barbed wire and under the scrutiny of armed guards. Living conditions in the centers almost preclude privacy for individuals, and family life is disrupted. Family meals are almost impossible in the dining halls, and children lack the normal routine home duties which help to build good discipline. One of the major worries of parents in the relocation centers is the way the children are "getting out of hand" as a result of the decrease in parental influence and the absence of the normal regimen of family economy and family life.

OUR FIRST MOVE

Feeling as deeply as we did, on March 11, 1943, we decided to write a rather comprehensive letter to Secretary Stimson summing up the status, progress, and problems at that time, along with some alternative possibilities and a recommendation for policy revision. The major portion of the letter follows:

The Honorable Henry L. Stimson
The Secretary of War
Washington, D.C.

Dear Mr. Secretary:

Now that the War Relocation Authority program is approximately one year old, it seems appropriate that we sum up the progress that has so far been achieved, take stock of the outstanding problems we currently face, and suggest some of the lines that the program might take in the immediate future.

As you know, the first steps leading to mass evacuation of persons of Japanese descent from certain areas in the Western Defense Command were taken in late February and early March of 1942 — almost exactly one year ago. Throughout most of March, the people of Japanese ancestry were permitted to leave the prohibited and restricted zones prescribed by the Western Defense Command and were allowed to resettle inland on their own initiative. In fact, it seems to have been the hope of the Western Defense Command in early March that a considerable portion of the people of Japanese ancestry might eventually be evacuated in this way. Assembly centers, I understand, were planned originally only for those people of Japanese descent who might be unable or unwilling to move out voluntarily.

Complications, however, soon developed. By the middle of March, the inland communities were protesting strongly against the influx of voluntary evacuees from coastal areas; and in some places violence appeared imminent. By the latter part of the month, it had become clear that voluntary evacuation would not be a feasible solution and that provisions would have to be made for quartering the entire evacuee population until orderly plans for their relocation could be developed.

Accordingly, the "freeze" order affecting persons of Japanese ancestry in the restricted areas was issued by the Commanding General on March 27 to take effect on March 29. At about the same time, plans for moving the evacuees into assembly centers were expanded and selection of sites for the ten relocation centers to be administered by the War Relocation Authority was begun. The movement of approximately 110,000 persons of Japanese descent, first to assembly centers and then to relocation centers, was completed about eight months later in November of 1942.

During the period while this mass movement was going forward, beginning in May of 1942, an intensive demand for labor developed in the agricultural areas of the West. In an effort to alleviate this problem, a program permitting the employment of groups of evacuees on western farms was developed jointly by the Western Defense Command and the War Relocation Authority in the latter part of May. Recruitment was started both in the assembly centers and in the few relocation centers which were operating at that time. Throughout the summer, as the fall harvest season approached and the demand for labor on western farms became increasingly acute, the recruitment procedure was speeded up and the whole movement intensified. By October nearly 10,000 evacuees had been recruited from assembly and relocation centers for work on western farms.

On the whole, this movement into the harvest fields was carried out with surprisingly little difficulty. Although we had anticipated the possibility of serious trouble in some areas, there were no incidents of major proportions and in most communities the Japanese Americans were well received and well treated. Despite a few minor incidents in some localities, it seems safe to say that the influx produced no more — and perhaps even less — social tension than the normal seasonal movement of migrant farm workers. And it is certainly significant that more than 2,000 evacuees who left the centers on temporary group leave during 1942 are still out working in agricultural areas of the West and have requested indefinite leave under the procedures developed last summer and fall.

These procedures were first announced by the War Relocation Authority on July 20 and later broadened (to include aliens as well as citizens) on October 1. As finally developed, they provide that any resident of a relocation center may apply for a permit of indefinite leave to take a job or establish normal residence outside the center and away from the evacuated area. Indefinite leave permits are being granted in all cases provided: (1) the applicant has an offer of a job or some other means of support; (2) there is reasonable evidence that the applicant will be accepted without difficulty in the community of destination; (3) there is no available evidence indicating that the applicant might endanger the internal security of the Nation; and (4) the applicant agrees to keep the War Relocation Authority informed of any change of job or change of address.

Already approximately 2,500 people have taken advantage of these procedures and have re-established themselves outside the centers, mainly in communities throughout the midwestern sections of the country. Like the seasonal movement to the harvest fields last spring and summer, this exodus of people going out on indefinite leave has been accepted in the main with tolerance and understanding. Opposition has been expressed by some individuals and groups who do not have accurate information about the status of the evacuees and by some who have deep-rooted prejudices against all people of Japanese descent. The great majority of people with whom we have dealt directly on the leave program, however, have been wholly favorable and many have expressed a positive desire to assist American citizens of Japanese ancestry and law-abiding aliens in re-establishing themselves in normal American communities. We have had excellent cooperation in nearly all quarters once the facts are understood.

On February 1, there were approximately 107,000 American Japanese still in relocation centers, another 20,000 or so outside the centers within the limits of the continental United States, and still another 160,000 in the Territory of Hawaii. With the exception of the few thousand evacuees who have left the relocation centers on indefinite leave, all the people in the latter two groups have lived continuously in normal American communities and have been free (except for the Department of Justice restrictions applying to the aliens) to conduct their affairs on the same basis as other residents of the United States.

From the beginning, the War Relocation Authority has been carrying out its responsibilities under Executive Order No. 9102 with three basic assumptions in mind. The first of these is that all evacuees of Japanese ancestry, except those who request repatriation and those who may be deported for illegal activities, will continue to live in the United States after the close of the war. The second is that the United States has no intention of conducting the war on a racial basis and that the relocation program should be carried out at all times in harmony with this principle. The third assumption is that all American citizens and law-abiding alien residents of the United States should be treated by the government, insofar as possible under wartime conditions, without racial discrimination.

With these basic assumptions — and especially the first one — in mind, many of the problems which have arisen in connection with the administration of relocation centers take on added significance. Some of the problems were anticipated in the early days of the program. Most of them, however, have become far more acute and widespread than we originally expected, and a few have developed which were not foreseen at all.

One of the most serious arises from the fact that we have thrown together in closely-packed, somewhat rudimentary communities thousands of people who have a common racial ancestry but who are highly heterogeneous in almost every other respect. Citizens are mixed in with aliens; the well-to-do with the poor; farmers with city-dwellers; the highly educated with the near illiterates; those whose cultural background is primarily Japanese with those who have never visited Japan and have no desire to go there. This mingling of people with widely varying economic status and cultural backgrounds under the conditions of relocation center life has created many conflicts and has intensified others which existed prior to evacuation. It has produced a widespread feeling of individual and collective insecurity and has led to frustrations, fears, and bitterness. It is, I feel, one of the fundamental causes lying behind nearly all the demonstrations that have occurred in assembly centers and relocation centers to date.

In the atmosphere of tension that prevails almost constantly at most of the centers, a few active agitators have been able to produce results out of all proportion to their numbers. They have been able to suggest, with considerable plausibility, that all alien evacuees will be deported to

Japan at the close of the war and have hinted that any show of cooperation with the United States government now will be considered evidence
of disloyalty in Japan after deportation. This kind of reasoning has
gained considerable acceptance among many of the older people and has
led them to bring counter-pressure on the younger citizen group whenever cooperation in the war effort becomes an issue. The recent experience with registration and enlistment is a specific case in point.

Another problem of serious proportions at the relocation centers is
the gradual breakdown in the pre-war structure of Japanese-American
family life. Older women who have spent virtually all their lives in hard
physical labor are now reduced to idleness and find time hanging heavy
on their hands. Youngsters who were formerly kept busy on the farm or
around the household have virtually no required duties except attendance
at school. Families eating in community mess halls and living in crowded
barracks with thin partitions (sometimes two small families in a single
barracks apartment) find privacy a virtual impossibility. In short, practically all the social and economic factors which tend to hold families
together in a normal community have been thrown out of gear. As a
result, many of the older people have found their parental control over
their children seriously weakened and the whole problem of family
discipline has increased. The Japanese American youngsters who established an admirably low record of juvenile delinquency on the Pacific
Coast prior to evacuation have already begun to form gangs at some of
the relocation centers and have displayed definite rowdy characteristics
at nearly all of them. Part of this, perhaps, can be explained in terms of
wartime neuroses and anxieties which have recently produced a sharp
increase in the juvenile delinquency problem in many of our larger
cities. But much of it, I feel, is directly traceable to the extraordinary
conditions of life at the relocation centers.

The economic situation at the centers is abnormal in two major
respects. On the one hand, there is no necessity to work; the minimum
essentials of life (food, lodging, and medical care) are and, under
conditions of detention, must be provided by the government. On the
other hand, there are no real opportunities for economic gain; the great
majority of those who do work at the centers are paid $16 a month
plus small clothing allowances. The result has been a kind of levelling-
off process. Hundreds of families who enjoyed comparatively high in-
comes before evacuation are now seriously depleting their reserves in
relocation centers while some of the poorer families are perhaps realiz-
ing a better standard of living and more economic security than ever
before. Under these conditions, large number of the evacuees, both old
and young, are becoming apathetic and are losing nearly all incentive
for achievement. Despite all our efforts to provide work for everyone,
the use of manpower at the centers remains highly inefficient and probably always will. The full potentialities of this labor force can be realized, I am convinced, only in normal pursuits outside the relocation
centers.

The problem of evacuee properties has been a vexing one since the early days of the program. From the beginning, we anticipated difficulties in connection with the management and disposal of these properties, but only recently have we come to appreciate the full scope and significance of the problem. Altogether there are about $200,000,000 worth of properties belonging to the evacuees, ranging from household furnishings and purely personal effects to real estate such as farm lands and hotels in the coastal cities. A considerable portion of the real property, particularly in the fruit and vegetable areas of the West Coast, is of such a nature that it can probably be handled with full effectiveness only by Japanese American families who have had long experience in this highly specialized type of farming. As long as the owners and operators remain in relocation centers, many of these farms, I am afraid, will never make their maximum contribution to the war effort.

Another problem is the growing drive against the citizenship of American-born persons of Japanese descent. This drive, spearheaded by certain small groups who seem to have interests other than the immediate problems of coastal defense, has continued over the past several months. If it gathers additional momentum, it may lead in these times of emotional stress to actions that would be out of keeping with our democratic principles — actions that might perhaps have serious international implications. Moreover, I cannot escape the feeling that the arguments of these groups will continue to have a superficial air of plausibility just as long as an official stigma remains attached, in the public mind, to all the evacuated people.

These are the outstanding problems which we now face. I have sketched them only rather briefly and have purposely omitted mention of some of our lesser difficulties. As we look ahead to the future, it seems to me we should analyze these problems and attempt to work out solutions for them in the light of several highly pertinent considerations. The first of these is that the danger of invasion has undoubtedly receded. Another is the increasing seriousness of the manpower problem. A third is the need for pushing food production and other production activities to the utmost. And a fourth consideration is the high desirability of eliminating, insofar as possible, all discriminatory actions against American citizens and law-abiding alien residents of the United States at a time when we are fighting abroad for the principles of freedom and democracy.

Keeping these things in mind, three possible plans of action suggest themselves for the immediate future.

Plan A would be simply to continue on our present course. Under this plan, we would push forward with our indefinite leave program and try to relocate as many qualified individuals as possible in agriculture or industry outside the evacuated area. We would also continue to provide seasonal leave for those who preferred to remain at the centers but who might wish to work temporarily in agriculture or other lines of activity in areas reasonably close to the centers. We would provide for army enlistment in special units such as the combat team and the intelligence school. And we would continue our efforts under special procedures to clear citizen evacuees for work in war plants outside the evacuated area.

If this course is maintained, I anticipate that over the next four to six months we may be able to relocate between 10 and 25 percent of the evacuees now in relocation centers. If we can gain the proper degree of public acceptance and if a sufficient number of evacuees are willing to face the public in unfamiliar areas, the volume may be somewhat larger. But in any case under Plan A, I feel certain we shall have to maintain ten relocation centers for some time to come.

Plan B would involve the removal of all those regulations and restrictions which now apply only to Japanese Americans and not to the American population at large. It would mean elimination of the evacuated area as such, immediate reinstitution of selective service for all male citizens of Japanese descent, and release from relocation centers of all evacuees except those who would be designated by a joint board representing the War Department, the Department of Justice, and the Office of Naval Intelligence. This board would examine the dockets of all questionable individuals and would recommend some for internment, others for exclusion from specific areas. This latter group would be treated much as we now treat individual excludees. The War Relocation Authority, in other words, would assist them in finding work opportunities and in re-establishing themselves outside the excluded area.

Plan C represents a middle-ground approach. It would not involve elimination of the evacuated area but would in all other respects resemble Plan B. Under this plan, all American-citizen evacuees cleared by the joint board mentioned above would be permitted to return to the evacuated area and would be recommended for work in war plants throughout the country. Parents of men in the armed forces and other members of their immediate families would be released from relocation centers and allowed to return to the evacuated area provided their record was otherwise good. Provision would also be made for release of veterans of the last war and perhaps others whose record was in no way open to question. The remainder of the evacuees (except those who might be designated by the joint board for internment or some other special type of treatment) would be handled much as we are now handling the entire group. Those who wished to return to private life outside the relocation centers and outside the evacuated area would be processed under the regular leave procedures. Those who wished to remain at the centers would be permitted to remain. Selective service would be reinstituted immediately for all American citizens of Japanese descent. Evacuees cleared by the joint board for work in war plants and for return to the evacuated area would no longer be subject to discriminatory restrictions and regulations.

My recommendation is that we adopt Plan C or something similar to it immediately and that we move toward the adoption of Plan B as soon as all real danger of West Coast invasion seems to be eliminated. I should greatly appreciate receiving your comments and recommendations.

The only portion of the above letter not included in the quote was a summary of our view of the advantages and disadvantages of each plan.

THE DISAPPOINTING REPLY

In view of the importance of the problem, we are herewith quoting Secretary Stimson's reply in full:

May 10, 1943

Dear Mr. Myer,

I have given careful consideration to your letter of March 11, 1943, in which you review the history of the evacuation of persons of Japanese ancestry from certain areas on the West Coast, and subsequent developments. Your letter also analyzes certain problems which the War Relocation Authority is presently encountering, and you outline three alternate plans in solution thereof on which you solicit my comments and recommendations.

While under Executive Order 9102 promulgated March 18, 1942, the War Relocation Authority has been charged with exclusive responsibility for the care and resettlement of persons of Japanese ancestry evacuated from the West Coast, the Army has been in contact with several aspects of the program at first hand. For instance, the Army ran the assembly centers to which the evacuees were initially transferred, pending construction of the relocation projects by Army engineers. The Army supervised the movement of the evacuees from their homes to the assembly centers and from the assembly centers to the relocation projects. Recently the Army teams visited the relocation centers to procure, in cooperation with the War Relocation Authority, the accomplishment of loyalty questionnaires. In addition, there have been from time to time numerous consultations between the War Relocation Authority and the War Department on such miscellaneous matters as attendance of Japanese evacuees at educational institutions, entry of evacuees into critical defense areas, and the maintenance of order in the relocation centers themselves. I am glad to give you the views of the War Department based on this accumulated experience.

A serious deterioration in evacuee morale has been noted in recent months. This unsatisfactory development appears to be the result in large measure of the activities of a vicious, well-organized, pro-Japanese minority group to be found at each relocation project. Through agitation and by violence, these groups gained control of many aspects of internal project administration, so much so that it became disadvantageous, and sometimes dangerous, to express loyalty to the United States. The fact that these groups were permitted to remain in power not only shook the confidence of the loyal ones in their Government, but also effectively stifled the expression of pro-American sentiment. It has been, and remains, the opinion of the War Department, already frequently expressed to you, that much trouble could have been avoided if these troublemakers had been removed from the relocation centers and placed in rigorous confinement.

To be sure, there were other reasons for the decline in evacuee morale, some of which you have touched upon in your letter. There is little incentive at the projects to work. Relations between parent and child are difficult, with the child no longer dependent upon his parents for shelter, for food, or for clothing. Absence of the normal outlets for youthful enthusiasm brings an increase in juvenile delinquency.

I am compelled, however, to the conclusion that failure to take aggressive action against those individuals who were actively working against the interests of this Government is a primary cause for the marked deterioration in evacuee loyalty. You will understand, of course, that my purpose is not to criticize, but to lay the basis for intelligent future action.

It is the War Department's considered opinion that the War Relocation Authority should take immediate steps to screen out from the centers and segregate in close confinement all individuals appearing to have pro-Japanese sympathies. This would include the already substantial number of individuals who have applied for repatriation, as well as the troublemakers. It is significant that the evacuees themselves propose segregation as a necessary step too long delayed, and volunteer the opinion that the situation will grow worse at an accelerated rate if action is not taken immediately. It seems clear to me that the problem of resettlement of persons of Japanese ancestry loyal to this country would be measurably simplified through segregation, as it would constitute an assurance to the American public that the bad actors had been effectively dealt with.

The importance which the War Department attaches to segregation renders premature any consideration of relaxing the restrictions in force in the Western Defense Command against persons of Japanese ancestry, as suggested in your Plans B and C. The War Department, however, is not necessarily committed to a policy of maintaining these restrictions for the duration of the war. The question can easily be reconsidered after the results of segregation have been observed.

In the meantime, the War Department will continue to do all it can to assist the War Relocation Authority in the permanent resettlement of all persons of Japanese ancestry loyal to the United States, so that their services may be profitably utilized in the war effort. In this connection, the reinstitution of general Selective Service procedures is being actively considered. The recent establishment by the War Department of the Japanese American combat team should prove helpful in procuring general public acceptance for loyal Japanese Americans. Similarly, the operations of the Japanese American Joint Board initiated by the War Department, will clear the way to the employment of many loyal Japanese Americans in war industry.

Sincerely yours,
/s/ Henry L. Stimson
Secretary of War.

CLARIFICATION OF WRA PROBLEMS

In view of previous developments and the condescending tone of the secretary's reply, we always had a feeling that the secretary relied rather heavily on the Western Defense Command for preparation of the reply. We also felt that the secretary, in view of his excellent record as a statesman and public servant over many years, would have used a somewhat different approach if he had been as close to the problem as some of the rest of us were.

Because of our deep concern about the problems that would be involved in a mass segregation program, because I felt that the suggested approach was negative, because I preferred the positive approach of aiding all unquestionably loyal evacuees to relocate anywhere they wished, and because of the obvious fact that the secretary did not have a full understanding of the problems involved or of our position, we prepared a rather detailed reply under date of June 8, 1943, which we quote in full:

The Honorable Henry L. Stimson
The Secretary of War
Washington, D.C.

Dear Mr. Secretary:

I wish to thank you for the support which the War Department has given the program of the War Relocation Authority generally. I value the advice and assistance I have received from Assistant Secretary Mc-Cloy and other members of your staff. Without the assistance of the War Department our task would be immensely more difficult, if not impossible, to perform. More and more I come to realize that the work of the War Relocation Authority, not merely as it touches the restricted military areas, but in many of its larger aspects, necessarily must lean heavily upon the War Department for assistance and guidance if it is to be successful.

For these reasons, particularly, I am disturbed to learn from your letter of May 10 the view held by the War Department on the related questions of evacuee morale, segregation of evacuees, and the treatment of evacuees believed to be disloyal. I have known for some time that the Western Defense Command held a point of view on these questions somewhat at variance with ours, but I had not realized until I read your letter and was informed of Mr. McCloy's recommendations to the Senate Military Affairs Committee that the point of view of the Western Defense Command on these questions appears to be settled War Department opinion.

To say that "the War Relocation Authority should take immediate steps to screen out from the centers and segregate in close confinement all individuals appearing to have pro-Japanese sympathies" in my judgment is to state the problem in over-simplified terms. To say that "it has been and remains the opinion of the War Department already frequently expressed to you that much trouble could have been avoided if these troublemakers had been removed from the relocation centers and placed in rigorous confinement" implies that the War Department has presented to this Authority a consistent approach to the problem of segregation, and that the War Relocation Authority has consistently ignored or opposed such suggestions.

I feel it is only fair to point out that if segregation could have been accomplished by the War Relocation Authority during 1942 and the early part of this year as easily as your letter implies, it could also have been accomplished by the War Department during the evacuation period. Substantially all the information about individual evacuees actually available to the War Relocation Authority prior to registration was available to the Army at the time of evacuation and later. If mass segregation on a fair and individual basis is so simple that the War Relocation Authority is to be criticized for not accomplishing it, it is difficult to see why a wholesale evacuation of all persons of Japanese descent was ever necessary. If the dangerous and potentially dangerous individuals may be so readily determined as your letter implies, it should have been possible to evacuate only the dangerous from the Pacific Coast area.

If military considerations other than the danger from disloyal individuals, such as danger of civil disorder, for example, prompted wholesale evacuation, then I suggest the Army had a second opportunity to effectuate segregation, that is, during the assembly center period when plans for removal to relocation centers were in preparation.

The earliest segregation proposals presented to the War Relocation Authority advocated removing certain broad classes from the evacuee population. The first specific suggestion was made by Lt. Commander K. D. Ringle, a Naval Intelligence officer who served for several weeks with the War Relocation Authority in the early summer of 1942. He suggested segregating Kibei who had resided for a certain number of years in Japan. Their parents and children would also, under Commander Ringle's suggested plan, be segregated. On August 23, 1942, we received the first formal suggestion from the War Department when General DeWitt made a similar recommendation. On September 9, 1942, he proposed that not only the Kibei but also the Issei be segregated and that repatriation be asked for both groups.

The War Relocation Authority, after full consideration, rejected the idea of segregating entire categories of the population. We felt, and still feel, that while we should probably look with particular care at the individuals who fall into certain specific categories, the arbitrary removal of an entire class would be unjust, unwise, and seriously damaging to evacuee morale. The evacuation process itself was such a categorical segregation involving, as has been acknowledged, many injustices to individuals. The evacuation was justified by military urgency, but military necessity would not justify segregation on a categorical basis as proposed to the Authority. The disloyal of the group were now in safe custody under military guard.

Moreover, there were practical considerations. Removal of the Issei en masse would have disrupted the majority of the families. There are in the centers some 40,000 American citizens under 20 years of age, most of whom are sons and daughters of aliens. At the time of evacuation General DeWitt had repeatedly reassured the evacuees that family composition would not be disturbed; in fact, the Western Defense Command put itself to great trouble to unite families during and immediately following evacuation to assembly centers. Removal of the Kibei, likewise, would have penalized many loyal citizens. In this connection it is relevant that a large proportion of the evacuees recruited for the special Army school at Camp Savage, Minnesota, and for the Navy language school at the University of Colorado are Kibei.

On October 5 General DeWitt presented to the Chief of Staff another recommendation, proposing both segregation and the retention of all evacuees in the centers for the purpose of a study to develop data for psychological warfare. This would have meant holding all evacuees in centers. Other recommendations were presented on October 9 and October 30. On December 30, in response to my personal request to Assistant Secretary McCloy, the War Department outlined the following comprehensive plan for segregation:

"(a) All evacuees who did indicate their desire to accept repatriation or were loyal to Japan.

"(b) All parolees from detention and internment camps now living in relocation centers.

"(c) All evacuees having an evaluated internal security police record during assembly or relocation center residence.

"(d) All evacuees who are listed and evaluated by the intelligence service as potentially dangerous and who are not included in the above mentioned categories.

"(e) Members of the immediate families of listed segregatees and groups (b) and (c) above where the segregatee is listed as a family head."

In items (c) and (d) of this proposal, the idea of "screening out" individuals, in addition to segregating entire categories, was proposed for the first time.

The War Relocation Authority believes that a plan of segregation based upon the examination of individuals through the customary processes utilized by intelligence agencies, or by hearings or other more or less formal process, represents a sound approach to the problem. Segregation is not, however, a simple procedure. It requires a great deal of background study and work among the population to be dealt with. It requires the building up of police and intelligence records and analysis such as has been proceeding since the registration program was carried out on the centers in February 1943.

Until the registration was effectuated the War Relocation Authority had no adequate basis for conducting a large scale segregation program based upon the examination of individual cases. The Japanese American population was turned over to the War Relocation Authority progressively from May to November, 1942. No basic records were supplied the Authority by the Army. We were denied the privilege of securing questionnaires from evacuees while they remained in assembly centers. We had no access to the intelligence records of the period prior to evacuation. We had no information about the individuals in our custody except that which was developed during the course of managing the centers. Since we did not have half the population until August 25, 1942 and did not secure all the remainder until November 1, 1942, we naturally were compelled to move slowly in approaching the problem of screening out the agitators. As a practical matter, we had to wait until the individuals made trouble in the centers. We had to locate them. It was essential that we make certain we had the right people before we moved, and then we did remove them from the centers.

In light of these facts I think the Authority can be accused of nothing more than exercising reasonable caution in dealing with this problem. In December, 1942, following the incident at Manzanar, we established an isolation center for the purpose of segregating trouble-makers. We also developed procedures in collaboration with the Justice Department for sending trouble-making aliens to internment camps operated by that Department. Under the procedures thus developed and through the collaboration of the Federal Bureau of Investigation, about 100 aliens and 55 citizens have been removed from the centers and placed in detention camps or the isolation center.

Now, on the basis of the information developed during registration, I feel that for the first time the War Relocation Authority has a reasonably adequate background of information on which to proceed with the process of screening out disloyal or potentially disloyal individuals.

While segregation of evacuees might have been accomplished during the process of evacuation and movement from assembly centers to relocation centers without adding materially to the frustration and insecurity the evacuees were obliged to experience, once they were settled in relocation centers it became evident that the only positive form of segregation is that involved in relocation of loyal individuals outside the centers. It is unfortunate that the outside relocation program has never been widely regarded as a process of segregation as, of course, it is. In fact, if one looks primarily at the welfare of the Japanese American population, it is the only process of wholesale segregation which has very much to recommend it.

At this point I should like to consider briefly the general subject of evacuee morale in relocation centers. Again, I regret to say, your comments regarding the situation appear to me to be an over-simplification of the problem. I do not minimize the influence of what you have called the "pro-Japanese minority group" in the centers. When this group has acted in such a way as to provide a basis for removal of individuals to the isolation center, or has justified other such action, we have taken it. But the fact is that many of the ostensibly pro-Japanese, the repatriates, for example, have generally not been a source of trouble in the centers, either by overt act or by agitation among the rest of the community. Agitation by the disloyal element plays a part in the problem but by no means the leading role. We would be making a serious mistake to assume that by taking out the disloyal we will solve the problem of morale among the remainder.

So far as we have been able to determine, morale in the centers generally develops through a series of stages and fluctuates. First, there is the period of initiating work, receiving evacuees, and getting the centers organized. Generally, this period has been characterized by a high degree of cooperation and hopefulness on the part of the evacuees. This period has ordinarily been followed by a period of increasing dissatisfaction and bitterness as the people settled down in their new location and began to contemplate their situation. In three or four centers the second period culminated in some kind of incident, but this was by no means universally the case. Generally, in the centers which started later, we were able, on the basis of the experience gained in the centers which started earlier, to anticipate such incidents. The cycle of development, however, was substantially the same in all centers. To be entirely objective, one must say that morale now and at all times in the past has varied from center to center, depending upon local conditions, in part the ability of the project management and in part on accidents of time and local circumstances. Speaking generally, however, morale in the centers is at the moment better than it has been at any time since the centers were established. This may in part be due to recovery of balance following the emotional strain of the registration.

Because of the importance you have attached to the activities of the disloyal element, I should like to return to that subject. I think it is elementary that the influence of agitators in any group of people depends more upon the receptivity of the group than upon the skill and energy of the agitators. The disloyal group, in my judgment, would have relatively little influence upon the majority of Japanese American population if they were not already badly demoralized as a result of the treatment they have received. We have definite evidence, for example, that the disloyal people have taunted the loyal and cooperative citizens about their citizenship and about how little it actually means when they can be forcibly removed from their homes and confined in what in physical respects are concentration camps, and in most cases forced to sacrifice property and a chance to earn a livelihood. Now, segregation may remove the subversive ones who do the taunting, but it cannot remove that realization from the loyal population. The real cause of bad evacuees morale is evacuation and all the losses, insecurity, and frustration it entailed, plus the continual "drum drum" of certain harbingers of hate and fear whose expressions appear in the public press or are broadcast over the radio. A segregation program which imposes additional restrictions on the disloyal, without removing the restrictions and reestablishing the rights of the loyal, will not accomplish very much in improvement of morale.

In saying this I do not wish to convey the impression we are unwilling to pursue a program of segregation based upon an appraisal of individual cases. We are willing to do so and are undertaking the necessary planning to launch such an undertaking, but I should not like anyone to overestimate the benefits to the evacuee population which will result from segregation. I agree that, in view of the importance which has been attached to segregation by the War Department and by other agencies and individuals who are guided by the War Department position in this matter, public acceptance of the loyal evacuees will no doubt be facilitated by a program of segregation. For this reason primarily we believe it will be worth the effort and demoralization it will entail.

I think I should point out in this connection that the WRA has never had the surplus center facilities with which to establish a segregation center of any size. Our desire to put relocation ahead of segregation rather than the other way around, as proposed by General DeWitt, arose in part from the desire to vacate living space so that segregation could be accomplished without moving all or nearly all the loyal evacuees in order to make room for the disloyal. In August, 1942, for example, we surveyed the country to find a center for repatriates. We found no facilities available and were given no hope that priorities to construct new facilities could be secured.

Now that relocation has reduced the population of the centers from a maximum of 107,000 to somewhat less than 100,000, with other evacuees leaving regularly on both seasonal and indefinite leave, we can look forward to making shifts which will release one or more centers for segregation purposes. The process will be a disrupting one, nevertheless. It will be virtually impossible, for example to effect wholesale segregation and at the same time meet the agricultural production quotas of the centers this year. Since our budget for food purchase contemplates $5,000,000 worth of food production, it is vital to the administration of the centers that the agricultural program be interfered with as little as possible. Similarly, our efforts to secure a maximum utilization of evacuees in seasonal agricultural labor outside the centers will undoubtedly be delayed, as will the indefinite leave program, and the school program, by the process of segregation. And finally, the constitutional problems inherent in the confinement of American citizens will be sharpened and brought more definitely into question when citizens are confined without leave privileges in segregation centers. I mention these points merely to make clear the fact that segregation has disadvantages. From the point of view purely of the Japanese American population, the disadvantages appear to outweigh the advantages.

However, if it will help to secure acceptance of the relocation program, we are willing to accept the consequences of segregation in the centers. Our real problem both in maintaining morale in the centers and in securing the relocation of evacuees arises not from the problems which segregation will solve, but from the public attitude often expressed that no Japanese can be trusted, from the point of view which engenders restrictive and discriminatory legislation, which seeks to deprive Japanese Americans of their citizenship, and to class all of them as enemies no matter what their individual records may be. Perhaps segregation will help us to deal with that point of view more effectively.

We have almost decided to use Tule Lake as the segregation center for a number of reasons — there are a rather large number of nonregistrants and repratriates there now. It has good facilities for subsistence food production, and it lies within the evacuated area where movement in and out of the center requires special permits and escorts which makes it undesirable as a center from which to relocate. Before we make public announcement we would be glad to have your opinion as to the use of this center for this purpose.

Sincerely,
/s/ D. S. Myer
Director

AN APPEAL FOR JOINT PLANNING

Shortly after this exchange of letters we announced detailed plans for the segregation process. For many weeks we were busy with the administration of centers under the chaotic conditions resulting from the movement of more than 15,000 people in and out of Tule Lake. On top of this we were moving ahead with our all-out relocation program, while at the same time fighting a rear guard action against the forays of the Dies committee, the Hearst Press, the *Los Angeles Times,* and their race-baiting supporters.

Because of our preoccupation with all these matters, we did not officially approach the question of easing the exclusion order again until October 16, 1943, when I sent a letter to Assistant Secretary McCloy, which was a follow-up of a discussion with him on October 5 having to do with our concern about the effects of court cases and the need for joint planning. The letter follows:

October 16, 1943

Hon. John J. McCloy
Assistant Secretary of War
War Department
Washington, D. C.

Dear Mr. McCloy:

This letter is for the purpose of summarizing in writing the statements made to you in your office on October 5, not only in the hope that it may clarify my own thinking but also that it may lead to a better understanding of the problems ahead.

The War Relocation Authority is now looking forward to an intensification of the relocation program, and plans are being made to expedite this program. As you know, we have nearly completed our analysis of the records of the total adult population in the relocation centers. We have also completed the major portion of the segregation program announced some months ago and instituted in July.

In making plans for the future we cannot overlook considering the problems involved in the ultimate return to the West Coast evacuated areas of those evacuees who may wish to return. Since responsibility for determining the need for evacuation rests with the War Department, it follows that it is also its responsibility to determine when the military necessity for total exclusion from this area no longer exists. Policy determinations in relation to the return of evacuees to the West Coast, and the planning and execution of the procedures, should be a joint activity of the War Department and the War Relocation Authority with the War Department taking the lead.

There are, of course, a number of alternatives to be considered in connection with the opening of the evacuated area to the return of evacuees. One would be to announce that there will be no return of any evacuees, except those for whom exceptions have already been made, until military operations have ceased. Another would be to outline a series of steps which would provide for the gradual opening of the area to certain groups of evacuees during the war period. As you know, the War Relocation Authority believes that the latter procedure is highly desirable.

However, it is not my purpose at this time to urge the immediate announcement of a particular policy. I do urge a joint reconsideration of the whole problem by qualified representatives of the War Department and the War Relocation Authority for the purpose of reviewing the whole problem. It should be the function of this committee to make recommendations concerning policy and to outline the general procedures of the War Department and the War Relocation Authority in the execution of any program that may be decided upon.

One of the major reasons for making this recommendation at this time is our concern about the possible development of court cases protesting the detention of evacuees or continued exclusion from the evacuated areas. As you know, the constitutionality of the use of the curfew in the early stages of the war has been sustained by the Supreme Court. While the question of the constitutionality of the evacuation has not yet been decided, it is our belief that the evacuation will be considered constitutional by the Court under the conditions existing at the time of the evacuation. On the other hand, we doubt whether continued detention and continued exclusion from the evacuated areas, under present military conditions, would be sustained by the courts. There are a number of reasons why we have arrived at this conclusion. Among them are two recent adverse decisions in the courts regarding exclusion from eastern areas. If we should have an adverse court decision as the result of a suit filed by an evacuee, and if our assumptions are sound, such action may lead to a very chaotic situation.

It is my hope that you and General Emmons will assign representatives to work with representatives of the War Relocation Authority in exploring the problem and to make recommendations. The decisions should be well thought through because the policies and procedures decided upon must be sound and logical, based on military needs and the practical problems involved from the standpoint of public relations. I would like to repeat that the policy determined upon should be jointly supported by the War Department and the War Relocation Authority.

Sincerely yours,
/s/ D. S. Myer
Director

My letter of October 16, 1943, was forwarded to General Emmons, who had taken over as commander of the Western Defense Command succeeding General DeWitt. Under date of November 19, 1943, we received from Mr. McCloy's office excerpts from General Emmons comments regarding my October 16 letter. These excerpts are pertinent to the discussions of that period. They are quoted as follows:

I have read Mr. Myer's letter to you with a great deal of interest. He stated to me that the Army's prestige is such that we could do things that he could not do and suggested that we were in a good position to handle public relations matters bearing on this subject. I recommend that the War Department confine its interests in this matter to military security. That we do not enter into any joint policies or agreements reference the return of the Japanese to the West Coast but that we do retain veto power. It is true that the Army evacuated the Japanese from the Coast but they did it because there was no other agency that could do it. In the meantime, the WRA has been organized and, as I understand it, it is their job to relocate evacuated Japanese and our job to determine what Japanese may be brought back into critical areas.

On the first of November the West Coast ceased to be classified as a theater of operations. That, coupled with the President's statement which you quoted, leaves us in a very weak legal position and that is the reason why I am going through all individual exclusion cases, except Japanese, with a view to permitting the return to the Coast of a large proportion of non-Japanese evacuees. I am also going through the mixed Japanese marriage cases. I can't give you a policy covering these cases as I think each one of them, and there are not very many, has to be handled on its merits, giving due consideration to humane reasons.

This Tule Lake situation has aroused a tremendous amount of anti-Japanese feeling on the West Coast. Newspaper reporters are concocting the wildest kind of stories and the papers are giving wide publicity to them because it is a popular issue. Of course, the politicians are riding along at full speed. I think it would be very good policy, therefore, to let this feeling subside before any considerable number of Japanese are returned to the Coast. I would like to suggest to Mr. Myer that it would be good policy for him to endeavor to obtain the support of Governor Warren and other Western States governors on a sound plan for relocating Japanese in these areas, both during and after the war. I am quite sure that if we ram down their throats any plan to return Japanese to the Western States, such political opposition would be aroused as to completely nullify even a perfectly sound plan.

Mr. Myer also suggested that he would like several officers detailed to the WRA to work with them in the solution of this problem. I would like to repeat my recommendation that the War Department take the attitude that this relocation problem is purely a civil matter and a responsibility of the WRA and that our only interest in the matter is that of military security.

On the matter of military security, I think the danger of plant sabotage has been over-emphasized at the expense of espionage. The danger of sabotage has been greatly reduced by reason of barbwire fences, plant guards, etc., and by the fact that most Japanese will be under constant surveillance by other races. Espionage, however, is still serious because knowledge of fleet and ship movements would be of real interest to the Japanese. Because of our proximity to the Mexican border, it would be easy to get this information to Japan.

On January 17, 1944, I again wrote Assistant Secretary McCloy pointing out that there was a misunderstanding on the part of

General Emmons and that while we felt joint planning was essential, we were not asking for a detail of army personnel to WRA. I suggested joint effort both in planning and execution of plans. I received no reply to this letter.

In the meantime orders were quietly revised so that Japanese-American soldiers and Nisei wives of Caucasians were allowed to return to the West Coast.

THE FINAL DRIVE

On March 6, 1944, less than three weeks after the transfer of WRA to the Department of the Interior, I wrote a memorandum to Secretary Ickes summarizing the communications that had passed between WRA and the War Department. I ended by stating that if the exclusion orders were revoked, except for Tule Lake, effective July 1, 1944, WRA could be liquidated by July 1, 1945, and Tule Lake could then be turned over to the Department of Justice.

Three days later I prepared another memorandum for Secretary Ickes, urging that we press for a War Department announcement of revocation of the exclusion orders not later than July 1, 1944, and that plans be jointly made by the Department of Interior, the War Department, and the Department of Justice. Ten important reasons were given for my recommendations.

On April 5, 1944, another memorandum entitled "Plan for Bringing the Relocation Program to a Conclusion" was forwarded to Secretary Ickes. In this one we recommended a three-point program for bringing the relocation program to a conclusion, with detailed reasons for the recommendations. The three-point plan was summarized as follows:

I. Revocation of the military order excluding persons of Japanese ancestry from the Pacific Coast of the United States, except as those orders apply to persons who have been interned or segregated.

II. Transfer of the segregation center from the War Relocation Authority to the Department of Justice within three months after announcement of this plan.

III. Development and execution of an orderly plan for liquidation of relocation centers and the War Relocation Authority as an organizational entity by July 1, 1945, this plan to include mandatory relocation of all evacuees now in centers, and development of appropriate procedures for the transfer of responsibility for provision of public assistance to evacuees requiring it after July 1, 1945, by appropriate permanent welfare agencies of the Federal or state governments.

On May 10, 1944, still another memorandum was forwarded to Secretary Ickes, containing WRA's recommendations as to the steps that should be taken in announcing and effectuating the revocation of the Pacific Coast military orders affecting Japanese Americans. This was a fairly detailed proposal setting forth the type of announcements to be made by the various agencies involved and the timing of these announcements.

This memorandum was drafted because we knew that the War Department, the Department of Justice, the Budget Bureau, and the Secretary of State all had agreed that it was time to act regarding revocation of the exclusion orders.

On June 2, 1944, Secretary Ickes sent the following letter to the president:

My dear Mr. President:

I again call your attention to the urgent necessity of arriving at a determination with respect to revocation of the orders excluding Japanese Americans from the West Coast. It is my understanding that Secretary Stimson believes that there is no longer any military necessity for excluding these persons from the State of California and portions of the States of Washington, Oregon and Arizona. Accordingly, there is no basis in law or in equity for the perpetuation of the ban.

The reasons for revoking the exclusion orders may be briefly stated as follows:

1. I have been informally advised by officials of the War Department who are in charge of this problem that there is no substantial justification for continuation of the ban from the standpoint of military security.

2. The continued exclusion of American citizens of Japanese ancestry from the affected areas is clearly unconstitutional in the present circumstances. I expect that a case squarely raising this issue will reach the Supreme Court at its next term. I understand that the Department of Justice agrees that there is little doubt as to the decision which the Supreme Court will reach in a case squarely presenting the issue.

3. The continuation of the exclusion orders in the West Coast areas is adversely affecting our efforts to relocate Japanese Americans elsewhere in the country. State and local officials are saying, with some justification, that if these people are too dangerous for the West Coast, they do not want them to resettle in their localities.

4. The psychology of the Japanese Americans in the relocation centers becomes progressively worse. The difficulty which will confront these people in readjusting to ordinary life becomes greater as they spend more time in the centers.

5. The children in the centers are exposed solely to the influence of persons of Japanese ancestry. They are becoming a hopelessly maladjusted generation, apprehensive of the outside world and divorced from the possibility of associating — or even seeing to any considerable extent — Americans of other races.

6. The retention of Japanese Americans in the relocation centers impairs the efforts which are being made to secure better treatment for American prisoners-of-war and civilians who are held by the Japanese. In many localities American nationals were not interned by the Japanese government until after the West Coast evacuation; and the Japanese government has recently responded to the State Department complaints concerning treatment of American nationals by citing, among other things, the circumstances of the evacuation and detention of the West Coast Japanese Americans.

I will not comment at this time on the justification or lack thereof for the original evacuation order. But I do say that the continued retention of these innocent people in the relocation centers would be a blot upon the history of this country.

I hope that you will decide that the exclusion orders should be revoked. This, of course, would not apply to the Japanese Americans in Tule Lake. In any event, I urge that you make a decision one way or another so that we can arrange our program accordingly.

Sincerely yours,
/s/ Harold L. Ickes
Secretary of the Interior

The President,
The White House.

At about this same time, on June 1, 1944, we received most disturbing news, namely, that the Japanese American section of the Office of the Provost Marshal General located in Washington, had had orders informally approved for removal to San Francisco by July 1, 1944. Major Harbert of that office stated that several factors led to the decision to move the office but that he was unable to discuss the more important reasons. After we had questioned Major Harbert at some length, however, it seemed clear that plans were being formulated within the army for some sort of selective return of evacuees to the West Coast and that they were thinking of a reprocessing of the entire Japanese American population in cooperation with the Wartime Civil Control Administration for the purpose of establishing eligibility to return. The presumption was that neither the leave clearance processing of the WRA nor the work of the Joint Board would be used as a basis for issuing permits to return.

Within the first week of June 1944 we received a proposal from General Emmons through the War Department which would permit the return of selected evacuees. This plan was similar in many respects to our plan C which we had recommended fifteen months earlier on March 11, 1943, before the segregation program was announced. In the meantime the situation had changed drastically. The military situation had improved and the leave clearance process was substantially completed. We felt that such a plan was impossible, and we told Undersecretary of the Interior Abe Fortas (later to become Associate Justice of the U. S. Supreme Court) that we strongly felt it would be better for the country and the evacuees to continue as we were — namely, with total exclusion of Japanese Americans — than to institute a procedure such as the Western Defense Command was proposing. Our memo of June 8 to the undersecretary read in part as follows:

1. By setting up a wholly new procedure to review the loyalty of individual evacuees, the plan disregards and inferentially discredits the leave clearance processing and segregation program of the War Relocation Authority. New forms, finger print charts, and applications are to be secured from all evacuees who wish to return to California. A staff of clerks and officers is to be put to work at the Presidio examining and passing upon these applications. I will not emphasize the frustrating and demoralizing effect this new processing will have upon the evacuees who already have reason to feel that they have been sorted, sifted, and classified beyond anything citizens of this country should have to endure. What is most objectionable in the proposal is the way it discredits the loyalty determinations of the War Relocation Authority.

It is difficult now for us to argue that persons who have been released from centers can safely be received in New York, Chicago and Denver when they cannot return to their homes on the coast. If this plan is adopted, it will be virtually impossible to argue that people who have been given leave from centers, but have been denied the right to return to California, are safe. The evacuees and the general public have a right to expect the United States Government to take a consistent position on the question of loyalty of individual evacuees. The problem with which the War Relocation Authority will be confronted if this proposal is put into effect is illustrated by the line of questioning taken by Congressman Mundt in the first Dies Committee hearing when he was considering the relationship of Joint Board clearance and leave clearance review by the War Relocation Authority to eligibility to enter the Eastern Defense Command. We were unable to give a wholly satisfactory answer to his question "If a person is safe to be relocated in Omaha, why is he not safe to be relocated in Baltimore?"

2. The relocation process will be further delayed. There is a great likelihood that if this plan is announced evacuees will stop relocating in other sections of the country until after their applications to return to the coast have been processed. On the basis of our experience and that of the Japanese American Joint Board, I have no confidence in the estimate that 1,000 family groups per week can be processed under the proposed procedure. Moreover, we know from experience that the failure of a single family member to secure clearance will probably delay or prevent relocation of the entire family group. Because of the evacuee reaction and the problem of community acceptance, I feel certain that the proposed procedure will seriously retard relocation and will be a powerful force toward the permanent institutionalization of relocation centers.

3. The administrative complications of the proposed procedure are serious and unjustified. Creation of a series of new boards, preparation of additional forms and records at the relocation centers and their review by an extensive clerical staff in San Francisco will not add enough knowledge to what is already known about evacuees to justify the work involved. But those complications are only the beginning. Policing the evacuated area will be very difficult. Evacuees who have received permits to return will have to be provided with a positive means of identification. There will be no practical way of preventing evacuees who have been released from centers but have been denied permits to return to the coastal area from entering the area without authorization. The virtual certainty that some evacuees will attempt to enter the area without authorization will invite local police officers throughout the coastal area to harass all the evacuees under the pretext of establishing identification. At best, the problem of identification will be a nuisance; at worst, it can be a very vicious form of persecution.

The basic weakness of this proposal can best be seen by comparing it with the plan suggested by the War Relocation Authority. We have proposed a clear-cut provision that all evacuees who are cleared to go anywhere can go home; all others are to be segregated and detained in segregation centers. Under such a plan there would be no need of positive identification of individuals in the evacuated area and no justification for continually checking the authorization of individuals residing in the area.

4. The legal position of the government in excluding some citizens of Japanese descent from the coastal area and detaining others would be actually weakened by the proposed plan. The insecure legal position in which the government finds itself is fairly adequately presented in the memorandum by Col. Joel F. Watson in the attached file, although Colonel Watson's conclusion that the proposed processing plan will satisfy the requirements of due process seems to me to be entirely unjustified by the facts of the situation. I have little confidence that the courts will sustain even the leave clearance regulations of the War

Relocation Authority and the related segregation program. I feel certain, however, that they will never agree that, in addition to the leave clearance processing, evacuees must also submit to a further loyalty review before being allowed to return to their homes. In short, once the government's action establishes the fact that it is no longer necessary, from a military point of view, to exclude all persons of Japanese descent, it will be very difficult to exclude any except after appropriate judicial process.

The Western Defense Command proposal underlines once more the administrative difficulties inherent in the division of responsibility within the Federal government for handling the Japanese American problem. The War Relocation Authority is responsible for the relocation of evacuees and for the exercise of such powers of detention of citizens as the government may have. It has been obliged, consequently, to determine criteria upon which it is willing to base the detention of any particular individual. The War Department, on the other hand, has always controlled the basic policy by virtue of its authority to order evacuation and maintain the exclusion area. For a time, the War Relocation Authority attempted to subordinate itself in a number of important questions of policy to the War Department. For example, we encouraged the establishment of a Japanese American Joint Board, hoping that it would be able to clear large numbers of citizen evacuees for work in war plants, but expecting to be guided to some extent by the recommendations of the Board as to leave clearance. We found that the Board, in fact, cleared very few people for war plants and instead was drawn more and more into general problems of determining loyalty of Japanese Americans. We soon found also that the Board, free of all responsibility for defending the act of detaining any individual evacuee, was less sensitive than we are to the problems of justifying such detention. We have felt obliged to grant leave clearance to a number of individuals on whom the Joint Board recommended denial.

In response to the letter of March 11, 1943, to which I have referred in the opening paragraph of this memorandum, the Secretary of War insisted that a program of segregation be carried out before consideration could be given to relaxing the exclusion orders. In part because of the War Department's interest in the problem, the War Relocation Authority carried out the segregation program.

On the other hand, I think it is fair to say that the War Department has seemed in some instances to give consideration to the recommendations of the War Relocation Authority in the determination of basic policy questions. At any rate, it has cooperated in a good many cases in carrying out administrative details of the Japanese American program. But on the basic question of determination of loyalty there has been and apparently there remains some difference in point of view between the two agencies. I think it is inevitable that this should be the case. Between any two agencies considering questions in which there is so much room for personal judgment, there is bound to be a difference. I know, in fact, that no two agencies concerned with the determination of individual loyalty in the Japanese American cases see all cases alike.

So long as the several agencies passing on the loyalty of individual evacuees are concerned with mutually exclusive problems, the variation in standards among them does not present an insoluble problem. It is not unreasonable to expect that some people will be considered safe for general relocation (a determination of WRA) but not safe for employment in a war plant (a determination of the Provost Marshal General), or on a merchant ship (a determination of the Coast Guard), but when two agencies pass judgment on eligibility for essentially the same purpose, problems arise very quickly. This we learned in our relations with the Joint Board during the period when evacuees were given leave clearance but were not allowed to relocate in the Eastern Defense Command without further Joint Board clearance. Until we revoked the "gentleman's agreement" under which this restriction was imposed, the relocation program was very seriously hampered.

In light of this experience, I recommend that we oppose the program presented by the Western Defense Command and urge in its place the program I presented to you in my memorandum of May 24, 1944. In effect, our plan proposes that General Emmons accept the findings of the War Relocation Authority as to the loyalty of the evacuees who have been given leave clearance.

Needless to say, I hope that the decision will be in favor of the WRA proposal. I think it is fair, reasonable, and gives proper weight both to the public relations and administrative problems involved in this question. The basic difference between our proposal and that of the Western Defense Command is the question whether a new sifting of the population is necessary. Even the Western Defense Command estimates 90% of the people who have been cleared by the War Relocation Authority and who have asked to return to the coast, will be accepted. The other 10%, I am certain, can be explained in terms of slightly different criteria for judging presumed loyalty, not by an application of new information and not because of any failure of the War Relocation Authority to exercise care in the granting of leave.

SETBACK AND SUCCESS

In spite of the fact that the War Department, the Department of Justice, the Interior Department, and the other interested agencies recommended in June that the time had come to rescind the West Coast exclusion order, someone in the office of the president decided that it should not be done before the November election in 1944. Nevertheless we did get the approval of the army allowing certain selected individual evacuees who applied for permits to return to the West Coast during the fall of 1944. By the time of the announcement of the revision of the exclusion order on December 17, 1944, about 2,000 evacuees already were in the exclusion area.

The revision of the exclusion order took effect on January 2, 1945. It was not a complete revocation.

Brigadier General William Wilbur, Assistant Chief of Staff in the Western Defense Command, was adamant regarding the continued exclusion of several thousand evacuees. Furthermore he insisted that these evacuees be detained in relocation centers or at Tule Lake until the WDC could process them by its own standards and methods. He was completely unimpressed by the thoroughgoing leave clearance records which the WRA and the Joint Board had developed.

With this development we realized that the move to the West Coast of the Japanese American section of the office of the Provost Marshal General was tied in with the vehement insistence on the part of General Wilbur and his group that they continue to process thousands of dockets. They took this position in spite of the fact that such a procedure would probably tie up 20,000 to 30,000 people because of family affiliations, in addition to the 8,000 to 10,000 that General Wilbur actually felt should be processed.

Finally, after much argument, General Wilbur definitely stated that there would not be more than 5,000 excludees, including those recommended for internment. We accepted his word as a commitment and quit arguing the matter. In spite of this definite commitment, the first list of excludees that was presented to WRA by the army included nearly 10,000 names. While this list was gradually reduced after further processing and hearings, it was a major deterrent in the final relocation plans for several thousand people between January 2, 1945, and September 4, 1945, at which time the War Department finally retired from the scene and left the processing of potentially subversive evacuees to the Department of Justice.

CHAPTER 13

The Beginning of the End

ON DECEMBER 8, 1944, nine days before the revocation announcement — which we, of course, knew was coming — we addressed a five-page confidential letter to all project directors (see Appendix J). Attached to this letter was *A Message from the Director of the War Relocation Authority* for distribution to center residents and also a *Summary of WRA Policies and Procedures for the Final Phase of the Relocation Program*. Additional copies of the two attachments were forwarded for distribution to the evacuees and to the staff upon notification from us. This distribution was authorized on December 17.

FINAL RELOCATION POLICIES AND PROCEDURES

The message to the evacuees, and the *Summary of WRA Policies and Procedures for the Final Phase of Relocation Program*, except for the property assistance portion (see Chapter 19), follow:

The lifting of the blanket exclusion orders by the Western Defense Command is undoubtedly the most significant event since evacuation both in the lives of the evacuated people and in the program of the War Relocation Authority. To the great majority of the evacuees, it means full restoration of the freedom of movement which is enjoyed by all other loyal citizens and law-abiding aliens in the United States. To the

War Relocation Authority, it signifies the beginning of the final phase of the relocation program.

Our prime objective in WRA, as always, is to restore the people residing in relocation centers to private life in normal communities. The lifting of the exclusion orders makes it possible to broaden the scope of this program and put it for the first time on a completely nationwide basis. Within the next few weeks WRA will establish field relocation offices at key points in the evacuated area and will extend assistance to those who have good reason to return. At the same time, we shall also continue our relocation offices and assistance for those who wish to locate in other parts of the country.

Although the WRA is now entering the final phase of its program, the relocation centers will not be closed immediately. All of them will remain in operation for several months so that all the residents will have reasonable and adequate time and opportunity for the development of sound relocation plans.

During the period ahead, many of the facilities at the centers will have to be sharply curtailed as the population declines. Schools, however, will be continued through the current school year. This will enable families with school age children time to plan their relocation so that the pupils may reenter school in their new communities at the beginning of the fall term. All the really essential services at the centers, including mess operations, housing, and medical care, will of course be provided until the time each center actually closes.

The re-opening of the evacuated area and the broadening of the relocation program come at a fortunate time for the evacuated people. Largely as a result of the splendid record which your sons, brothers, and husbands have achieved in the armed services, the American public has come increasingly to a recognition of the essential good faith and loyalty that characterize the great majority of people of Japanese descent. Today the evacuees as a group have more friends and supporters throughout the Nation than at any previous time. They are being accepted in hundreds of communities as fellow-workers, friends, and neighbors. The removal of the restrictions that formerly applied in the West Coast area underscores this growing public acceptance and should help to bring about even more widespread recognition of the fact that the great majority of the evacuees are loyal and law-abiding people.

It is fortunate, too, that the WRA program enters its final phase at a time when there is a good demand for workers in war plants, in civilian goods production, in service occupations, and on the farms. Both from the standpoint of the national welfare and the evacuees' long-range economic security, it is highly important that the people now residing at the relocation centers make the transition back to private life at a time when employment opportunities are still plentiful.

Recognizing that there are a number of people in the relocation centers who have not been able to relocate previously because they are incapable of self-support, the War Relocation Authority is now making intensive efforts to meet this problem by mobilizing facilities and resources that are available for public assistance in normal communities throughout the Nation. Special funds have been provided by Congress through the Federal Security Agency for the assistance of needy people who have been displaced from their homes by restrictive governmental action. All evacuees — both citizens and aliens — who are in need of such assistance are eligible to apply for it under the terms of this Federal law. In addition, old age assistance and grants to certain other types of handicapped people are available to both citizen and alien evacuees as they are to all persons who can qualify under the regular programs of the Federal Security Agency. In the development of individual or family relocation plans at the centers, the Welfare Section will give special attention to those who may need some form of public assistance after relocation. In all cases of this kind, the specific needs of the family or individual will be presented in advance of relocation through the WRA field office to the appropriate agency in the community of proposed resettlement. Wherever individuals or families find themselves in need of public assistance after relocation, the WRA field offices will help to facilitate arrangements with the appropriate state or local agency. In view of the funds that are available and the arrangements that are being made, the War Relocation Authority feels wholly confident that no evacuee will be deprived of adequate means of subsistence by reason of the closing of the centers.

It is possible that some evacuees who have relocated outside the evacuated area will now wish to avail themselves of the opportunity of returning to their former homes. The final decision as to whether this is the best thing to do rests with the individual relocatee. Many have homes, business connections, or close personal friends in the evacuated area and will be anxious to get back to them. On the other hand, many relocatees have found new friends and much greater opportunities, both social and economic, than they enjoyed prior to evacuation. There is every indication that these greater opportunities will continue for most persons. The WRA believes that all relocatees should carefully consider all factors before breaking their present connections and moving back to their old home communities. It should be remembered that the entire West Coast area has undergone a tremendous change since evacuation. Hundreds of thousands of war workers have moved into the area. Housing is difficult to obtain and living conditions are extremely complex and expensive. Many relocatees will find that it will be much easier and more advantageous to have Center family members join them in their present location than to dislocate themselves again to return to something new and untried.

If after careful consideration and investigation the relocatee decides to return to his former home he should see his local relocation officer. The Authority will furnish the usual types of relocation assistance to such people provided they have a sound plan for resettlement in the evacuated area and provided that certain other requirements, such as those of the War Manpower Commission, are met. This assistance will be available for the duration of the relocation program and there will be no need to make hasty decisions in order to qualify for it. It will be available only in the field and cannot be obtained if the evacuee returns to a relocation center or the evacuated area without the approval of the relocation officer.

Those relocated evacuees who have close family relatives still residing at the centers and who need to consult with these family members in the development of relocation plans may apply at the nearest WRA field office for permission to visit the center. However, in view of the War Manpower Commission regulations governing job transfers and the congested transportation facilities in the vicinity of the centers, it is exceedingly important that all relocated evacuees desiring to return to the centers at this time actually obtain such advance approval. Those who attempt to come back without it may be denied admission to the center and may become ineligible for all future relocation assistance.

More detailed information on the policies and procedures which the War Relocation Authority will follow in the final phase of its program, insofar as these have now been determined, is contained in the attached bulletin. As additional policy decisions are made and procedures further clarified, every effort will be made to provide the essential information both to the people at the relocation centers and to those who have relocated.

In conveying this message to you, I want to express my sincere appreciation of the fine, cooperative attitude which has been displayed by the overwhelming majority of the evacuated people over the past two and one-half years under the most trying of circumstances. All of you who have already left the relocation centers or who will be leaving in the next several months have my very best wishes for a successful and satisfying life in the communities where you choose to make your homes.

Summary of WRA Policies and Procedures
for the Final Phase of the Relocation Program

Now that the blanket exclusion orders have been lifted, the War Relocation Authority has made a number of basic policy decisions covering the immediate future of its program. These decisions are:

(1) WRA assistance will now be made available for relocation in the evacuated area on the same basis as elsewhere.

(2) All relocation centers will be closed within a period of six months to one year after the revocation of the exclusion orders. No center, however, will be closed without three month's advance notice to the residents.

(3) Essential services at the relocation centers — food, housing, and medical care — will be provided until the centers close. Schools will be

maintained at the centers through the end of the present school year.

(4) Relocation in areas outside the evacuated zone will continue.

(5) WRA assistance will be extended, within certain prescribed limits, to evacuees who have previously relocated and who now wish to return to the evacuated area.

(6) There will be no further processing of evacuees for leave clearance and leave permits will no longer be necessary for relocation. Relocation assistance, however, will be made available only to those whose relocation plans are approved by WRA.

(7) Arrangements will be made with appropriate state and local agencies to provide public assistance throughout the country for those evacuees who are incapable of self-support.

Welfare Assistance to Relocatees

Public assistance is available under this program to evacuees who need medical care, money for rent or groceries, or money for emergency living expenses. Those needing such assistance should consult the nearest public welfare office or the nearest field office of the War Relocation Authority. They should be prepared to describe their financial resources in some detail. Depending on the individual situation, the welfare office may provide personal help in solving the problem or may furnish cash resources for the purchase of the needed goods or services. Cash grants of this kind are available on the basis of actual need even though the applicant may not be a resident of the community where he is making application, even though he may be employed, and even though he may have property which is not in expendable form.

Special aid for the aged, the blind, and needy children is available to relocating evacuees, as it is to all other persons in these categories, under Federal programs which are administered by state agencies. For more detailed information on these types of assistance, evacuees should consult the nearest public welfare office or the nearest field office of the WRA.

Assistance for dependents of servicemen is now being extended under the Dependency Allowance and Allotment Act. Relocated evacuees desiring detailed information about such assistance should consult the nearest office of the American Red Cross.

Social insurance may now be obtained by evacuees over 65 years of age whose employers withheld part of their salary for this purpose prior to evacuation. Those who believe themselves eligible for such insurance should consult the nearest field relocation office or the welfare section of the center for the name and address of the nearest field office of the Bureau of Old Age and Survivors Insurance of the Social Security Board. Full particulars may be obtained by writing or visiting the latter office. The applicant should furnish the Social Security Board office with his Social Security number and with essential information about his pre-evacuation employment.

Miscellaneous Information

Travel permits must be obtained by all alien evacuees before the travel is actually undertaken. Aliens at the relocation centers going out on relocation either to the West Coast or elsewhere may obtain permits covering travel to the original point of destination by applying to the relocation office at the center. All those outside the centers desiring to travel either back to the centers or to another community should apply for a permit at the office of the United States Attorney for the district in which they are currently residing. Within five days after reaching the point of destination on any type of travel, alien evacuees must report their new address to the Alien Registration Division, Immigration and Naturalization Service at Philadelphia, Pennsylvania, and to the Federal Bureau of Investigation field office mentioned in the alien's certificate of registration. If there is any further change of address, the same requirements apply.

Travel to Hawaii and Alaska is controlled by the War Department. Evacuees wishing to go to either of these territories should apply to the Office of the Provost Marshal General, War Department, Washington, D.C.

Frozen funds are not affected by the lifting of the exclusion orders. Alien evacuees eligible for relocation throughout the United States whose assets have been frozen and who now wish to regain possession of them should consult the nearest office of WRA. In justifiable cases, arrangements will be made for taking the matter up with the Foreign Funds Control Division of the Treasury Department.

Legal residence of evacuees in the states from which they were evacuated has not been affected by reason of their having lived in a relocation center. Those who have relocated and who have acquired legal residence in other states, however, can regain legal residence in the states of the evacuated area only in accordance with the provisions of the state law.

Voluntary evacuees who have never resided in relocation centers and who have an approved plan for returning to the evacuated area are eligible for relocation assistance (if they request it) on the same basis as persons who have been relocated from WRA centers. For this purpose, a voluntary evacuee is defined as a person of Japanese ancestry who left the evacuated area in response to government urging between February 16, 1942 and the date when voluntary movement from that area was prohibited by military order (March 29, 1942 in the case of Military Area No. 1; June 2, 1942, for the remainder of California) or who later departed by special permission of the Western Defense Command. Application should be made at the nearest field office of WRA.

Deportees and parolees now residing at relocation centers may relocate under sponsorship arrangements approved by the Department of Justice, and are eligible for relocation assistance on the same basis as other evacuees. Full particulars may be obtained from the relocation office at the center.

Government property at the relocation centers which is surplus to the needs of center operations will be disposed of through the regular established procedures of the Treasury Department. WRA has no authority to make such property available to evacuees either through sale or any other arrangement.

Gate control will be maintained at all relocation centers even though leave permits are no longer required of those going out on relocation. All evacuees leaving or entering the center will be expected to report at the gate.

Address cards will be furnished, as previously, to all relocating evacuees in order that they may report arrival at their destinations and subsequent changes of address. There are many situations where the WRA will wish to communicate promptly with evacuees regarding restoration of personal property and similar matters, or where the Authority will be called upon to furnish the address of a relocated evacuee to friends, relatives, and business associates. It is highly advisable, therefore, for all evacuees to keep the WRA constantly informed of changes of address as long as the field relocation offices remain in operation.

On December 18, 1944, at the same time we were announcing plans to close all centers, the Supreme Court ruled in connection with the Korematsu case that the West Coast evacuation was constitutional; however, strong dissent was expressed by Mr. Justice Murphy, with additional dissent by Justices Roberts and Jackson for different reasons. (See Chapter 20.)

The Court also ruled in the Endo case that WRA had no authority to detain a concededly loyal American citizen. We of course welcomed the Endo decision.

At the time revocation of the exclusion orders was announced, about 80,000 people were still residing in WRA centers. Within this group approximately 10,000 people were to be detained for an indefinite period because of General Wilbur's insistence that they be reprocessed, and about 10,000 more were immobilized because of close family ties with the detainees. Fortunately most of these were at Tule Lake. The 60,000 who were immediately eligible for relocation within the 12-month period comprised a group about twice as large as the number that we had assisted to relocate over the preceding two and a half years.

One of the first essential steps in relocation procedure was to establish field offices on the West Coast. During early 1945, area offices were established in Los Angeles, San Francisco, and Seattle. About twenty-five district offices were set up in other communities for the purpose of preparing the way for relocatees and assisting their resettlement within or return to the evacuated area. It was a matter of both resettlement and return. Some of the evacuees went back to the communities from which they had been evacuated; others chose localities where they had not been living at the time of evacuation.

EVACUEE DISBELIEF, FRUSTRATION, AND OPPOSITION

WRA had realized for many months that it was most important that the relocation job be completed, if possible, while the war was still in progress, because jobs and housing would be much easier to secure. In this connection it should be recalled that in 1944 and 1945 there were widespread expectations and predictions of a major economic recession for the post-war era. Few at that time were forecasting the boom that actually took place in the late 1940's.

Among evacuees and friends of evacuees, pressures began to build up against the planned total liquidation. In view of this development, we announced the following reasons for the liquidation policy:

1. Center living was bad for the evacuees. It did not provide an atmosphere in which children could develop in the normal American pattern. It was generally destructive to good work habits, tended to weaken the sense of responsibility on the part of family heads, and did not provide normal family living conditions. For their own welfare, the evacuees needed to get back into the life of the usual American community. This could be accomplished only by closing of centers.

2. The country, still at war, needed the skills and the manpower represented by the center population.

3. The Congress would undoubtedly question the necessity of appropriating funds to continue centers (and such questions were raised in connection with our last budget).

4. As long as the evacuees remained concentrated in centers, they were more vulnerable to campaigns directed against them by their enemies. The very fact that they were set apart tended to heighten the impression that their loyalty was in question.

5. Since centers were to be liquidated, it should be done during the wartime period of high employment when relocation opportunities were favorable.

In spite of our announcement of what seemed to us perfectly logical reasons for liquidation, strong opposition continued to develop from evacuees and from their friends and enemies outside the centers.

The basic reaction of the evacuees within centers was one of disbelief. Rumors began to fly that the Gila River and Poston centers would be continued. This rumor probably grew out of our announcement regarding the continuation of our agriculture programs there because of the winter vegetable crops. Other rumors stated that the Department of Justice was opposing the plan for closing all centers, and hopes grew that the department might be expected to continue two or three centers under its own administration. Activity increased within the various community councils during December and January. Surveys were conducted to determine the thoughts of the residents, and block meetings were the order of the day.

On February 16, 1945, an all-center evacuee conference was held in Salt Lake City under auspices of the community council from Central Utah. Thirty representatives from seven centers attended. Manzanar and Tule Lake were not represented. The week-long conference developed into a searching study of the problems facing center residents. The conference sentiment was fairly evenly divided among three groups. One group sought to enlist the support of various public and private agencies, arguing that if they could secure a sufficiently wide audience on the outside they could obtain increased government assistance. Another pressed vigorously for full restitution of evacuation losses before relocation. The third group favored resettlement but saw insurmountable difficulties. The members of the first group gained control and were able to exert a constructive influence. They argued for increased relocation assistance rather than a strongly worded protest against center closing.

Out of this meeting came a "statement of facts," as the evacuees saw them, and a list of twenty-one recommendations. It was designed for consumption by center residents, by the public, and by WRA, which to them represented the United States government.

The "statement of facts," which served as a preamble to the twenty-one recommendations, was as follows:

1. Mental suffering has been caused by the forced mass evacuation.

2. There has been an almost complete destruction of financial foundations built during over a half century.

3. Especially for the duration, the war has created fears of prejudices, persecution, etc., also fears of physical violence and fears of damage to property.

4. Many Issei (average age is between 60 and 65) were depending upon their sons for assistance and support, but these sons were serving in the United States armed forces. Now these Issei are reluctant to consider relocation.

5. Residents feel insecure and apprehensive toward the many changes and modifications of WRA policies.

6. The residents have prepared to remain for the duration because of many statements made by the WRA that relocation centers will be maintained for the duration of the war.

7. Many residents were forced to dispose of their personal and real properties, business and agricultural equipment, etc., at a mere trifle of their cost; also they drew leases for the "duration," hence nothing to return to.

8. Practically every Buddhist priest is now excluded from the west coast. Buddhism has a substantial following, and the members obviously prefer to remain where the religion centers are located.

9. There is an acute shortage of housing, which is obviously a basic need in resettlement. The residents fear that adequate housing is not available.

10. Many persons of Japanese ancestry have difficulty in obtaining insurance on life, against fire, on automobiles, on property, etc.

The twenty-one recommendations may be summarized as follows. Some had to do with such items as the need for grants and/or loans (both short-term and long-term), the expenses for investigation of relocation possibilities, OPA (Office of Price Administration) priorities for equipment, return of properties, hostels, new housing, reinstatement of civil servants, and business licenses. Others involved the need of local relocation offices, protection or aid to students, work opportunities, union membership, powers-of-attorney for property management from soldier sons, old peoples' homes, release of frozen assets, release of parolees, indemnity for victims of violence, compensation for property losses, and a number of other less urgent items.

All of the recommendations were carefully considered, and carefully drawn replies were made. In some cases WRA had already planned for the things requested; in many other cases the answer had to be "no," in spite of our understanding of the problems presented by the conferees and our feelings of compassion toward them.

The preceding facts and summary of recommendations provide a thoroughgoing index of the evacuees' concerns, with one major exception. The 8,000 elderly bachelors, most of whom had been migrant farm workers for years, and many of the older women, who had spent years of hard toil in the home and on the farms, found center life, after a period of adjustment, much more pleasant than the daily grind of toilsome field work. These elderly men enjoyed the less arduous jobs in centers and the time for playing goh, while many of the older women enjoyed the flower arrangement and English classes as well as the time and the opportunity to visit with their neighbors. In short, institutionalization had set in rather quickly, and for many the new environment with all of its shortcomings was found to be more pleasant than the thoughts of another readjustment.

During the early weeks of 1945 I made it a point to visit each of the centers to explain our plans and our reasons for the liquidation program to the residents. On February 19, 1945, during the very week that the Salt Lake City meeting of center representatives was in session, I made a speech to the residents of the Minidoka, Idaho, center. After my speech and an extended question-and-answer period were over, the farm manager came to see me with an appeal from his farm crew who wanted to meet with me at breakfast, in their separate mess hall near the farm, on the following morning.

I agreed to meet with the crew. After a hearty farm breakfast these elderly men, mostly of the migrant labor type, gathered around their spokesman who told me in no uncertain terms that they liked it here and that they were going to stay. I spent an hour and a half trying to explain why it was impossible, but they persisted. I pointed out that there would be no mess hall, no wages, no services of any sort, and that they would find it rather bleak and lonesome under those conditions. They were adamant to the last, and when I left them they were still insisting that they were going to stay.

OUTSIDE OPPOSITION

The group who finally dominated the Salt Lake conference in mid-February were right when they insisted that they could get outside support if they tried. In view of all the difficulties that they had faced and the problems (both real and imaginary) yet to be faced, many people of good will were touched by their pleas. As a consequence we were faced with the fact that several people who had been among our key supporters up to the time of revocation either opposed our policies publicly or privately expressed to us strong doubts about them. Some felt that we were hard-hearted and unrealistic, particularly when we were urging people to go home to areas where gunfire into houses had been reported. Many did not understand that we had worked out a thoroughgoing program to provide for those who were old or ill and would need adequate welfare aid.

There was much pressure upon Undersecretary Abe Fortas to order a change in policy and to keep two or three centers for the elderly and the welfare cases. Even Herbert Wechsler and the late John Burling of the Department of Justice urged a change and also urged the transfer of Tule Lake to the Department of Justice.

By June or July the pressure was so great that two recommendations were made to Secretary Ickes. One was that we postpone the previously announced time of closing centers, because of the feeling that we would not be able to meet our quotas. Fortunately Secretary Ickes ruled that we should proceed. He added, however, that a review would be made of progress on September 1, and if we had not been able to meet our quota of relocatees by that time he would consider the matter further. We missed our estimate by less than 100, so there was no need for further review.

The second recommendation was that Assistant Secretary Oscar Chapman and John Burling of the Justice Department visit some of the centers (including Gila River, Poston, and Manzanar) to review the situation there and bring back recommendations. H. Rex Lee accompanied the delegation as representative of WRA's Washington office.

Unfortunately a few of our own staff were opposed to liquidation for various reasons. Most of these were lower echelon people. The only two project directors who were in opposition were Roy

Bennett of Gila River and Ralph Merritt of Manzanar. Ralph Merritt was one of our most efficient project administrators, but he loved the Owens Valley, the location of Manzanar; he was well established there, and he wanted to stay. Both of these gentlemen, as well as others, were of course consulted by the delegation. Fortunately Oscar Chapman, who headed the delegation, did not recommend any immediate change in policy after he and Burling returned to Washington.

During the early months of 1945 Alan Barth of the *Washington Post* editorial staff, who had written more than a dozen excellent and knowledgeable editorials about the evacuation, the court cases, and the WRA, was greatly disturbed by the terrorism and the possible danger to returning evacuees. He and I had many discussions, and on several occasions he was on the point of writing an editorial in which he would have taken issue with our policies. Fortunately I was able to persuade him to hold off until the situation eased. So the critical editorial was never written. Instead he wrote an editorial entitled "Job Well Done," which appeared on March 28, 1946, and is one of my prize possessions. (See Appendix N.)

As so often happens, there were strange bedfellows. The people of good will who out of compassion opposed our closing of centers were joined by race-baiters and by persons with economic interests who opposed liquidation of the centers and return to the West Coast for less altruistic reasons. The Hood River story, which was an example, has been presented in Chapter 11.

CHAPTER 14

Problems and Frustrations of the Returnees

ONE OF THE FIRST MOVES made by terrorists in California to scare off the returning evacuees occurred on January 8, 1945, when an attempt was made to dynamite and burn the fruit packing shed of a returnee in Placer County. This incident was followed by about thirty other attempts by terrorists to frighten the returning evacuees away from their homes. Most of these involved shooting incidents in which the shots were directed at the corners and other portions of evacuee houses with long-range rifles to try to frighten the residents into leaving. These were the incidents that concerned Alan Barth and many other good people so deeply — not to mention the deep concern felt by evacuees and by WRA.

MEETING THE RACIST OPPOSITION

Late in 1945 we prepared a memorandum entitled *The WRA Campaign Against West Coast Racists,* which summarized our approach to the problems. It is quoted here in full.

In the late fall of 1944, when WRA knew that the mass exclusion orders would soon be revoked and that most people of Japanese ancestry would shortly be free to return to their former homes, the agency began laying plans for an intensive campaign to combat prejudice and protect the rights of the evacuees in the former exclusion zone. WRA anticipated that there would be resistance and discrimination directed against the returnees in many sections of the West Coast but felt strongly that these manifestations of prejudice could be broken down and gradually made ineffective. The methods which it developed for this purpose are adaptable to almost any similar campaign against racial prejudice whether carried on by a governmental agency or by private groups.

Methods of Meeting the Opposition

The basic strategy of the WRA plan was to keep a reasonably constant flow of evacuees moving into the various communities of the exclusion zone. WRA felt that this approach was necessary for three main reasons. In the first place, it was essential to have some evacuees return in order to provide a focal point for the campaign against racial intolerance — a group around which the friendly forces could rally and organize their efforts. Unless such a group was physically present in the evacuated area, it would be like battling racial intolerance in a vacuum. Secondly, the agency was faced with the problem that a great many people sincerely friendly to the evacuees were advising them to remain in centers until after better public attitudes could be built up; in order to counteract this type of attitude, WRA had to take the initiative in encouraging evacuees to return. Finally, the Authority had only a limited amount of time available for the liquidation of its program and thus had to keep the evacuees moving constantly out of centers.

Shortly after the exclusion orders were formally revoked on January 2, 1945, WRA began establishing field offices in all the major West Coast communities where significant numbers of evacuees were likely to return. Through these offices the Authority encouraged the formation of local committees of fair-minded citizens who were concerned about racial prejudice and anxious to assist the returning evacuees in their problems of community adjustment. Such committees were eventually formed in practically all of the principal West Coast communities and they played a major part in the campaign against racial intolerance.

The techniques which WRA used in the beginning to break down prejudice in the West Coast area were the same ones which had already proved their effectiveness in other sections of the country. Factual information about the Japanese Americans was supplied to the local citizen committees for use in countering the lies and the misinformation which were being disseminated by the hostile groups. The record of Japanese Americans in the Army and in supporting war activities was emphasized in the press, over the radio, and in public speeches. A direct appeal was made to the basic American sense of fair play and to the respect for cherished American traditions of racial justice.

These methods helped to pave the way for return of the evacuees in community after community up and down the West Coast. But after the return had begun to take on significant volume in the spring of 1945, new problems arose and new techniques had to be devised to meet them.

The most serious of these problems was the wave of terrorism and threatened violence which prevailed particularly in the rural sections of California throughout the spring and reached its height toward the end of May. Most of the terrorism took the form of shooting attempts and threatening telephone calls or visits. In some cases, these incidents were undoubtedly perpetrated by strongly prejudiced individuals acting on the spur of the moment. But in most instances, there is considerable evidence to suggest that the terrorism was part of a planned campaign aimed at frightening away the Japanese American agriculturalists and thus making their lands available to Caucasian competitors.

In tackling the problem of terrorism within the evacuated area, WRA worked in close collaboration with the State and local law enforcement agencies. A detailed system of reporting incidents was established so that the necessary information would be made available by the appropriate WRA field office both to the county law enforcement officials and to the office of the Attorney General of the State within a few hours after the incident occurred. Civic-minded groups interested in the welfare of the evacuees were encouraged to talk with the local law enforcement officials and insist upon prompt and vigorous action.

Meanwhile the WRA national office in Washington, through its Current Information Section, made a special effort to keep the spotlight of publicity focused on the terrorism in California. As rapidly as incidents occurred they were brought to the attention of the leading wire services and of major newspapers in the East and Middle West which had displayed an active and sympathetic interest in evacuee problems. In this way the Authority kept the issue of anti-evacuee terrorism in California alive and brought the pressure of an aroused nationwide public indignation to bear on the situation. The climax in this particular campaign came on May 24 when Secretary of the Interior Harold L. Ickes, acting on the suggestion of WRA, issued a public statement denouncing the terrorists and calling for more vigorous local law enforcement. This was followed by a large number of editorials in papers throughout the country, including several in California, demanding that the terrorist elements on the West Coast be brought under effective control. By midsummer the terrorism had dwindled off to comparative insignificance.

Some of the other, less dramatic problems were actually more difficult of solution. In the Pacific Northwest, for example, there was a well-organized attempt to boycott the handling of evacuee farm produce in the vegetable markets of Portland and Seattle. After WRA had made several unsuccessful efforts to eliminate this discrimination by direct consultation with the produce handlers and with Dave Beck and other officials of the International Teamsters' Union which obviously played key role in the boycott, the Authority eventually sent a marketing specialist into the area to assist the evacuees in finding other outlets for their products. Eventually the boycott was rendered ineffective and quietly dropped. In at least one case, Harold Fistere, our area officer in Seattle, arranged with some local community committee men to drive an evacuee truck to markets while the evacuee sat in the back and appeared to be only a helper.

Another type of boycott that was tried in several West Coast communities involved the posting of "No Jap Trade Wanted" signs in the windows of retail shops and stores, and a general effort to drive the evacuees out of the community by refusing them goods and services. Such boycotts, of course, had to be quite comprehensive in order to be effective. Consequently WRA focused its primary efforts not on a mass drive against the entire boycotting group but rather on a few key merchants. The help of the local citizens group was enlisted in persuading some of the retailers to remove the signs from their windows. Evacuees were encouraged to go into some stores in defiance of the signs and thus learned that the signs had been posted in many windows because of community pressures rather than any real hostile feelings on the part of the individual shopowner. And in a few extreme cases the evacuees were advised to do their retail buying in some nearby town rather than in the community of their residence. This latter method proved particularly effective at Hood River, Oregon, where most of the boycotting merchants changed their tune when they saw evacuee business going to the stores in the adjacent community of The Dalles.

A number of other manifestations of anti-evacuee prejudice were encountered and were dealt with on an individual basis. As one case in point, there were a number of alien evacuees who experienced difficulty in obtaining licenses for the operation of certain types of commercial establishments or for the practice of their professions. In these cases, WRA attorneys attached to the field offices were sent in to talk with the local licensing boards and point out the hazards of withholding permits on such a patently discriminatory basis. In the majority of cases, these efforts were ultimately successful.

The final drive in WRA's campaign against West Coast discrimination was built around the group of American Army officers who had served with the Nisei in combat and who undertook a speaking tour throughout the West Coast region on behalf of the evacuated people.

In June of 1945 Robert Cozzens, Assistant Director in San Francisco, and I made a trip all the way up the San Joaquin Valley of California from Los Angeles to the north of Sacramento. Our main purpose was to visit returned evacuees and especially those whose homes had been shot into. After making a large number of visits we found only one family among those threatened by shots which had decided to move. This was near Lancaster in the Los Angeles area. All others were determined to stay and most seemed at that time not to be perturbed about their future. Two incidents during this trip stand out in my memory.

In one case we stopped at a fruit farm where the packing boxes from Poston, Arizona, were still piled up in the back yard, and the whole family, old and young, were out in the orchard picking plums. We located the Issei father, who called the others in to meet us. When I greeted the mother, who was the last one in, I asked if she was glad to be home. Her response was a quick and emphatic "No!" When I asked why not, she took only three more words: "Too much work!" The reply was not untypical and, all things considered, it was a wholly understandable reaction.

The other visit was to the Kishi family in the northern part of the valley, whose house had been shot into. As we drove into the yard a beautiful young Nisei girl appeared, putting the bread box out to sun. Her name was Mamie. We introduced ourselves and explained our visit. Mamie invited us into the house, and at our request she showed us the bullet holes high up near the ceiling.

In the meantime Mamie's younger sister had joined us, and I began noticing that Mamie had a Boston accent. When I asked where she had acquired her accent, the young sister jumped with glee and said, "See, we've been telling you that you had an accent." It developed that Mamie had relocated earlier to Boston and had gotten a job as salesgirl in a Boston department store. When I asked if she was glad to be home, she said "No," except that it was nice to see her folks. I then asked, "How about your friends?" She said, "I have no friends here now except the family; my friends are in Boston." She said she had made many friends there, that she had many invitations out to dinner, and she guessed because she was different many people had been nice to her and had entertained her. This was easy to believe, because Mamie was most attractive. When we asked why she had come home, she gave us the expected answer — that the parents had asked her to come. She said, however, that after they were completely settled she hoped to return to Boston. Whether she did go, I never have learned.

In spite of terrorism, attempted boycotts, and advice from well meaning friends of the evacuees to wait awhile, relocation proceeded on schedule. We had planned for 16,000 relocatees by June 30, 1945. We fell short of this quota, but not by much.

FRIENDLY OPPOSITION AND FIRM ACTION

By June 1945 terrorism was no longer a major problem, but instead there was a rising tide of so-called friendly opposition, especially from Los Angeles and the San Francisco Bay area. We were sure that some of this had been stimulated by alert young Nisei who had relocated throughout the country and who were enjoying the financial advantage of having their parents maintained at government expense in relocation centers. In any case the friendly opposition persisted throughout the summer, at times using great ingenuity in trying to prevent WRA from carrying out its scheduled center closings.

Large volumes of mail were addressed not only to WRA but to the secretary of the interior and the president. Resolutions were passed, and critical articles were written for liberal journals such as *The Nation* and the *Christian Century*. This type of campaign accounts for the deep concern that Undersecretary Fortas showed during this period regarding our center closing policy.

In spite of opposition, friendly and otherwise, we were able to move forward with the support of Secretary Ickes. We realized that hundreds of evacuees were determined to stay until the final closing, and this prospect was worrisome. Because of problems of transportation, housing, and other required services, we were deeply concerned about bottlenecks and inability to cope with any large bulges in the movement, as contrasted with a reasonably smooth and even flow. With this in mind, we announced on June 22 the closing of the Canal Camp at Gila River in Arizona and Units II and III at Poston by October 1. Three weeks later, on July 13, we announced the schedule for closing of all centers except Tule Lake between October 15 and December 15. Closing dates were as follows: Granada Center in Colorado October 15, Minidoka in Idaho and Central Utah November 1, Gila River in Arizona and Heart Mountain in Wyoming November 15, Colorado River (Poston) in Arizona and Manzanar in California December 1, and Rohwer in Arkansas December 15. The Jerome Center in Arkansas had been closed on June 30, 1944.

Three other steps became necessary in order to convince some of the evacuees and other persons that we really meant what we said. First, project directors were authorized to curtail services that were interfering with relocation. At the same time, we announced the scheduling of persons in dependency or welfare status who had been accepted by public welfare agencies. If housing was not available, the district offices attempted to provide it. The last step was to issue Administrative Notice No. 289 on August 1, 1945, which provided that each project director should schedule departures during the last six weeks of his center's existence for all of those who had not previously made plans on their own.

Everyone was given a choice of relocation area, but those who had not chosen by the time of this final scheduling were to be sent back to the point from which originally evacuated. In only a few cases was this necessary. Some of the older Issei at Granada and Minidoka refused to go and were physically boosted onto trains. As was expected, Order No. 289 provoked much discussion both inside and outside of centers, but it worked. Fortunately about two weeks after the issuance of this order, the Japanese government surrendered and the war was over.

On September 4 the Western Defense Command retired from the reprocessing scene and left any further processing to the Department of Justice. At this point we were able to see real light at the end of the tunnel, even though it took seven more months to empty the last center, at Tule Lake.

HOUSING PROBLEMS

During the last six months of 1945 two of the most difficult problems that we had to meet in order to keep to our schedule, and at the same time do it as humanely as possible, were housing and transportation. From the first of July until December 1, Rex Lee, Chief of the Relocation Division, spent about 90 percent of his time on the West Coast; much of it was devoted to finding and negotiating for housing.

Housing was a difficult problem in all parts of the country in 1945, but the shortage was particularly acute on the West Coast at the time evacuees were returning. Throughout the war there had been a tremendous influx of new workers into that part of the country. In the first half of 1945, war activities had shifted to the

West Coast as the European conflict neared its end and military efforts were increasingly directed toward the Pacific.

Most of the comparatively few center residents who had owned their own homes on the West Coast had retained title to them, but quite often it was difficult to regain possession. Where these homes were rented, it was necessary to follow OPA eviction proceedings, and some evacuees were hesitant to evict for fear such action might stir up public hostilities. Others found that their property had been vandalized, and they encountered difficulty and delay in effecting repairs.

The large majority of returnees simply required some sort of shelter which they could rent. Slums, which had housed many in "Little Tokyos," were now occupied by others; flimsy shacks, formerly occupied by farm workers, were beyond repair or already in use.

Immediately after the lifting of the exclusion order, extraordinary efforts were put forth by friendly groups in California to establish hostels that would provide temporary housing for returnees. The hostel movement had started early in the relocation program but was vastly expanded later. The War Relocation Authority assigned part of its staff to stimulate and assist local clubs, church groups, and sometimes individual evacuees, to operate these refuges, which were planned as nonprofit rooming houses.

In order to serve the greatest number, some hostels placed a limit on the length of time individuals could remain. Increasing rentals after a specific period was another effective method of spreading the benefits to a maximum number of individuals. As liquidation progressed, the West Coast hostels became an integral part of the program. Many of the most successful operators were returned ministers of various denominations who secured churches, schools, or other buildings and established hostels.

To further encourage this movement, the Authority initiated in April a policy of lending necessary equipment, including such items as chairs, beds, mattresses, china, and cooking utensils. We stipulated that hostels using this equipment should be open to all evacuees. By June 30, some 50 hostels were operating in 25 cities over the country, nearly all of them in the area of the original evacuation. By the end of the year, 110 hostels were operating in California alone. While some of these hostels could be classed as little more than shelters, and offered only a temporary solution to the housing needs of returnees, they made it possible for people to establish a base in their home communities from which they could seek employment and permanent housing.

WRA's West Coast field offices also concentrated on finding employment opportunities that would include housing. Perhaps the outstanding achievement of this type was accomplished in the San Jose district, where a large influential growers' association purchased considerable demountable housing of excellent quality which was transported to farms of association members and set up there to house returning evacuees.

Efforts were also made by church and other friendly groups to canvass in many localities and neighborhoods for individual families. While some housing was found in this manner, the results obtained were disappointing as compared with the effort expended. Individual evacuees were sometimes able to find housing for friends and relatives, and there was evidence of a great sense of responsibility and mutual aid being shown within the group with respect to housing needs and problems. In many instances returned evacuees took other evacuee families into their homes for a period. Efforts to secure housing in advance of the arrival of the returnee to the community were generally fruitless, although various attempts were made to accomplish this.

During this period closer liaison was established with the National Housing Agency and two of its constituent agencies, the Federal Public Housing Authority and the Federal Housing Administration, both in Washington and in their regional and district offices.

Some of our WRA people talked with the head of the National Housing Agency shortly before the lifting of the exclusion order and inquired whether it would be possible to set up a special program for the housing of evacuees returning to the West Coast. The reply was that the National Housing Agency was having a difficult time providing for the housing needs of war workers and the armed forces and would therefore be opposed to any program which called for the use of special funds to provide housing for returning evacuees. As housing was one of the limiting factors in the West Coast war effort, the head of the National Housing Agency stated that he believed there was absolutely no chance of obtaining the legislation needed for special evacuee housing. The cooperation of federal housing agencies was promised, however, within the framework of the regular housing pattern existing on the West Coast.

Although the NHA and the FPHA expressed their willingness to help, they were limited in their ability to be of assistance because of provisions in the Lanham Act which specified that only war workers were eligible to occupy war housing. Early in July, however, the Congress passed an amendment to the Lanham Act which put families of servicemen and veterans on a parity with war workers as eligible tenants of war housing. Because of the large number of Nisei soldiers and veterans, it was anticipated that this amendment would be of some help in housing resettlers.

VJ Day on August 14 brought immediate cancellation of war contracts and suspension of war production, and on August 29 the National Housing Agency issued new instructions concerning eligibility to occupy war housing. These provided that "distressed families without housing, who have been dislocated or displaced as a result of the war or its orderly demobilization, may also be admitted as an aid to the orderly demobilization of the war effort." Evacuees were made eligible by this order, and the West Coast regional housing authorities agreed to do everything in their power to assist evacuees to take advantage of these new regulations. In Washington and Oregon, the NHA actually assumed responsibility for housing returnees and succeeded in providing housing for large numbers of them. This solved the major problems in these two states.

As early as June it had become apparent that the WRA would have to take some extraordinary measures to meet the housing crisis in a few of the California districts. Consequently, the chief of the Relocation Division went to the West Coast the first of July to explore all possibilities for housing. Renewed emphasis was placed on the acquisition of suitable hostels. A general survey was made of all army, navy, and Coast Guard installations with the hope of obtaining sufficient temporary barracks to solve the problem in the more crucial areas.

By late July sufficient installations had been located in the San Francisco Bay area and in the Los Angeles area to meet the most immediate needs. However, the Authority experienced considerable difficulty in negotiating the acquisition of these installations. In some instances, the owners of the property on which the installations were located had been trying for months to recover their property and objected strenuously to its use by another government agency, especially one which proposed to house returning evacuees. In other instances, communities in which the installations were located opposed the use of the installations for housing evacuees.

Finally, the Western Defense Command turned over to WRA the first big block of temporary housing. This was located at South Fort Funston, a part of the San Francisco Harbor defense system. Sufficient barracks were turned over to the Authority there to house approximately 500 persons. Shortly thereafter, the Lomita Air Strip in Los Angeles County was turned over to the Authority on a permit to use. This installation was capable of housing approximately 500 persons. Soon thereafter, five other installations, located in Los Angeles County, were purchased from the Army Engineers. These installations had a total capacity of approximately 700 persons. The Santa Ana Air Base in Orange County provided, on a permit to use, sufficient barracks to house more than the number of residents returning to Orange County. The Army Air Transport Command in Sacramento turned over sufficient barracks at Camp Kohler to house returnees needing housing in Sacramento.

While these barracks were being acquired, WRA negotiated an agreement with the FPHA office in San Francisco to take 100 veterans or service-connected families into public housing in San Francisco, 100 such families in the Los Angeles area, and 25 such families in the San Diego area. At the same time FPHA agreed to make available dormitories at Hunters Point in San Francisco sufficient to house 800 persons, and in Marin County, just across the Bay, sufficient dormitories to take care of 1,000 persons. FPHA also entered into an agreement to manage for WRA, on a reimbursable basis, all the temporary housing which had thus been acquired. Finally FPHA agreed to convert the barracks into temporary family living quarters at WRA expense.

In general these steps went a long way toward solving the immediate housing crisis. Although the situation remained very acute in Los Angeles County, FPHA finally agreed to lend more than 450 unused trailers to be used to supplement housing at five of the existing army installations. With the acquisition of these trailers, sufficient housing was in sight to meet the temporary needs of all residents returning to the county who did not have other housing resources.

Planning for the housing needs for the evacuees was complicated considerably by the fact that many evacuees used the housing crisis as an excuse for not relocating. In a survey made of San Francisco Bay residents who wished to return, over 2,100 stated that they could not return unless housing was furnished. Consequently, arrangements were made at Fort Funston, Hunters Point, and Marin City dormitories to house approximately 2,100 people. When relocation to that area was completed, only 800 had moved into the housing provided. In the San Diego area, out of 110 families indicating that they needed emergency housing, only about 15 moved into the housing provided. It was apparent that many evacuees had housing in sight prior to the survey of housing requirements but had hopes of obtaining better or cheaper housing. When it was found that the federal housing was not better or cheaper, the evacuees turned to their own resources.

In a few rural areas no housing resources could be found, and in these instances many evacuees requested the loan of tents. WRA borrowed 250 tents from the army and lent most of these in rural communities, pending the time the evacuees could erect or find their own housing.

By the time the last relocation center was closed on November 30, approximately 250 veterans or service-connected families had moved into public housing; approximately 100 persons were in Camp Kohler, Sacramento; 100 in Fort Funston, San Francisco; 100 in the Santa Ana Air Base; 2,000 in the six temporary installations in Los Angeles County; and in addition to this, approximately 4,000 were in hostels.

TRANSPORTATION PROBLEMS

Transportation was a critical problem but, thanks to the ingenuity of WRA's executive officer, Malcolm Pitts, and his friendly relations with the Washington representatives of the American Railway Association, everyone was moved on schedule.

Because of the generally critical transportation situation, careful and detailed plans were formulated for transporting the evacuees from the centers to their destinations. In conferences with the Office of Defense Transportation and the American Association of Railroads, plans were made for the use of special cars along regularly scheduled runs, as well as special trains to definite points on the West Coast.

In mid-July 417 people left Rohwer, Arkansas, on a special train that had been chartered by the center to take evacuees back to various points in California. This was the first special train movement and the first mass movement of returnees to the evacuated area. It was anxiously watched by both WRA personnel and evacuees, particularly in regard to its effect on public attitudes and community sentiment on the West Coast. Many persons, both within and outside of the Authority, had advised against such large-scale arrivals, fearing that they might occasion large-scale public opposition.

The train left Rohwer amid a great deal of excitement both among the travelers and among those being left behind. During a stopover in St. Louis, the local resettlers' committee and representative evacuees then living in St. Louis met the train and provided sightseeing trips and entertainment for the travelers. Reception committees also welcomed the evacuees at their destinations and provided transportation for them to hostels or to their homes. There was no disturbance or incident anywhere along the way. This first special train movement was adopted as a pattern for many similar mass movements in the months to come.

Group movements were thereafter encouraged by the Authority, especially as it was discovered that many evacuees were actually afraid to make the return trip alone but lost this fear when traveling and arriving at their destinations in groups. The chartering of such special trains and coaches, in addition to making the completion of the relocation program a physical possibility, gave a tremendous psychological impetus to relocation. The railroads gave complete cooperation to WRA by providing the needed equipment for group movements. With the shift of the war effort to the Pacific, the demands on the western railroads had reached unprecedented heights. Only their efficiency and cooperation enabled WRA to carry out its program on schedule. Most of the state and local officials were helpful, Governor Earl Warren of California especially so. He responded effectively each time we requested his aid.

We had magnificent cooperation from the top-level Social Security Board staff and from most of the state and local agencies in the handling of welfare cases. If we did run into trouble, as we did in a couple of counties in California, the state and federal staff members came to the rescue and straightened matters out quickly.

CLOSING THE RELOCATION CENTERS

Most centers closed from two days to two weeks ahead of schedule. Two closed on time; and Rohwer, the last one scheduled, beat the deadline by two weeks. Center closings were a herculean task for the appointed staff. There was confusion, of course, and some discomfort on the part of evacuees. For some of the aged and a small number of weaker individuals, the closing days were periods of real mental distress. However, for the great majority of the residents, the end of a long period of tension and indecision came as a welcome relief.

CHAPTER 15

Completion of the Relocation Program

WITH THE CLOSING of the relocation centers, the first phase of the relocation program was completed. There remained the jobs of assisting the last thousands who had left the centers to secure initial settlement in the communities to which they had gone and of making certain that communities were adequately prepared to give such continuing services as might be needed after WRA closed offices.

FINAL RESETTLEMENT ASSISTANCE FROM WRA

The Authority continued to give travel assistance to those evacuees who had left relocation centers for eastern points prior to the lifting of the exclusion order and who now wished to return to their former homes on the West Coast. Transportation continued to be available both for the individuals and for their household goods up to February 28, 1946. Between the closing of the last relocation center and the last date on which such travel assistance could be given, there was a considerable increase in the number of persons availing themselves of this service, but the majority of the resettlers did not do so, choosing to remain in the communities in which they had relocated.

The Director and the Chief of the Relocation Division spent the first three weeks of December 1945 visiting the larger relocation areas on the West Coast to determine what major problems remained. In general, conditions were found to be satisfactory. Community acceptance had improved greatly. The majority of the evacuees were happy to be back home and were making a good adjustment. Employment was readily available, although within a restricted range of occupations. Housing remained the most difficult problem but was available for all returnees on at least a temporary basis. It was decided to keep most district offices on the West Coast open until May 1, and the area offices open until May 15, 1946. These were the latest dates that could be considered, since the Authority's entire program was to be liquidated by June 30. For the fiscal year beginning July 1, no operating appropriations had been requested.

District officers were instructed to conduct intensive interviewing programs among the evacuees to determine their remaining problems. This interviewing program was intended to include every evacuee insofar as possible and was to ascertain housing needs, employment problems, medical and social problems, and any instances of racial discrimination. It was recognized that some hardship cases were not known to the Authority, and this interviewing program was intended to find and assist these families. Area offices were given authorization to recommend special grants for furniture and household equipment as needs were found to be genuine and urgent.

This program was carried through with considerable success in the San Francisco and Seattle areas. In the San Francisco area alone, families representing approximately 30,000 people were interviewed and their problems worked out by relocation officers. In the Los Angeles area the acute housing problem occupied the full time of most staff members, and only known hardship cases were interviewed. In the Seattle area the majority of families were interviewed.

In addition to assisting families to find adequate shelter, the Authority's housing job included the disposal of temporary housing installations it had obtained in California through joint arrangement with the War Department and the Federal Public Housing Authority. While the Director and the Chief of the Relocation Division were on the West Coast in early December, a program for the liquidation of these temporary housing sites was agreed upon.

WRA personnel in districts where the housing problem was most acute were given the specific responsibility of locating housing for specified families. Relocation officers with agricultural backgrounds were assigned to help farm families, and specialists in urban and domestic employments were delegated to take care of the others. In general the plan was to find employment that would provide or include housing for the family unit. Between December 1945 and March 1, 1946, the staff worked hard at carrying out this plan, and with considerable success in some districts.

Fort Funston was completely emptied by the first week in December, and Camp Kohler by March 15. However, at Hunters Point and other installations in southern California, some difficulties were encountered. When the San Francisco office was closed on May 15, approximately 117 families still remained in these dormitories. WRA transferred sufficient funds to the FPHA to convert the dormitories into family units.

In southern California efforts to move families into individual units met with less success. While a great many job and housing opportunities were found, especially in domestic and agricultural work, a large percentage of the evacuees preferred to remain in the housing installations despite their inadequacy. Many families were receiving full support from the local welfare department and expressed the belief that they could live better on relief than they could on the wages offered by domestic and farm jobs which provided housing.

Some families were reluctant to give up the group living to which they had become accustomed after nearly four years in relocation centers. Arguments advanced by the Authority's staff that it would be to the advantage both of the individual families and of the entire group for them to leave these installations fell on deaf ears. Little success was had up to March 1 in moving out many of these families. Evacuees frequently told relocation officers that they would continue in these installations until the latter were closed, at which time they would attempt to find something else.

The Authority was faced with a difficult situation. It had to dispose of these installations before going out of existence on June 30. The families resident in them refused to move. The Chief of the Relocation Division went to the West Coast to try to work out a definite program for providing other housing for people remaining in these installations. Negotiations were entered into with the FPHA and the county of Los Angeles. The county of Los Angeles finally agreed to take care of 250 persons needing domiciliary or other institutional care, out of the 2,100 persons then living in the six temporary installations.

FPHA agreed to house the 367 persons in veteran or service-connected families by moving them into more permanent public housing projects. FPHA also agreed that if WRA would provide funds for tearing down the barracks at Winona site in Burbank and would assemble at the Winona site 300 of the FPHA trailers then scattered among the six installations, FPHA would take this trailer project over and operate it as a standard FPHA trailer camp. WRA was also to provide the funds to FPHA to bring these trailers up to standard. FPHA further agreed that if WRA would find individual placements for 150 trailers, FPHA would rent these trailers to employers or other persons willing to provide housing for evacuee families.

Under these arrangements at least 1,000 persons were housed at the new trailer camp in Burbank. These, plus the 250 the county was to assume responsibility for, and the 367 persons in veteran or service-connected families, made a total of 1,617 persons of the total of 2,100 persons residing in WRA installations in Los Angeles County. The remaining 483 persons could be accommodated in the 150 trailers to be placed out on rental or by moving to alternative housing which some of them had.

FPHA, the county of Los Angeles, and WRA were pleased with this arrangement and were sure that it was the best that could be done considering the extreme stringency in regard to housing existing in the locality. Each of the types of housing to be furnished would be far superior to that existing in the temporary installations. However, the program was no sooner announced than WRA began to receive complaints from the evacuees living in the installations and from some other persons friendly to the evacuees, charging that these additional moves were unnecessary and that the evacuees were being pushed around. Some ill-advised well-wishers counseled the evacuees to sit tight in the temporary installations and refuse to move. It was necessary to complete the Winona project with a great deal of speed and move the service-connected persons and those needing domiciliary care in a very short time in order to meet the deadline for closing of WRA operations on the West Coast.

During April and continuing into May, the Los Angeles WRA staff devoted almost full time to the problems involved in assisting the people to move. In spite of the opposition and the difficulties involved, by May 15 all installations except the Lomita Air Strip had been closed. There remained at Lomita approximately 130 persons who were scheduled to move to two private trailer camps. These camps were habitable but not complete. WRA suggested that the residents move so that WRA could assist before closing its office. However, the Bureau of Public Assistance of Los Angeles County advised the evacuees not to move until all facilities at the trailer camps were complete. WRA therefore closed its offices and left the evacuees in Lomita under the sponsorship of Los Angeles County.

LOCAL RESETTLEMENT COMMITTEES ESTABLISHED

In planning the closing of field offices throughout the country, sufficient time was allowed to assist in completing the initial readjustment of the last resettlers to leave the centers and to develop plans for continued services to resettlers after these offices were closed. It was decided that area offices would close on May 15, 1946, with the exception of the New Orleans office, which was to close on April 1. District offices were to close on a staggered schedule based on the number of resettlers in the district and the time that the office had had to prepare for their continued social adjustment. By April 15, all district offices outside of the evacuted area were closed. The major district offices on the West Coast remained in operation until May 1 with the Los Angeles district office remaining open until May 15.

The first indications earlier in 1945 that WRA was planning to end its field services and complete all its operations by mid-1946 brought protests, from some sources, that the Japanese population would require continuing federal assistance after that date. As director, I took the position that such continuing services as might be needed for this one segment of the population were not a function of the federal government and particularly not of a temporary wartime agency. I believed that these problems could be handled by established agencies and by volunteer individuals already familiar with the evacuee and his problems and willing and able to continue assisting him.

To assure that there would be no let-down after WRA folded its tents, a Relocation Division memorandum was issued in September 1945 instructing relocation officers that the mobilizing of community organizations for continued aid to evacuees should be a major item in their liquidation programs. This memorandum suggested that in each community where a substantial number of evacuees had resettled, the district relocation officer should arrange for a meeting of interested community public agencies, private organizations, and concerned individuals, including of course the resettlers themselves. The purpose of these meetings was to have the community analyze the immediate and long-term needs of the resettlers and develop the machinery necessary to meet these needs.

As a result of final community organization work undertaken by WRA's field staff, there was at the closing of the Authority's program an effective local organization carrying on many of its services to resettlers in almost every community having any sizable number of Japanese living in it. In those few cases where communities did not actually develop an organization primarily concerned with the local Japanese population, organizations of broader scope agreed to include the problems of the Japanese in their long-range programs, and concerned individuals agreed to continue to assist resettlers in meeting any difficulties which might arise. In larger cities strong organizations were functioning with assistance to the evacuees as their primary concern. In some localities these organizations were made up largely of resettlers, with local people agreeing to assist in their specialized fields. In other cities committees were made up largely of representatives of churches, welfare agencies, and business and professional men, with only a small resettler representation.

It was presumed that in general such committees would continue to exist and function as long as there was need for them. However, by the spring of 1946, many such groups were finding almost no calls being made upon them for service, and some committees found that there would be no need for their continuing beyond the end of the year.

CHAPTER 16

The Closing of Tule Lake Center

As HAD BEEN CHARACTERISTIC of the life of the Tule Lake Center since it became the segregation center in the fall of 1943, the closing months of its existence were full of stress and strain and anxiety. However, the present anxiety was different from past anxiety at Tule Lake or, in fact, from that at any time at any other center.

The tensions arose mainly from the fact that the majority of the people were anxiously awaiting word from the Department of Justice as to whether they would be released and allowed to take up their lives again in the United States or whether they must be deported to Japan. The majority awaiting this news were renunciants who had requested and were in the process of having mitigation hearings designed to release renunciants through a rehearing process; the remainder were a small number of segregated parolees and people under deportation order as illegal entrants, treaty traders, or students with expired visas.

The renunciants could await mitigation hearings or they could request repatriation; they were to be repatriated if they requested it or otherwise they were to be turned over to the Department of Justice for movement to an internment camp.

The possibility of a decision to repatriate voluntarily to Japan added further to the state of uncertainty of many families, although in some cases it solved difficult problems. The decisions reached by and for these several categories of people would determine the future of the members of their families. In many cases, the families had already relocated.

NON-DETAINED RESIDENTS

On January 1, 1946, there were 7,269 persons of Japanese ancestry still resident at Tule Lake. Approximately 2,300 of these were free to relocate and were required to do so before February 1, the announced closing date of the center. This number did not include the 1,071 dependent children of those detained. These people made their plans with the relocation advisers and received all the assistance ordinarily rendered to evacuee resettlers. Approximately 1,600 left during the first half of the month, and during the latter part arrangements were made for the majority of the welfare cases. For all, their departures had been carefully scheduled to take best advantage of the available transportation. Special cars were arranged for the 80 percent returning to California, while the other persons took regular trains to their destinations in other states. Only 93 "free" individuals remained after February 1, and all of these had legitimate reasons for staying — such as health reasons or dependence on detained family members.

The project director wrote on February 8: "Tule Lake Center closed the books on the first and original phase of its relocation program with a population of 5,045 the night of January 31st." He stated that 8,714 persons had relocated from the center since January 1, 1945, including all who had been released from a detention status by the army or by the Department of Justice, except the above-mentioned 93 persons.

RENUNCIANT HEARINGS

It had been planned that Tule Lake would finally close its gates after all evacuees had departed by February 1. However, when the Department of Justice announced on December 10 that it would hold hearings for all renunciants who requested the opportunity to show cause why they should not be deported, the WRA agreed to keep the center open for the additional time required to hold the hearings, process the results, and allow those released to make preparations for their departure. The date was therefore extended to

February 15, then March 1, and finally March 20. During this period there were no center activities beyond the bare essentials, and people just waited.

When the hearing board officers of the Department of Justice began to arrive at the project on January 1, 1946, a total of 3,161 applications already received through the block managers were transmitted to the officer in charge of the hearings or to the officer in charge of the Immigration and Naturalization Service contingent at the center. Eventually only 107 of the renunciants did not request hearings. Between January 7 and February 6, hearings were held on 3,186 cases, each of the petitioners appearing before one of fifteen hearing officers with any witnesses he might desire and an interpreter if needed. The hearing form, with the recommendation of the hearing officer either (1) to hold for internment and possible deportation or (2) for release, was then forwarded to Washington for review and final decision by the attorney general.

Of the 3,186 persons who requested hearings, 2,780 were given releases to relocate anywhere in the United States, and 406 went to the Department of Justice internment camp at Crystal City, Texas. Most of these latter had been rejected for sojourn in the United States. However, the decisions were not absolutely final, and a few had not yet received word from Washington at the time of train departure. After reaching Crystal City, several more were released.

In approaching the renunciant hearings, the hearing officers of the Justice Department came to understand the complicated circumstances which had led to the renunciations and to realize that this decisive step had been taken in a state of confusion and under pressure and not, in most cases, because of any real loyalty to imperialist Japan. The officers therefore seemed to reserve recommendations for deportation mainly for those who had spent years in Japan and who lacked the mitigating circumstances of immediate relatives in the United States. Those whose loyalty records seemed clouded were also rejected.

The renunciants involved in hearings, meanwhile, circulated rumors about the numbers being recommended for rejection or about "tough-minded" hearing officers. There were few discussions on other subjects. Tensions rose and fell as small events and rumors took effect, and the project doctors noted an increase in intestinal upsets and stomach ulcer cases coming to the hospital. As release notices came through, those whose names were included were almost hysterical with joy and relief. One man was seen sitting on his doorstep in tears, waving his release and saying, "This is the happiest moment of my life."

People who received their release notices were only too glad to be out of the center within the five days allotted for relocation planning. This was not difficult, because after the "free" individuals had left on January 31, the relocation office immediately began planning on an if-and-when basis with the renunciants and their families who hoped to be released later. Most needed only a few hours of final processing and packing before they could leave. The week ending March 16, with 1,085 persons relocating, was close to the heaviest load for any week at any center.

Most of those who were rejected but who felt that their cases were not markedly different from some who had been cleared, made efforts to obtain another hearing or a changed judgment either by writing directly to the attorney general or having other people write in their behalf. These people felt that they had not been able to give the hearing officers their full story. Many of the rejected renunciants, and those still waiting for final word, joined the ranks of a group of 1,300 attempting to test the validity of the renunciation orders in the federal courts.

REPATRIATES

On January 12 it was announced that the third ship carrying repatriates would sail for Japan during February. Those who wished to go were asked to sign up with the Immigration and Naturalization Service. It was made clear that the movement was purely voluntary and that anyone could ask that his name be removed if he changed his mind.

Since the previous ship had arrived in Japan, many letters had been received from earlier repatriates, along with newspaper stories of interviews, describing the rather discouraging conditions that the unsuspecting repatriate frequently encountered.

As time went on, it became increasingly evident that the decision of the older members of the family generally influenced the young people. In one case a family of seven immediately withdrew from the repatriation list when the grandmother died. In another case a renunciant who had been cleared by the Department of Justice for release took the repatriation train at the last minute after receiving word from his parents in Japan that they needed him.

The repatriation train departed from Tule Lake for the Navy Landing at Long Beach, California, on February 19, with 439 persons aboard. However, a family of five, after boarding ship, changed their minds and remained in Los Angeles. Included in the repatriate list was only one man who was involuntarily deported by the Department of Justice for illegal entry and for whom no writ of habeas corpus had been presented. The majority of the renunciants who went were from the 107 who had not requested mitigation hearings.

On February 23, the ship sailed with 202 United States citizens (194 under 20 years of age, and 8 who were 20 years or older), 114 renunciants, and 116 aliens, making a total of 432 persons from Tule Lake. In addition, one person from Gila River and one from Granada had joined family members at Tule Lake to repatriate, making a total of 434 persons who sailed.

DEPORTEES AND SEGREGATED PAROLEES

Early in January 47 persons were still being held at Tule Lake as segregated parolees. Beginning on January 21 their cases were heard before a Special Alien Board of the Department of Justice, composed of the dean of the University of California Law School and two lawyers. These hearings were of the same type as those given internees at the Department of Justice internment camps. For nearly two months thereafter these men had no word of their fate. Then on March 18, two days before the center closing, releases for the majority came through. In the following days the remainder also received releases and relocated at once, their families having gone out ahead of them. Only one was given an "interim" release to have much-needed surgery. Two who were listed for release had already repatriated to Japan.

Also at Tule Lake were about 30 persons who were held by the Department of Justice under deportation orders. Most of them had had the status of treaty merchants, but when the commercial treaties with Japan were abrogated in late 1941, these persons had lost their status and had become deportable. The majority were released from Tule Lake when a waiver of the usual $500 bond was arranged, although two remained in Department of Justice custody and were sent to San Francisco to be held for deportation.

On March 20, with a train scheduled to leave for the internment camp at Crystal City at 5 P.M., 554 people were still in the center, detained either by the Department of Justice or by family members. All were hoping that more releases would come in. Sixty releases arrived during the final twenty-four hours. Forty-seven of these came before 11 A.M., the time at which the people were to gather to undergo complete search of their persons and belongings by the guards of the Immigration and Naturalization Service. Eleven releases came in the afternoon after baggage had been loaded on the train and seats had been assigned. Some receiving releases had been given no previous notification, while others were already on the rejected list. Names had to be announced over loudspeakers, and plans were changed at a moment's notice. Everyone wondered whose name might be called next — or if there would be any more.

During the day, 102 people were relocated — put on buses and taken to Klamath Falls to catch a train for wherever they wanted to go in the United States. Three more left during the night. The last two persons left at 4 A.M. for Chicago. On the scheduled 5 P.M. train to Crystal City, 447 persons left, 41 of them family members, the youngest a 6-day-old baby. One renunciant departing on this train said, "Well, I'm paying for the greatest mistake of my life — listening to other people."

On January 1, 1946, the resident population at Tule Lake was 7,269, with 34 persons on short-term passes; on February 1 the population was 5,045, with 1 short-term pass; on March 1 the population was 2,806, with 2 short-term passes.

After everyone had left, on March 20, the lights went off around the perimeter of the Tule Lake center. On March 21 the population was zero.

After the last resident had left the Tule Lake Center, the remaining members of the appointed personnel concentrated their efforts on preparing the final reports and records for the center and on preparing the physical facilities for disposition. The property was inventoried and turned over to the designated disposal agencies. The buildings which still remained to be cleaned were put in stand-by condition.

On May 4 the Tule Lake center was turned over to the Bureau of Reclamation.

CHAPTER 17

The Last Days of the WRA

DISTRIBUTION OF RELOCATEES

WITH THE CLOSING OF THE TENTH and last relocation center, a total of 109,300 people had departed from these artificial communities and gone back into normal life. This number included 2,355 men who had gone directly into the armed forces from the centers. A total of 25,778 men and women of Japanese ancestry had been inducted into the armed forces of the United States as of December 31, 1945. Of this number, over 13,000 were from the mainland and the remainder from Hawaii. Many of these servicemen had been discharged by the end of 1945, but a large number later served with the occupation forces in Japan and in Germany.

At the time of completion of the WRA program in 1946, about 50,000 evacuees were living in areas away from the West Coast, and roughly 57,000 had returned to regions from which they were evacuated. This latter figure included some 5,600 who returned from other states with travel grants from the WRA. (February 28, 1946, was the last date on which requests for transportation assistance were accepted.) The majority of the total returning were from Illinois, Colorado, and Utah — states which had received the most substantial number of resettlers.

Other than the Pacific states, nine states each received more than 1,500 resettlers — Illinois 11,200; Colorado 5,300; Utah

5,000; Ohio 3,900; Idaho 3,500; Michigan 2,800; New York 2,300; New Jersey 2,200; and Minnesota 1,700.

Before the evacuation, California had a population of 93,717 people of Japanese ancestry. In March 1946 the evacuees who had returned numbered approximately 48,600. The comparable figures for Washington were 14,565 and about 5,900, and for Oregon 4,071 and 2,800.

Of a total of 120,000 people of Japanese ancestry who at some stage were the responsibility of the War Relocation Authority between 1942 and 1946, a total of 4,724 repatriates and expatriates sailed for Japan on five different dates — 4 persons on June 11, 1942; 314 on September 2, 1943; 423 on November 25, 1945; 3,551 on December 29, 1945; and 432 on February 23, 1946. Of the 4,724 total number, 1,659 were alien repatriates; 1,949 were American citizens, all but about 100 under 20 years of age, mostly children under 15 years of age accompanying repatriate parents; and 1,116 were renunciants. Of this latter group, 930 were between the ages of 20 and 35 years and were quite likely Kibei who had had most of their education in Japan. This group of 1,116 renunciants who actually went to Japan was only about 20 percent of more than 5,700 who had applied for renunciation of their American citizenship earlier.

In view of all of the bitterness, frustrations, and pressures that these 120,000 people were subjected to, it is quite remarkable that fewer than 4 percent of the total decided to cast their lot with Japan. Of this limited number 1,800 were youngsters 18 years of age or under who felt that they had no choice except to accompany their parents. The fact that so few renounced in spite of the pressures is a testament to their training and life in America. We believe it is also due in part at least to WRA policies.

On May 21, 1959, United States Attorney General Rogers was quoted in the *Washington Post* as saying that there were "5,766 Nisei who renounced their citizenship and 5,409 have since asked that it be returned. Only 357 failed to apply for a return of their citizenship in the United States. So far 4,978 have recovered status as U.S. citizens." This was all but 431 of those who had requested that their U.S. citizenship be returned.

In view of these figures some of the 1,116 renunciants who

returned to Japan must have succeeded in recovering their citizenship, along with more than 4,000 who remained in the United States.

IMPROVED PUBLIC ATTITUDES

On the whole, the attitude toward the Japanese Americans throughout the country continued to improve. The long series of acts of terrorism toward evacuees returning to the West Coast was definitely ended. Only one such incident took place during this later period. The plate glass window of a store owned by a Nisei ex-serviceman in a small California town was smashed by stones on the night of January 29.

On the positive side, sentences were meted out by California courts to several who had attacked resettlers earlier. In places such as Hood River, Oregon, and Auburn, California, where sentiment had at first been strong against the evacuees, the "No Japs Wanted" signs slowly disappeared from the windows of shops and restaurants, and the people began to be accepted far better than had been anticipated.

The futility of further protest as a means of discouraging resettlement in the areas of evacuation had become apparent. The lessening of war emotions and the record of the Nisei in uniform had also played their part in furthering better acceptance.

Nisei veterans continued to be the recipients of numerous military decorations for feats performed beyond the call of duty (see Chapter 11). The Nation's highest honor, the Congressional Medal of Honor, was posthumously awarded to Private First Class Sadao S. Munemori, and the seventh Presidential Citation was given to a unit of the 442nd Combat Team. It was also announced that the Marine Corps, in accordance with the change of policy of the Navy, would accept Nisei enlistments.

Civilian Japanese Americans were also the recipients of many honors. One Nisei received a fellowship for work in atomic research, another for work in the field of race relations. Two young Nisei won the National Essay Contest and the Daughters of the American Revolution Citizenship Essay Contest. The president of the Japanese American Citizens League was awarded the Selective Service Medal.

A restriction against the aliens was removed on January 7,

1946, when Attorney General Tom C. Clark announced that they need no longer carry special identification cards or make special reports of changes of address or employment.

There still remained, however, some manifestations of discrimination. These were, mainly, refusals to grant business and fishing licenses, escheat prosecutions on the basis of alien land laws, use of restrictive covenants to negate real estate transactions, and other minor affairs where individuals or organizations were more or less directly affected economically by competition with persons of Japanese ancestry. All these discriminations were, however, strongly contested, some by test cases in court, through the combined efforts of socially minded individuals and organizations, certain cooperative state officials, and WRA.

During the final period conferences were held in West Coast cities and additional community committees were organized and began to function. In all, at least eighty-seven organizations in almost as many communities throughout the country were ready to help the evacuees in such basic problems as housing, education, welfare, legal aid, and general community adjustment. The committees were composed of local people representing church, welfare, civic unity, and other interested groups.

In Los Angeles, which had been the headquarters of several organizations that had concerned themselves with the welfare of the evacuees, the Community Resettlement Committee, composed of representatives from several private and state organizations, was ready to assist in problems arising there, including housing, welfare, employment, and legal, civil and human rights. The Japanese American Resettlement Committee was similarly organized in San Francisco, as were other committees in thirty-seven other communities throughout the state.

Besides these communities which had major responsibilities for planning and coordinating community services, 222 community agencies had committed themselves to provide services to the resettlers, and fifty-eight local groups were composed entirely of resettlers themselves.

CLOSING AND LIQUIDATION

Between January 1 and May 4, 1946, the district field offices scattered over the country were closed. Their property was transferred as surplus to the designated disposal agencies, and all their records were forwarded to the area office taking over their work. On April 1 the Southern Area Office closed, and on May 15 the other eight area offices finished their work. The property was declared surplus, the leases canceled, and the records forwarded to the Washington Office of WRA to be prepared for the Archives and for the University of California Library at Berkeley.

By May 23, 1946, the WRA had disposed of the 100 million dollars worth of government property that had been under its jurisdiction, except for a small amount of movable property held until June 30 by the Washington office. A large part of the movable assets of the agency, valued at 35 million dollars, was inventoried and declared surplus during this period. After the various bureaus of the Department of the Interior had selected the items they desired, and a small portion had been turned over to the Federal Public Housing Authority in the Los Angeles Area, the remainder was declared surplus to the regional offices of the disposal agency, the War Assets Administration.

The fixed assets of the WRA, valued at 65 million dollars, were all declared to the Washington office of the War Assets Administration, which office in turn declared them to the disposal agencies of the departments interested. Appendix R lists the agencies that took over the ten relocation centers and the refugee shelter, and the dates when the properties were released by the WRA.

During this final period of WRA, its personnel section continued to be occupied with the job of assisting WRA personnel to find other employment, where such help was desired, Four Civil Service Commission representatives explored openings in different areas of the United States. At the same time, personnel technicians continued to interview the WRA people, at Tule Lake and in the field offices, to determine whether they wished to have help with their future placement and to find where their interests and abilities lay. Every effort was made to match reported openings with the needs of the WRA staff. Summaries of all job opportunities were sent to the field so that field personnel could know of the vacancies and personally apply for the jobs. This work was finished about the middle of May.

Early in April an interviewing program was started in the Washington office to determine the needs of the personnel who were still with the central office. Placement officers at the same time were in touch with federal agencies in Washington in an effort to place the employees.

By June 30, 1946, approximately 3,000 people — all but the 80 employees who would continue with the liquidation unit — had been terminated. By June 1 about 2,200 had found employment in other fields. Of this total the majority transferred to other federal service, many going to bureaus and divisions within the Department of the Interior, to the National Housing Agency, and to UNRRA. The remainder went into private employment.

In order to carry out the final liquidation of WRA, a "War Agency Liquidation Division" was set up. This division functioned for about a year after June 30 under the Office of the Secretary of the Interior. The budget recommended to Congress for this unit, under a supplemental estimate of the Department of the Interior, was $173,000. Approximately 80 persons were employed.

The unit had at its head a chief of the division; also there were an attorney and an administrative assistant. The finance section was the largest, its purpose being to liquidate the outstanding obligations of the Authority. These obligations numbered about 40,000 and represented between 1.5 million and 2 million dollars, mostly in transportation requests and bills of lading for the transportation of evacuee property. The records section completed the consolidation of records and file material, the biggest part of the job being to prepare the evacuee records for disposal in the National Archives. These evacuee record files were used by the property section in their work of servicing requests from evacuees concerning property and claims for losses and damage. The personnel section completed the carry-over of personnel transactions, such as the transmitting of leave and retirement records to other agencies and to the Civil Service Commission.

In order to make a final appraisal of the end results of the resettlement activities of the Authority, three social science analysts composed a study group in the liquidation unit to investigate evacuee adjustment after relocation, study the new distribution of the evacuee population, and analyze the effects of the evacuation on the evacuees and on the country. A preliminary survey of evacuee adjustment on the West Coast was made during this period by one of the community analysts. The report on this and the work by the study group added the final chapter to the records covering the work of the agency.

REPORTS AND RECORDS

It was realized very early by those in charge of WRA that its program was unique in American history and that it would be to the advantage of future historians as well as to students of government, public administration, and the social sciences to have a complete documentation of its activities. Throughout the swift-moving life of the WRA this idea was carried out, and it culminated during the period of preparation of final reports covering most of the major aspects of the program.

Each of the centers prepared and sent into Washington a final report, consisting of accounts by the project director and by each person in charge of a program or an activity. These reports covered the many aspects of the management of a center from the point of view of the person actually engaged in the specific work, and usually contained an evaluation of the successes and failures of that particular part of the program. Similar reports were prepared for each area and field office. The personnel of the Washington office turned in over-all reports on the activities in which they had been engaged, stressing the problems of the central office in administering the program.

These functional and operational records of the agency's activities were deposited in the National Archives at the end of June. At the same time a complete duplicate set of these records was sent to the library of the University of California at Berkeley where it would be available to students. A less complete record was sent by the Berkeley library to the library of the University of California at Los Angeles. Under similar arrangements, surplus records of WRA's administration of the Emergency Refugee Shelter at Fort Ontario, Oswego, New York, were sent in June to the library at Columbia University in New York.

A complete file of the photographic record of WRA, with the negatives, was also prepared and transmitted to the National Archives. Duplicates were sent to the depository libraries.

In addition to the archival records, special reports, monographs, and statistical records were prepared by members of the WRA staff for public dissemination. They do not cover a full review of the agency's activities or findings but were selected because they record important aspects of an unprecedented type of government activity.

PART 4

The Summing Up

CHAPTER 18

Summary of WRA Relations With Other Government Agencies

ONE OF THE MOST DIFFICULT problems that the War Relocation Authority faced during its four years was in its relations with other government agencies. Because of the nature of the job to be done by WRA, and because of the tense emotional situation that existed particularly throughout 1942 and 1943 regarding people of Japanese ancestry, government administrators at all levels were generally cautious, to say the least, and in some cases actually antagonistic in their dealings with us. In a few cases they were understanding and cooperative.

Both in the problems affecting the operation of the relocation centers and in the problems involved in the relocation of people of Japanese ancestry into normal communities, the government agencies — federal, state, and local — played an important part. The War Department was concerned with policies affecting the movement of people and controlled the policy in the West Coast area and certain other areas in the country. The Coast Guard and the navy in their control of movements in shore areas and on ships also had regulatory authority that affected the program. All intelligence agencies of the national government had some interest in the program. They were concerned with security information about the people involved and with the employment of people with special ability. Many agencies were concerned with employment — the United States Employment Service and the Civil Service Commission from the standpoint of rendering employment assistance, and other agencies from the standpoint of potential employers. Several agencies were involved in providing services that WRA required. For example, the Quartermaster Corps of the United States Army handled most of the purchases of food for the relocation centers. Numerous federal, state, and local agencies were responsible for law enforcement, issuing licenses, and similar services.

THE DEPARTMENT OF JUSTICE

Within the Department of Justice, WRA dealt with several divisions: the Enemy Alien Control Unit, the Immigration and Naturalization Service, the Federal Bureau of Investigation, the Criminal Division, and the Civil Rights Division.

The Enemy Alien Control Unit, under the general supervision of Edward Ennis, was cooperative and understanding at all times, particularly in 1942 and 1943. However, early in 1944, we had many differences of opinion with Herbert Wechsler, the assistant attorney general in charge of the War Division, and these differences of opinion continued throughout the period of Mr. Wechsler's tenure, which ended in August or September of 1945. WRA strongly disagreed with the procedure for handling hearings relating to renunciation of citizenship, the categorical detention of all people who had requested renunciation, and the possible deportation of all such people. There was also a definite difference of opinion on the WRA's plan to close the centers within a year after the exclusion orders were lifted. Most of these arguments are well documented in a series of memoranda from me to the secretary of the interior, and from the secretary of the interior or the undersecretary to the attorney general.

Our relationships with the Immigration and Naturalization Service were excellent throughout the entire period of our program. Ugo Carusi, the chief, was most cooperative, as was Willard Kelly, who was in charge of the custodial program within the Service, and with whom much of our liaison was carried on. We had little difficulty in working out a sound solution of any problem affecting the two programs.

Our contacts with the other two divisions were limited. The

Criminal Division was concerned with court cases affecting evacuees. Rather continuous contact with the Civil Rights Division was required during the last two years of the program in the many cases where we felt civil rights were being violated in the exclusion zone.

OTHER AGENCIES

We had close relations with the State Department in regard to the maintenance of regulations at the centers which might affect our obligations under the Geneva Convention agreements governing prisoners of war or wartime internees. Although the evacuees were not, strictly speaking, either prisoners of war or internees, their status was at least roughly comparable, and our treatment of them undoubtedly had some bearing on the welfare and prospects of United States servicemen and civilians in the hands of the Japanese. Generally speaking, the representatives of the State Department were cooperative and understanding. No serious differences were encountered in working out our negotiations with them, or with either the Spanish Embassy or the Swiss Legation representing the interests of Japanese nationals in the United States.

The Alien Property Custodian and the Foreign Funds Control Unit handled the blocked accounts of enemy nationals relating to property and funds. Consequently, we had frequent contacts with both agencies. The relationship was excellent throughout, and we encountered no difficulty. We found both agencies cooperative, once they understood the facts regarding the many problems involved in the WRA program.

We had a close working relationship with the War Refugee Board because of its concern with the European refugees who were under our custody in Fort Ontario, Oswego, New York. This relationship is well documented in the final reports of the Authority in regard to the refugee program.

RELATIONSHIPS ON EMPLOYMENT

A most important group of agencies having effect upon our program were those concerned with the recruitment of war service employees. In the spring of 1942 we worked out an eminently satisfactory program with the Civil Service Commission, which placed virtually no special restrictions on the employment of American citizens of Japanese ancestry who were relocated from the relocation centers. Immediately following the attack by the investigators and staff of the Dies Committee in the latter part of May 1943, however, the Civil Service Commission, without consulting us, changed the rules and regulations in such a manner as to require special investigation of every person of Japanese ancestry in advance of actual employment by a government agency. This greatly handicapped our relocation program and discriminated against American citizens of Japanese ancestry.

In our efforts to cooperate with the United States Employment Service, we gained the general support of the officials of that agency in Washington regarding the employment of persons of Japanese ancestry in wartime production. In many of the communities throughout the country, the United States Employment Service was most helpful; in other communities its service was uncertain; and in some areas it was completely ineffective. Because of the tremendous demand for agricultural workers, we worked very closely with the Department of Agriculture and the state extension services in the placement of evacuees in seasonal employment on farms, particularly in the irrigated intermountain area. Generally speaking, however, we were able to maintain good relations with these agencies, and thousands of evacuees were employed through their cooperation.

A wide variation in the attitudes of the different government agencies existed in respect to the employment of evacuees. Soon after Pearl Harbor, several intelligence agencies, including the Office of Strategic Services, the Federal Communications Commission, the Office of War Information, and Military Intelligence, began recruitment of persons of Japanese ancestry who had a good understanding of the Japanese language. The War Department recruited a large number of such persons, many of them Kibei, for intelligence work in the Pacific several months before opportunity was provided for the more thoroughly U.S.-oriented Nisei to enlist in the army long before the draft was made applicable to persons of Japanese descent.

Four important federal agencies were most adamant in their refusal to employ people of Japanese ancestry — the War Manpower Commission, the Department of Agriculture, the Navy, and the State Department. Many other units of the government did employ people of Japanese ancestry in various capacities, particularly as stenographers, clerks, or translators.

INTELLIGENCE RELATIONSHIPS

Because of the very nature of the program, it was essential that we work closely with all of the intelligence agencies of the government. Early in the program we requested the officials of the Federal Bureau of Investigation to conduct the screening of evacuees in relocation centers. They indicated that they could not do so because of a shortage of personnel and great wartime responsibilities. The FBI did, however, check its records and provide all information available in the cases of more than 70,000 people under our supervision. The bureau also conducted investigations in relocation centers, which we requested from time to time. In late 1942 and early 1943, J. Edgar Hoover, upon the request of the director of the WRA, assigned one man, Mr. Myron Gurnea, to visit all of the centers to make a study of internal security problems and the handling of the internal security program. Mr. Gurnea did not limit himself to the request, but made a study of all phases of center activities and made recommendations accordingly. Some of the recommendations on internal security matters were helpful, but most of those dealing with other matters were of dubious value.

Early in the program, we experienced considerable difficulty in the relocation centers because FBI agents came into some of the centers and, without revealing their mission, removed evacuees, in some cases without even reporting whom they were taking. When this kind of activity was brought to the attention of the FBI Washington office, it was agreed that agents would not thereafter go into a center without notifying the project director and reporting their mission to him. Although the FBI officials were often helpful, we found them sensitive to public or congressional criticism, either direct or implied. Because of a rather strained relationship that arose between WRA and the liaison officer of the FBI, we relied less and less on that agency as the program progressed.

The FBI took on the task of investigating Nisei and other evacuees for the Civil Service Commission under that agency's revised policy of requiring investigation of government employment. Because WRA was badly in need of stenographic help for the Washington office, we recruited 25 or 30 Nisei stenographers who had been trained in the center high schools and found living quarters for them in the Washington, D.C., area. Shortly thereafter I had a report that a real problem had developed because the FBI agents were following their normal pattern of investigation of these Nisei, which consisted mainly of visits to five or ten neighbors to inquire about the loyalty of the employees. These Nisei of course were complete strangers in the neighborhood, and furthermore people became aroused in some cases because they had learned from the investigators for the first time that there were Japanese in their midst. In several cases the neighbors brought pressure on their landladies and the Nisei had to move.

When I learned of this problem I called Mr. Ladd, Assistant Director and our liaison in the FBI, to point out the fact that this form of investigation accomplished absolutely nothing except to create trouble for the Nisei and for WRA. I requested that they use our investigative information and revise their methods because of the special situation. In my conversation I became irked because I was up against a stone wall. The agency did not take kindly to anything smacking of criticism of its methods. As a result of my call, we received from Mr. Ladd a sizzling two-page memorandum about our criticism; it concluded by telling us that FBI would do no more investigating of WRA employees and that the Civil Service Commission was being so notified.

Within a few days I received a call from one of the commission employees asking us to call upon the FBI to continue the service because the CSC was so hard pushed for investigators. As a result of this call I went to see Mr. Tamm, who was acting director of the FBI at the time. I humbly explained our problem and requested that the FBI continue the service for the Civil Service Commission. The atmosphere was chilly, and the answer was a frigid "No." This further widened the gulf in our FBI relationship.

Our relationship with the Office of Naval Intelligence was, on the whole, excellent and helpful. We cooperated by providing all information requested and by permitting ONI agents to come to the centers. The ONI, in turn, allowed us to see reports sent in from its field offices and upon request provided information regarding individuals, as did the FBI. The ONI designated an active member of the Japanese American Joint Board, which operated for several months under the supervision of the War Department.

The Office of Military Intelligence had much less information, generally speaking, regarding people of Japanese ancestry, than did the Naval Intelligence at the beginning of the program, and, as a consequence, was not in position to be equally helpful. As has already been indicated, the Military Intelligence recruited a large number of evacuees from the relocation centers for further training in language schools. Our relations with Colonel Kai Rasmussen, who was in charge of the language school, and the members of his staff, were excellent and most helpful.

The Secret Service, presumably in view of its responsibilities for safeguarding the president, requested information regarding the evacuees in Washington, D.C., and in the surrounding areas of Virginia and Maryland. This information was regularly provided.

In the case of merchant seamen, the navy objected for many months to seamen of Japanese ancestry sailing on vessels out of any port, even on the East Coast. After much negotiation, however, it was finally agreed between the navy, War Department, and Coast Guard, that the Coast Guard would be responsible for the screening of seamen of Japanese ancestry who wished to be employed in the merchant marine. While the rules and regulations established by the Coast Guard were rigid, they were uniformly applied, and within a short time many of the Nisei who were trained seamen were able to render service in the merchant marine.

Early in 1943 we developed a working agreement with the National Youth Administration, approved by the director of that agency, for training a large number of young Nisei in NYA training centers preliminary to job placement outside the centers. This program was agreed to and established in March 1943 and had just gotten well under way when the campaign of the investigators of the Dies Committee started. With the appearance of front-page newspaper items in the *Washington Star* during the last two or three days of May 1943, which charged WRA with releasing saboteurs and espionage agents willy-nilly, the director of NYA, without regard to prior commitments and without consulting WRA, ordered his regional offices to abandon all training activity that involved persons of Japanese ancestry. This decision was a severe disappointment to the evacuees who had accepted the program in good faith and also to staff members of WRA who had helped to promote the program. We were unable to secure a reversal of this unfortunate decision.

Throughout the program, we had close working relations with the Office of Indian Affairs and with the Bureau of Reclamation.

Three of the relocation centers were on lands belonging to the Bureau of Reclamation, and two of the centers were located within the bounds of Indian reservations. The Bureau of Indian Affairs served as the agent of WRA in administering the Poston center throughout the first eighteen months of the program. The relation with these two agencies was generally excellent. While there were a number of differences of opinion with the Bureau of Indian Affairs, which are well documented in the correspondence of the WRA, there were no significant differences between the Bureau of Reclamation and WRA.

We had excellent relations with the Bureau of the Budget, owing partly to the fact that the director of the Bureau was responsible for selecting both directors of WRA; and, during the first two years of the Authority, while it was an independent agency, he kept closely in touch with its program and policies. The excellent relationship was due also to the fact that Mr. Samuel Dodd, Mr. W. Barton Greenwood, and other members of the Budget Bureau committee which handled our appropriation estimates were helpful and understanding and went to great lengths to inform themselves about the problems involved. These men made several trips to the relocation centers and held numerous conferences with the director and other key officials of the Authority from time to time.

STATE AND LOCAL AGENCIES

During the early part of the program all the western governors, excepting Governor Ralph Carr of Colorado, were strongly opposed to the resettlement of persons of Japanese ancestry in their respective states. Most of these governors, however, reversed their positions within a short time because the pressure of the farm people for evacuee seasonal labor. Individual governors who continued to be adamant about relocation in their states included the governor of Arkansas and the governor of Arizona. But outside of the public statements and an occasional protest to members of Congress, we had little difficulty with state governments generally.

It was necessary to maintain contact with state and local law enforcement officers in areas where evacuees were relocated in order to secure their cooperation in enforcing the laws equally and without discrimination. Generally speaking, we encountered little antagonism with local officials and secured support from the majority of them. It is true there were cases, particularly in many counties on the West Coast, where there was little effective activity when evacuees were returning and running into trouble early in 1945. But later on nearly all of these officials measured up to their responsibilities in enforcing the law and protecting the returnees.

Certain county boards of supervisors on the West Coast and in other parts of the country passed resolutions which appeared to us to be un-American in content, and certain other state and local agencies responsible for issuing special licenses discriminated against the evacuees by establishing requirements which were impossible to fulfill or by refusing to grant licenses to aliens. Generally speaking, federal, state, and local officials were probably more sensitive to what they thought were political pressures against the evacuees than were people in private industry. This, perhaps, was to be expected. On the other hand, many public officials were most courageous and helpful in trying to eliminate the restrictions and discriminations against the people of Japanese ancestry.

It was the tendency of most federal agencies to adopt the attitude that they had no responsibility for the evacuees; when a problem affecting Japanese Americans fell in the general field of their responsibility, they tended to turn it over to the WRA for solution, even though in the executive order establishing the WRA the federal agencies were charged with the responsibility for assisting in the program. This attitude was very general throughout the first two years of the program.

As we moved toward the end of the program we readily secured the assistance of many agencies — federal, state, and local — partly because of the exceptionally fine record made by the Nisei in the armed forces and partly because of better understanding by the public of the problems involved.

FRUSTRATIONS WITH THE WAR DEPARTMENT

The War Department, under Executive Order 9066, had the authority and assumed the responsibility for the evacuation and for establishing regulations relating to the removal and the movement of people in the Western Defense Command as well as in other areas of the country. In line with this responsibility, the department established rules and regulations that had a drastic effect upon the people under the general supervision of WRA. For example, no one could return to California or to certain areas of Washington, Oregon, or Arizona without the specific permission of the Western Defense Command. This was true even in cases of emergency. In addition, the War Department was responsible for guarding the external boundaries of the relocation centers and thus was in position to control certain policies that drastically affected the program in the centers and particularly the relationship with the evacuees.

The provost marshal general's office was responsible for safeguarding war plants and military installations throughout the country. As a consequence, this branch of the War Department was in position to determine who should and who should not work in war plants and also to determine the definition of a "war plant" or "military installation."

Because the officers of the Western Defense Command were categorical in their handling of the evacuation and the rules relating to the evacuated zone, their actions were generally arbitrary, particularly during the period of 1942 and 1943. In the guarding of the relocation centers, certain rules and regulations that were established by General DeWitt were opposed by WRA. One example was the general order that all packages received through the mail or otherwise by evacuees in the California centers and in the evacuated zone in Arizona should be examined for contraband. In spite of our protest, this regulation was put into effect and maintained for many months before it was rescinded.

On matters affecting the engineering construction of the relocation centers, and on matters relating to the physical plants which the army provided, the War Department officials were generally cooperative. On matters relating to the movement of people of Japanese ancestry in and out of the evacuated zone, and on matters affecting restraints of these people, they were generally arbitrary. Exceptions were made, but they were infrequent and minimal in scope.

As we moved toward the time when the Exclusion Orders were to be lifted, most of our dealings were with Brigadier General William Wilbur, who was Assistant Chief of Staff, first to General Bonesteel, Commander of the Western Defense Command, and later to General H. C. Pratt, General Bonesteel's successor. During this period we argued strongly for a clean-cut revocation order with no further responsibility to be maintained by the military, and for turning over to the Justice Department the responsibility for determining who should continue to be interned or excluded from the defense area. This was not agreeable to General Wilbur. Consequently, when the mass exclusion was revoked, the WDC continued to exclude thousands of individuals, thus affecting relocation drastically. Furthermore, on the basis of the WDC's evaluation of individual evacuee records, and refusing to accept facts developed by WRA or by the Department of Justice, the WDC insisted on the detention of several hundred persons in relocation centers and at Tule Lake.

During a period of several months it was evident that most of the actions by the War Department and the Western Defense Command regarding the evacuees were guided by General Wilbur, and these actions were arbitrary and categorical in the extreme.

The story regarding the effects of the provost marshal general's rules and regulations relating to employment of people of Japanese ancestry in war plants is well documented in a series of letters addressed to the Secretary of War over the signature of Secretary Ickes. Suffice it to say here that the execution of the regulations varied, depending on the interpretation of the local area corps officers. Thus, by a combination of reviews required by the provost marshal general's office and by the Western Defense Command, Nisei were practically prohibited from working in war plants throughout the first several months of the war.

The insistent and unrealistic pressures by the Western Defense Command for a segregation program by WRA appeared to us uncalled for in view of the fact that they could have carried out the oversimplified program which they recommended while the evacuees were still in assembly centers. The handling of the registration and the loyalty questionnaires was planned by the adjutant general's office, and the plans were completed and put into execution before WRA was consulted. While some changes were agreed to on the basis of WRA representations, in several centers the program caused trouble that might have been alleviated if there had been joint planning from the start.

The Western Defense Command pressed strongly for the evacuation of several thousand Issei and Nisei from Hawaii. Fortunately Admiral Nimitz and General Emmons did not agree.

The comparatively small Hawaiian contingent that was evacuated to the mainland consisted mostly of strong-armed toughs who had been placed in isolation on Sand Island. They were therefore generally referred to as the "Sand Island boys." General Emmons came to Washington and requested that we take about 1,000 evacuees off their hands. I told him that we were in the business of relocation and unwilling to accept any evacuees not eligible to relocate on the mainland. He assured me that these people would qualify. This, however, proved to be untrue. The Hawaiian evacuees were sent to the Jerome and central Utah centers, and we soon realized after they arrived that we had a bunch of very tough young men. When the segregation files were complete, most of them were segregants instead of relocatees, and they went to Tule Lake. These hardnosed toughs were the nucleus for the strong-armed squad that served the purposes of the group in power at Tule Lake in early November of 1943.

After the joint board was abandoned the adjutant general's office took over the files; over our protest they moved the revised unit of the office from Washington to San Francisco to join up with the continuing force which had been maintained there by the Western Defense Command for more than two years, even though they had presumably turned over the responsibility for the evacuees to WRA.

HELP FROM THE QUARTERMASTER CORPS

During the entire existence of the relocation centers, we had an excellent working relationship with the Quartermaster Corps of the army, which procured most of the items of food needed by WRA as well as medical equipment and supplies. The service of the Quartermaster Corps constitutes one of the happier chapters in the long book of our relationships with other government agencies.

CHAPTER 19

Evacuee Property

BY THE TIME WRA first assumed full responsibility for the protection of evacuees' real and personal property in August 1942, evacuation-incurred property problems had become snarled and material losses had already reached disturbing proportions.

INITIAL CONFUSION

Several factors contributed to the property problems which WRA inherited:

1. The absence of any property safeguards whatever for several weeks after evacuation was a foregone conclusion.

2. Delay by the West Coast military authorities in providing property protection, after an order from Assistant Secretary of War McCloy had made such protection a definite responsibility of the Western Defense Command.

3. Property protection measures were inadequate to counteract initial losses or halt those which mounted throughout the period of exile.

4. Division of responsibility existed in the initial stages among the Federal Reserve Bank of San Francisco, the Office of Alien Property Custodian, and the Farm Security Administration, each with differing policies and none of them strong enough to prevent initial hardship.

5. Wartime hate, prejudice, and greed opposed the recognition of rights and privileges of the minority and created indifference on the part of many West Coast law enforcement authorities to destruction and pilferage of evacuees' property.

Many initial losses occurred before evacuation. Many families had been left destitute following the FBI raids in December and the rounding up of several thousand Issei. Other Japanese sold goods and property at sacrifice prices to persons who threatened to report them to the FBI if they refused offers to buy. Special police finally had to be stationed in the fishing village of Terminal Island, in Los Angeles Harbor, to protect families of interned aliens. Junk and secondhand dealers were buying furnishings valued from $50 to $200 for $4 and $5 by telling panicky families that the government intended to seize their household belongings. Since no official statements were made in this period, victims were strongly inclined to believe the rumors of the moment.

On February 20, the day after evacuation was authorized, Assistant Secretary of War McCloy sent a memo to the Western Defense Commander in which he instructed:

. . . Where they [the evacuees] are unable to protect physical property left behind in military areas, the responsibility will be yours to provide reasonable protection, either through the use of troops or through other appropriate measures.

In his final report the WDC Commander explained the delay which occurred in carrying out this responsibility.

. . . Prior to March 10 the General Staff . . . had not engaged in any extensive planning or preparation for the [evacuation] program. The tactical duties imposed upon it were such that it was unable to do so and at the same time meet the responsibilities imposed on the Headquarters by the essentially military aspects of its missions.

On March 15, however, the WDC head delegated authority to the Farm Security Administration "to institute and administer a program which will insure continuation of the proper use of agricultural lands voluntarily evacuated by enemy aliens and others designated by me, and which will insure fair and equitable arrangements between the evacuees and the operators of their property." Unfortunately, there was a further delay of several weeks before this delegation of authority actually became effective.

Still a fledgling organization at the end of March, WRA delegated to the Treasury Department the authority given to the Director by Executive Order 9102 "to assist persons removed under . . . [executive order] in the management of their property." This authority was subsequently redelegated by the Secretary of the Treasury to the Federal Reserve Bank of San Francisco, which became generally responsible for protection of urban evacuee properties.

On March 11 the Western Defense Command created the Wartime Civil Control Administration, which set up 48 "control stations" through which those about to be evacuated were processed. Stations were staffed with representatives of the Federal Reserve Bank of San Francisco, the Farm Security Administration, and the Federal Security Agency. Financial assistance with evacuation problems was offered by Federal Security only to those who were destitute. Both Federal Reserve and Farm Security encouraged evacuees to make their own arrangements, wherever possible, for disposition of their property. Both stressed rapid liquidation of assets, since there were no facilities for storage of movable property or disposition of automobiles during "voluntary" evacuation.

The army prohibited evacuees from taking automobiles to reception centers. If an evacuee car-owner did not wish to dispose of his vehicle privately, he could sell it to the army, or store it with the Federal Reserve Bank, at owner's risk, without insurance, in open spaces such as assembly centers. Under this policy the cars suffered rapid deterioration, and the owners became increasingly disturbed. By late fall of 1942, according to a Federal Reserve Bank report, all but 117 of the 2,000 cars thus stored had been sold to the bank. Then, the report states, the army, "in consideration of the national interest during wartime, and in the interests of the evacuees themselves, decided to requisition these [117] vehicles."

FEDERAL RESERVE BANK PROGRAM

In April 1942, after evacuation had become a controlled movement, military authorities instructed the Federal Reserve Bank of San Francisco "to provide warehouse facilities in a manner which would not exhaust or burden facilities of that character already in existence," and to make every effort "to keep the number of warehouses at a minimum to limit guarding costs." Since the evacuees had been encouraged earlier to make their own arrangements, fewer than 3,000 family heads took advantage of government storage, and they did so only as a last resort.

In an effort to forestall the victimizing of evacuees by unscrupulous creditors, the president of the San Francisco Federal Reserve Bank issued a special regulation on March 18, the very day WRA was being created in Washington by executive order of the president. Under terms of this FRB regulation any evacuee who felt that he was in danger of being victimized could apply to the bank to have his property "frozen" and thus made ineligible for any kind of transaction except under special licenses issued by the bank.

This system of protection, if vigorously exercised, might well have prevented some of the worst of the evacuee property losses. Actually, however, the bank relied chiefly on the power of "moral suasion" to prevent unfair transactions and exercised the freezing power on only one occasion. The authority was obviously considered a dangerous weapon in a property-minded nation. On handing over its property responsibility to WRA toward the end of 1942, Federal Reserve also delegated its freezing power. But losses had already been sustained; the time for effective application of freezing controls was past.

FARM SECURITY PROGRAM

In a final report to the Western Defense Command on the protection of evacuee agricultural properties, the Farm Security Administration stated the dimensions of the problem. Before evacuation, FSA indicated, Japanese-operated farms on the coast comprised two percent of all farms. Averaging 42 acres in size, however, they involved only three-tenths of one percent of the total farm acreage. While the average value of all West Coast farms was $57.94 per acre, with one out of four acres in crop production, Japanese-operated farms, with three out of four acres planted, averaged $279.98 an acre. Intertilled truck, fruit, and specialty crops were often planted and harvested several times a year. Japanese grew 90 percent of the area's strawberries, 73 percent of the celery, 70 percent of the lettuce, half the tomatoes, the majority of the snap beans, cauliflower, and spinach, and millions of dollars worth of carrots, cantaloupes, and other fruits and vegetables.

FSA's primary concern was to keep nearly 7,000 evacuee-operated farms, involving roughly a quarter of a million acres, in active production during a period of tremendous food requirements. Because many of the evacuee farm properties were so comparatively small, Farm Security found it convenient to encourage the formation of corporations, which would operate a whole group of evacuee holdings under lease, and "to make loans of considerable size to such corporations." Typical leases between evacuees and the corporations agreed that the evacuee owner should receive 50 percent of the net proceeds from the sale of crops after operating expenses had been deducted. In spite of such provisions in individual contracts with the owners, however, FSA viewed the entire income of a corporation as subject to crop mortgage and, accordingly, demanded full repayment before any lessor's interests should be recognized. Thus some evacuees received nothing because of poor crops on someone else's land. Individually leased farms were subject to the same FSA policy of collection without regard to the emergency circumstances.

In August 1942, Farm Security turned over all its responsibility connected with evacuee farm properties, except for control of its loans and collections, to the WRA.

WRA EVACUEE PROPERTY POLICY

When WRA inherited the property problems of the evacuees in August 1942, the agency set up an Evacuee Property office headquartered, not in Washington, but in San Francisco. Property conservation became a prime consideration in WRA's handling of both real estate and movable goods. The Authority could readily see the damage already done by earlier policies of quick liquidation and was determined to minimize such losses in the future to the greatest possible extent.

Because evacuees had been encouraged to make their own arrangements for storage of personal property in the months prior to WRA's assumption of property responsibility, the nineteen warehouses which the Federal Reserve Bank turned over to the Authority contained only 38,693 individual parcels belonging to 2,983 families. Others who had not sold their household effects in panic or desperation had stored the goods in vacant stores, churches, houses, garages, or other outbuildings on their vacated land. Some had reserved a room in a house rented to a tenant for the duration, with a verbal agreement that the reserved room would remain unmolested until the owner could recover the goods stored therein. It became increasingly evident that goods stored in vacant stores and

Appearance of a San Francisco sporting goods and hardware store at the time of its owner's return home from a war relocation center. Above, the store area. Below, the storage room behind the store area. The living quarters at the rear of the premises also were ransacked. (Haas & Associates photos, San Francisco)

churches or left with neighbors were not adequately safeguarded. Losses were steadily mounting from fire, theft, and vandalism. Local law enforcement agencies all too frequently provided inadequate protection.

In January 1943 WRA established procedures under which evacuees could have privately stored property moved at government expense to one of the WRA warehouses which were leased in key cities of the evacuated area. Great numbers of evacuees took advantage of this safer storage, but not before costly losses had been sustained.

As the relocation program developed, further changes were needed in the original regulations regarding storage and movement of household goods and business equipment. In the middle of January 1944 a conference was held in San Francisco involving WRA's property, transportation, and legal personnel from centers, and from the Washington, San Francisco, and area offices. More thorough investigation, reporting, and documenting of fraud, vandalism, pilferage, fire damage, and management lapses were urged upon property supervisors in the evacuated area. Transportation procedures were amended to permit the cost of packing of evacuee property at the centers at government expense, and the 500-pound limit on personal property shipments was eliminated as of March 4, 1944. New provisions allowed free transportation of 5,000 pounds of fixtures, equipment, tools, or machinery necessary to business enterprise if a family were unable to procure substitute equipment in the new area.

During the liquidation period of 1945 and 1946, WRA had to alter policy frequently to carry out its dual aim of giving all possible service to returning evacuees and at the same time terminating its property program. The deadline for emptying government warehouses on the West Coast, which was originally set for February 28, 1946, had to be extended to March 15. The reason for this was that many evacuees were living either in temporary quarters such as hostels or "special projects" or were doubled up with other families and in neither case were able to accommodate their personal property. Special consideration beyond final deadlines was given in genuine hardship cases. An important function of WRA during this period was arranging with local agencies, organizations, and firms which would continue some type of property assistance after WRA service ended.

After first circularizing bilingual newspapers, WRA moved from its warehouses and sold at public auction unclaimed property in all cases where the owner was unidentified or could not be located or failed to request or refused shipment by the authorized closing date. The last of the warehouses was closed toward the end of April, and the movable property program was formally terminated.

In 1943 the evacuee property offices began an exhaustive land ownership survey in the evacuated area, which was not completed until 1945. All county recorders' records were searched and all parcels of evacuee-owned land were identified, classified, catalogued, and mapped. The survey revealed a total of 5,788 evacuee holdings in forty-four counties of the three Pacific States. Of 3,742 urban properties, 3,267 were in California; of 2,046 rural holdings, 1,715 were in California.

Throughout the exclusion period WRA's main real property functions were:

1. Finding lessors for commercial, agricultural, and residential property, and buyers for evacuees wishing to sell real estate;

2. Effecting settlement of claims for or against evacuees;

3. Adjusting differences arising out of inequitable, hastily made, or indefinite agreements;

4. Securing accountings for amounts due evacuees and facilitating collections;

5. Determining whether property was being satisfactorily maintained.

When the exclusion ban was lifted and WRA's liquidation program announced, the property problem shifted to one of helping the evacuees to reoccupy their properties in the former prohibited zone. Many hasty leases merely specified vaguely that they were to be effective "for the duration." Others stating the "duration of hostilities" permitted the tenant to hold out for the end of hostilities with Japan. "Duration of the war" clauses were interpreted by some leaseholders to extend to the time when the president should proclaim the end of the national emergency. Few leases named a termination date. Some lessors had made only oral contracts.

Gradually, however, the great majority of these problems were straightened out, and nearly all evacuee property holders who still retained title or had adequately drawn leases were able to regain possession of their homes. The most significant fact is that the number of Japanese homeowners in the West Coast region was sharply reduced between 1942 and 1946. According to a WRA survey, the number of Japanese-owned or Japanese-leased farm properties in the evacuated area dropped from the nearly 7,000 tabulated by FSA at the time of evacuation to a little over 2,000 after the repeal of exclusion. The most important reduction was in leased farms. The mortality among urban property ownerships and leaseholds, which has never been adequately tabulated, was undoubtedly less drastic but quite substantial.

The loss of hundreds of property leases and the disappearance of a number of equities in land and buildings which had been built up over the major portion of a lifetime were among the most regrettable and least justifiable of all the many costs of the wartime evacuation.

FINAL PROPERTY SERVICES

In the document entitled *Summary of WRA Policies and Procedures for the Final Phase of the Relocation Program,* which was made available to the evacuees, the property assistance portion was set forth as follows:

Transportation of household goods and personal effects, like travel assistance, will hereafter be available to all relocating evacuees whose relocation plans are approved by WRA. This will include transportation (1) from a WRA warehouse in the evacuated area to a point of relocation anywhere in the United States (except that those relocating within a reasonable trucking distance of the warehouse will be expected to provide their own delivery service), (2) from a relocation center to a point of relocation anywhere in the United States, (3) from a railhead in any community outside the evacuated area to a point of approved relocation within the evacuated area, and (4) from a railhead in the evacuated area (in cases where properties are now in private storage) to a point of approved relocation anywhere in the United States. As previously, the WRA will provide assistance and materials for the crating of such property both at the WRA warehouses in the evacuated area and at the relocation centers. However, those evacuees whose goods are being moved from a point of private storage within the evacuated area or from a point of previous relocation outside the evacuated area will provide their own crating facilities and deliver the property at the nearest railhead. At the receiving end, properties of relocating evacuees will be delivered at the railhead nearest the point of relocation.

WRA warehouses in the evacuated area will be maintained for a period of not more than three months after the closing of all relocation centers. Evacuees who have property in storage at these warehouses and who return to the evacuated area will be required to remove their goods from the warehouses within a period of 60 days after their return.

Other types of property assistance will continue to be available through the Evacuee Property Offices and the Assistant Solicitor's office in the evacuated area as well as through the Evacuee Property Officers and the Project Attorneys at the relocation centers. Such service will be maintained within the evacuated area for a period of not more than three months after all relocation centers are closed. However, when an evacuee returns to an area in which his property is located, assistance will not be given beyond a 60-day period.

Contraband property, such as cameras and radios, previously surrendered by citizen evacuees to the United States Government may now be returned to the owners. Citizen evacuees should make application to the War Relocation Authority on prescribed forms (WRA-156 and WRA-260) supplying whatever identifying information or receipts they may have. Contraband property surrendered by alien evacuees cannot be recovered at the present time.

One of the most despicable and regrettable acts by the state of California was the initiation of escheatment action against a large number of Japanese families on the alleged basis that the land was owned by aliens in spite of the state's Alien Land Law which was enacted in 1913. These cases were brought late in the war period while some of the defendants were still excluded from California. Some of them were started as late as 1946.

There was little that WRA could do to aid the evacuees except to notify the defendants of the state's intent and to assist them in securing legal aid through the attorney referral system that our San Francisco office had devised.

The California Legislature voted an appropriation of $200,000 for use by the attorney general in the enforcement of the Alien Land Laws and in bringing escheatment action against presumed violators. At least 80 cases were initiated during the war period while the evacuees were excluded from California and 50 of these cases were still pending in 1946. A number of farms escheated to the state and were sold. While the individuals who lost their lands could not get them back because they had been sold, the California Legislature, in an attempt at fairness, did appropriate money sometime later to pay for the lands escheated.

Before completion of our WRA program, we drafted an evacuee claims bill which Secretary Krug of the Department of the

Interior presented to the Congress in 1946 with recommendations for enactment.

The bill as finally enacted authorized the Department of Justice to consider claims of persons of Japanese ancestry for damage or loss of real or personal property or other impairment of assets that arose from or was a natural and reasonable consequence of the evacuation and exclusion program.

Our WRA property officer had estimated that about $200,000,000 worth of property was owned by the evacuees at the time of evacuation. The bill did not become law until July 1948. Thereafter the majority of the claims were adjudicated and settled by the Department of Justice under the authority granted by November 10, 1950. The Justice Department settled 26,552 claims totaling $36,874,240. Some of the larger claims, however, had to be brought before the Court of Claims for adjudication. Eight suits brought an additional settlement of $1,600,000. The last to be settled was the claim of the Koda family of California; judgment on this claim came in the latter part of 1965. The settlement was in the neighborhood of $362,000. The total claims paid by the United States under the act amounted to $38,474,140, which of course did not cover all losses.

PROPERTY AND POSTWAR ECONOMY

The prewar economic welfare of the Japanese Americans of the West Coast states depended largely upon Japanese-operated farms. The growing of crops and the marketing of fresh produce required the services of nearly two-thirds of the working force. The evacuation destroyed the economic structure of the prewar Japanese communities of the West Coast. Not more than six out of ten returned to their former homes. About one-fourth of the prewar farm operators retained property to which they could come back. However, except for these and the few who left business establishments with competent and trustworthy managers, most of the former farm operators and agricultural businessmen found it necessary to start again from the beginning. The great majority of those farmers who were operating on leased lands lost their leases, and many reverted at least temporarily to working as farm laborers for other operators. The able-bodied had no difficulty in finding jobs, but many of the older Issei who came back were too old for productive labor. Many of them were living with friends and doing light work to pay for their keep, while some in the cities were working as dishwashers or doing odd jobs.

There was some shifting into areas that offered least resistance or provided a friendly atmosphere. The Santa Clara Valley, for example, had an estimated population of 6,250 Japanese people by mid-1946, against a prewar population of 3,773. In most areas, of course, the population was much less than prewar. In the Imperial Valley only 25 farm operators out of a prewar 212 had returned, and most of these were prewar landowners.

Many former businessmen established new businesses in cities such as Chicago, Denver, Cleveland, and Washington, D.C. Other notable changes were evident on the coast. There was an increase in the employment of women, both Issei and Nisei, along with a decline in the relative economic importance of the Issei men as compared with the Nisei who were maturing. Of course many more Japanese Americans were receiving public welfare assistance than in the prewar period, but it is interesting to note that by the close of 1946 the number on relief was less than half what it had been twelve months earlier. Generally, those who had been prewar operators and who were reduced to working for someone else were hoping to regain their former status within a year or two, and many of them undoubtedly did. As I drove through the Santa Clara Valley and in the area around Watsonville, California, in 1957 and saw the large acreage of strawberries, I was sure that some of them, at least, had made it back.

While some of the Nisei perhaps were temporarily handicapped because of loss of wartime profits, property losses, and lack of anticipated inheritances, I feel that over a period of years many of them are much further ahead in many ways than if there had been no relocation program.

CHAPTER 20

Constitutional Questions, Court Cases, and Other Legal Aspects

THE EVACUATION of 112,000 persons of Japanese ancestry, their continued exclusion from the West Coast from the summer of 1942 until January of 1945, and their detention for varying periods of time in assembly centers and relocation centers, inevitably raised extremely grave questions as to the consistency of such a program with the requirements and the prohibitions of the Constitution of the United States. The fact that two-thirds of the evacuees were citizens of the United States by birth sharpened these very grave issues.

Did the federal government have constitutional power to evacuate all these people from their homes and their jobs, and compel them to leave the West Coast? Even the women and children? Even those who were citizens? Could it do so without charging any of them with having committed any crime, and without any trial or hearing? Could the government follow the order to vacate the West Coast with enforced detention in an assembly center? Could the government thereafter, without consulting the evacuees, transport these people from the assembly centers to relocation centers under military guard and thereafter incarcerate and forcibly detain the evacuees in the relocation centers? What about the constitutional rights, in particular, of those evacuees who were citizens of the

United States and who insisted throughout these activities that they were patriotic, loyal to the United States, and willing to fight in the armies of the United States to prove that loyalty?

The many constitutional issues can be reduced to three basic questions:

1. Was the evacuation valid under the Constitution?

2. Was detention in assembly centers and relocation centers valid under the Constitution?

3. If it were to be assumed that the original evacuation was constitutional, because it was compelled by an overriding military necessity, how long did the military necessity continue to be sufficiently grave to justify continued exclusion; did such continued exclusion remain valid all the way through until December 1944 when the exclusion orders were finally revoked?

It is best to consider these constitutional questions in the order in which they have been listed.

There are two important reasons why the administrators of the WRA program felt compelled to think through these searching questions of constitutional authority. In the first place, the evacuees were deeply shocked by the fact of evacuation, and unable to determine what implications the evacuation carried for their future residence in the United States as citizens or as lawfully resident aliens. WRA had to provide to the evacuees and to itself answers to these questions that would provide a rational and moral basis for its relocation program.

In the second place, WRA had to be prepared to answer these same questions when propounded by congressional investigating committees, by groups attacking the relocation program, by citizens whose support it sought to mobilize, and by litigants in the courts.

WAS EVACUATION CONSTITUTIONAL?

It is radically important to make a distinction at the outset between the question of whether a given governmental action was valid under the Constitution and the question of whether that action was wise or proper. A governmental action — an increase in tariff schedules, the establishment of price control or consumer rationing, the prohibition of gambling, the evacuation of all persons of Japanese ancestry from the West Coast, or whatever — may be both a wise policy and a constitutional policy, or it may be a wise policy but not one permitted under our Constitution, or it may be an unwise policy but one that is permitted under our Constitution, or it may be a policy that is both unwise and prohibited by our Constitution. This would seem to be an elementary idea, hardly worth emphasizing, but for the fact that, again and again, persons convinced that the mass evacuation was unwise, unsound, and unfair, leaped unthinkingly to the conclusion that a policy of which they so strongthly disapproved as *unwise* must necessarily, therefore, be also *unconstitutional.*

Some of the important questions that were considered before arriving at a decision regarding constitutionality were:

1. Was the situation in existence in the spring of 1942 controlling, and was evacuation at that time within the power of the federal government?

2. Was the extremely broad power to wage war conferred upon the federal government by the Constitution broad enough to cover the decision to carry out the evacuation?

3. Could the government show that the mass evacuation was a military necessity?

4. Were the facts available, to the responsible military commander, in the spring and summer of 1942 sufficient to enable him to conclude that a mass evacuation was a military necessity?

After a thorough consideration of these questions and all of the available facts, the WRA lawyers and the federal government took the position that the responsible military commander could have reasonably decided, in the spring of 1942, that such a mass evacuation could be considered to be a military necessity. Later a majority of the Supreme Court agreed with this view and held that the evacuation was constitutional at the time it was ordered.

THE HIRABAYASHI CASE

The first case to reach the United States Supreme Court on any of these constitutional questions was *Hirabayashi* v. *United States,* decided by the Court in 1943 [320 U. S. 81]. The only question presented to the court in this case was the validity of a curfew order by the military commander, affecting all persons of Japanese ancestry in the evacuated area prior to their removal from their homes and requiring them to remain in their homes between 8 P.M. and 6 A.M. Gordon Hirabayashi, a citizen, intentionally violated the curfew order; when prosecuted under the Act of Congress that made it a misdemeanor to violate an order of the military commander, he argued in court that the military commander must impose curfew on all citizens or on none.

The Supreme Court unanimously sustained the curfew order, and in doing so was aware that it soon would also be called upon to consider the evacuation orders themselves. Were it not for the fact that the Court foresaw the problem it would face when asked to consider the validity of evacuation, the curfew problem would probably have been simple for the court to dispose of. It was the anticipation of the questions to be later raised concerning evacuation and detention that caused Justices Douglas, Murphy, and Rutledge to write special concurring opinions, even though they joined in the unanimous opinion and decisions of the Court.

Chief Justice Stone said, for the entire court:

> Distinctions between citizens solely because of their ancestry are by their very nature odious to a free people whose institutions are founded upon the doctrine of equality. For that reason, legislative classification or discrimination based on race alone has often been held to be a denial of equal protection. . . . We may assume that these considerations would be controlling here were it not for the fact that the danger of espionage and sabotage, in time of war and of threatened invasion, calls upon the military authorities to scrutinize every relevant fact bearing on the loyalty of population in the danger areas. Because racial discriminations are in most circumstances irrelevant and therefore prohibited, it by no means follows that, in dealing with the perils of war, Congress and the Executive are wholly precluded from taking into account those facts and circumstances which are relevant to measures for our national defense and for the successful prosecution of the war, and which may in fact place citizens of one ancestry in a different category from others.

Mr. Justice Douglas added:

> Since we cannot override the military judgment which lay behind these orders, it seems to me necessary to concede that the army had the power to deal temporarily with these people on a group basis. Petitioner therefore was not justified in disobeying the orders.
>
> But I think it important to emphasize that we are dealing here with a problem of loyalty, not assimilation. Loyalty is a matter of mind and of heart not of race. That indeed is the history of America. Moreover, guilt is personal under our constitutional system.

Mr. Justice Murphy, after emphasizing that the Constitution does not permit discriminatory action against any group of citizens on grounds of race, added:

In view, however, of the critical military situation which prevailed on the Pacific Coast area in the spring of 1942, and the urgent necessity of taking prompt and effective action to secure defense installations and military operations against the risk of sabotage and espionage, the military authorities should not be required to conform to standards of regulatory action appropriate to normal times. Because of the damage wrought by the Japanese at Pearl Harbor and the availability of new weapons and new techniques with greater capacity for speed and deception in offensive operations, the immediate possibility of an attempt at invasion somewhere along the Pacific Coast had to be reckoned with. However desirable such a procedure might have been, the military authorities could have reasonably concluded at the time that determinations as to the loyalty and dependability of individual members of the large and widely scattered group of persons of Japanese extraction on the West Coast could not be made without delay that might have had tragic consequences. Modern war does not always wait for the observance of procedural requirements that are considered essential and appropriate under normal conditions. Accordingly I think that the military arm, confronted with the peril of imminent enemy attack and acting under the authority conferred by the Congress, made an allowable judgment at the time the curfew restriction was imposed. Whether such restriction is valid today is another matter.

In another concurring opinion, Mr. Justice Rutledge emphasized that the Court's decision in Hirabayashi would *not* mean that the discretionary actions of military officers are beyond judicial review.

THE KOREMATSU DECISION

Then at last, in 1944, the Supreme Court decided the question of the constitutionality of evacuation, in *Korematsu* v. *U. S.* [323 U. S. 214].

On October 11 and 12, 1944, the Court heard oral argument in the Korematsu case; on the second day (October 12) the Court went immediately from oral argument in the Korematsu case to hear oral argument in the first (and only) case in which it considered the validity of the WRA relocation program and the temporary detention involved in that program; this was the case of *Ex parte Mitsuye Endo* [323 U. S. 283]. The Court delivered its decision in both cases on the same day, December 18, 1944.

Deciding the Korematsu case, the Supreme Court was no longer unanimous. Mr. Justice Black delivered the Court's opinion, speaking for six judges of the Court. Justices Roberts, Murphy, and Jackson dissented.

Korematsu, an American citizen, was convicted in a federal district court for remaining in San Leandro, California, contrary to Civilian Exclusion Order No. 34. The Circuit Court of Appeals affirmed.

Mr. Justice Black said:

Some of the members of the Court are of the view that evacuation and detention in an Assembly Center were inseparable. After May 3, 1942, the date of Exclusion Order No. 34, Korematsu was under compulsion to leave the area not as he would choose but via an Assembly Center. The Assembly Center was conceived as a part of the machinery for group evacuation. The power to exclude includes the power to do it by force if necessary. And any forcible measure must necessarily entail some degree of detention or restraint whatever method of removal is selected. But whichever view is taken, it results in holding that the Order under which petitioner was convicted was valid.

It is said that we are dealing here with the case of imprisonment of a citizen in a concentration camp solely because of his ancestry, without evidence or inquiry concerning his loyalty and good disposition towards the United States. Our task would be simple, our duty clear, were this a case involving the imprisonment of a loyal citizen in a concentration camp because of racial prejudice. Regardless of the true nature of the assembly and relocation centers — and we deem it unjustifiable to call them concentration camps with all the ugly connotations that term implies — we are dealing specifically with nothing but an exclusion order. To cast this case into outlines of racial prejudice, without reference to the real military dangers which were presented, merely confuses the issue. Korematsu was not excluded from the Military Area because of hostility to him or his race. He was excluded because we are at war with the Japanese Empire, because the properly constituted military authorities feared an invasion of our West Coast and felt constrained to take proper security measures, because they decided that the military urgency of the situation demanded that all citizens of Japanese ancestry be segregated from the West Coast temporarily, and finally, because Congress, reposing its confidence in this time of war in our military leaders — as inevitably it must — determined that they should have the power to do just this. There was evidence of disloyalty on the part of some, the military authorities considered that the need for action was great, and time was short. We cannot — by availing ourselves of the calm perspective of hindsight — now say that at that time these actions were unjustified.

In his dissent, Mr. Justice Roberts said:

This is not a case of keeping people off the streets at night as was Kiyoshi Hirabayashi v. United States, 320 U. S. 81, 63 S. Ct. 1375, 87 L.

Ed. 1774, nor a case of temporary exclusion of a citizen from an area for his own safety or that of the community, nor a case of offering him an opportunity to go temporarily out of an area where his presence might cause danger to himself or to his fellows. On the contrary, it is the case of convicting a citizen as a punishment for not submitting to imprisonment in a concentration camp, based on his ancestry, and solely because of his ancestry, without evidence or inquiry concerning his loyalty and good disposition towards the United States. If this be a correct statement of the facts disclosed by this record, and facts of which we take judicial notice, I need hardly labor the conclusion that Constitutional rights have been violated.

Mr. Justice Roberts added:

The Government has argued this case as if the only order outstanding at the time the petitioner was arrested and informed against was Exclusion Order No. 34 ordering him to leave the area in which he resided, which was the basis of the information against him. That argument has evidently been effective. The opinion refers to the Hirabayashi case, supra, to show that this court has sustained the validity of a curfew order in an emergency. The argument then is that exclusion from a given area of danger, while somewhat more sweeping than a curfew regulation, is of the same nature — a temporary expedient made necessary by a sudden emergency. This, I think, is a substitution of an hypothetical case for the case actually before the court. I might agree with the court's disposition of the hypothetical case. The liberty of every American citizen freely to come and to go must frequently, in the face of sudden danger, be temporarily limited or suspended. The civil authorities must often resort to the expedient of excluding citizens temporarily from a locality. The drawing of fire lines in the case of conflagration, the removal of persons from the area where a pestilence has broken out, are familiar examples. If the exclusion worked by Exclusion Order No. 34 were of that nature, the Hirabayashi case would be authority for sustaining it. But the facts above recited, and those set forth in Ex parte Mitsuye Endo, supra, show that the exclusion was but a part of an overall plan for forceable detention. This case cannot, therefore, be decided on any such narrow ground as the possible validity of a Temporary Exclusion Order under which the residents of an area are given an opportunity to leave and go elsewhere in their native land outside the boundaries of a military area. To make the case turn on any such assumption is to shut our eyes to reality.

In his dissent Mr. Justice Murphy said:

This exclusion of "all persons of Japanese ancestry, both alien and non-alien," from the Pacific Coast area on a plea of military necessity in the absence of martial law ought not to be approved. Such exclusion goes over "the very brink of constitutional power" and falls into the ugly abyss of racism.

In dealing with matters relating to the prosecution and progress of a war, we must accord great respect and consideration to the judgments of the military authorities who are on the scene and who have full knowledge of the military facts. The scope of their discretion must, as a matter of necessity and common sense, be wide. And their judgments ought not to be overruled lightly by those whose training and duties ill-equip them to deal intelligently with matters so vital to the physical security of the nation.

At the same time, however, it is essential that there be definite limits to military discretion, especially where martial law has not been declared. Individuals must not be left impoverished of their constitutional rights on a plea of military necessity that has neither substance nor support. Thus, like other claims conflicting with the asserted constitutional rights of the individual, the military claim must subject itself to the judicial process of having its reasonableness determined and its conflicts with others interests reconciled. "What are the allowable limits of military discretion, and whether or not they have been overstepped in a particular case, are judicial questions."

Mr. Justice Murphy added:

The main reasons relied upon by those responsible for the forced evacuation, therefore, do not prove a reasonable relation between the group characteristics of Japanese Americans and the dangers of invasion, sabotage and espionage. The reasons appear, instead, to be largely an accumulation of much of the misinformation, half-truths and insinuations that for years have been directed against Japanese Americans by people with racial and economic prejudices — the same people who have been among the foremost advocates of the evacuation. A military judgment based upon such racial and sociological considerations is not entitled to the great weight ordinarily given the judgments based upon strictly military considerations. Especially is this so when every charge relative to race, religion, culture, geographical location, and legal and economic status has been substantially discredited by independent studies made by experts in these matters.

The military necessity which is essential to the validity of the evacuation order thus resolves itself into a few intimations that certain individuals actively aided the enemy, from which it is inferred that the entire group of Japanese Americans could not be trusted to be or remain loyal to the United States. No one denies, of course, that there were some disloyal persons of Japanese descent on the Pacific Coast who did all in their power to aid their ancestral land. Similar disloyal activities have been engaged in by many persons of German, Italian and even more pioneer stock in our country. But to infer that examples of individual disloyalty and to justify discriminatory action against the entire group is to deny that under our system of law individual guilt is the sole basis for deprivation of rights.

In his dissent Mr. Justice Jackson said:

Korematsu was born on our soil, of parents born in Japan. The Constitution makes him a citizen of the United States by nativity and a citizen of California by residence. No claim is made that he is not loyal to this country. There is no suggestion that apart from the matter involved here he is not law-abiding and well disposed. Korematsu, however, has been convicted of an act not commonly a crime. It consists merely of being present in the state whereof he is a citizen, near the place where he was born, and where all his life he has lived.

Even more unusual is the series of military orders which made this conduct a crime. They forbid such a one to remain, and they also forbid him to leave. They were so drawn that the only way Korematsu could avoid violation was to give himself up to the military authority. This meant submission to custody, examination, and transportation out of the territory, to be followed by indeterminate confinement in detention camps.

A citizen's presence in the locality, however, was made a crime only if his parents were of Japanese birth. Had Korematsu been one of four — the others being, say, a German alien enemy, an Italian alien enemy, and a citizen of American-born ancestors, convicted of treason but out on parole — only Korematsu's presence would have violated the order. The difference between their innocence and his crime would result, not from anything he did, said, or thought, different than they, but only in that he was born of different racial stock.

Justice Jackson added:

It would be impracticable and dangerous idealism to expect or insist that each specific military command in an area of probable operations will conform to conventional tests of constitutionality. When an area is so beset that it must be put under military control at all, the paramount consideration is that its measures be successful, rather than legal. The armed services must protect a society, not merely its Constitution. The very essence of the military job is to marshal physical force, to remove every obstacle to its effectiveness, to give it every strategic advantage. Defense measures will not, and often should not, be held within the limits that bind civil authority in peace. No court can require such a commander in such circumstances to act as a reasonable man; he may be unreasonably cautious and exacting. Perhaps he should be. But a commander in temporarily focusing the life of a community on defense is carrying out a military program; he is not making law in the sense the courts know the term. He issues orders, and they may have a certain authority as military commands, although they may be very bad as constitutional law.

But if we cannot confine military expedients by the Constitution, neither would I distort the Constitution to approve all that the military may deem expedient. This is what the Court appears to be doing, whether consciously or not. I cannot say, from any evidence before me, that the

orders of General DeWitt were not reasonably expedient military pre-
cautions, nor could I say that they were. But even if they were permissible
military procedures, I deny that it follows that they are constitutional. If,
as the Court holds, it does follow, then we may as well say that any military order will be constitutional and have done with it.

And he concluded as follows:

My duties as a Justice as I see them do not require me to make a
military judgment as to whether General DeWitt's evacuation and detention program was a reasonable military necessity. I do not suggest that the
courts should have attempted to interfere with the Army in carrying out its
task. But I do not think they may be asked to execute a military expedient
that has no place in law under the Constitution. I would reverse the judgment and discharge the prisoner.

The finding in the Korematsu case perfectly illustrates the
tendency to generally support military judgments during a war.

THE CONSTITUTIONALITY OF DETENTION

There was never a question regarding the legality of detaining
aliens of an enemy country during the war.

The question of detaining American citizens did raise questions of legality. The WRA was faced with three distinct questions:

1. Did the government have constitutional power to detain
all the evacuees while they were being sorted to determine which
might be dangerous to the internal security if released?

2. Did the government have constitutional power to detain
admittedly nondangerous evacuees until the Authority was satisfied
that they had a means of support and that the community into which
they wished to go could receive them without danger of violence?

3. Could the government constitutionally detain those citizen-
evacuees deemed potentially dangerous, and for how long?

Since, during the first two years following the evacuation, there
had not been any court decisions upon which we could base our
support for a wide-open policy of allowing evacuees to relocate anywhere they wished, and since the Justice Department (which would
have to be our representative in court) advised against the adoption
of a wide-open policy, we in WRA decided for reasons already
stated that our leave policy adopted in 1942 must be realistic. We
established leave clearance procedures which required: (1) a leave
clearance permit after a review; (2) prospects of employment or

self-support; (3) a general receptiveness of the community where the individual wished to settle; and (4) a willingness to keep the WRA informed of changes in employment or address.

It was felt that all of these steps were essential to the evacuees' acceptance outside of centers and that these provisions were in the interest of relocatees if they were to be properly accepted and serviced. This procedure meant that an applicant could be cleared for outside relocation within a short time if there was no derogatory information that might affect the leave clearance.

THE MITSUYE ENDO CASE

In any case we proceeded under the leave clearance procedures until the Supreme Court on December 18, 1944, delivered its opinion in the case of *Ex parte Mitsuye Endo* [323 U.S. 283] (1944), which happened to come just a few hours after the announcement by the army that the West Coast exclusion orders were being revoked. This was a case that WRA had hoped would be tried much sooner, and we also hoped for the decision that was agreed upon by all members of the court, even though there were different reasons, that Miss Endo must be ordered released at once.

We had urged the Solicitor General on several occasions to proceed with the case, but at each meeting he insisted that we make the case moot by allowing Miss Endo to go without conforming to any of the provisions of our leave policy. We continued to argue that we wanted the court to act for the reason that we were quite certain of the outcome and that we wanted the backing of a Supreme Court decision in order that we might abolish any further need for leave regulations for anyone like Miss Endo who was free to relocate.

Quite obviously the Solicitor General felt just as sure as we did that the case would go against the government and he did not want to argue a case where the outcome was so clearly against the government's position. When the ruling did come it came too late to help, because of the army's action in lifting the ban on the West Coast a day or two previously.

In fact there is no doubt in my mind that the prospect of a ruling against the validity of detention in the Endo case was one of the major factors which finally persuaded the War Department to revoke the exclusion orders.

Mitsuye Endo was an American citizen. She was evacuated from Sacramento, California, in 1942 and moved to the Tule Lake Center. In July 1942 she filed a petition for a writ of habeas corpus in the U.S. District Court asking that she be discharged and restored to liberty. The District Court denied the petition in July 1943. She appealed to the Circuit Court of Appeals in August 1943. Shortly thereafter she was transferred from Tule Lake to the central Utah relocation center at Topaz.

The remaining facts are stated in the following extracts from the opinion of the court delivered by Mr. Justice Douglas:

Mitsuye Endo made application for leave clearance on February 19, 1943, after the petition was filed in the District Court. Leave clearance was granted her on August 16, 1943. But she made no application for indefinite leave.

Her petition for a writ of habeas corpus alleges that she is a loyal and law-abiding citizen of the United States, that no charge has been made against her, that she is being unlawfully detained, and that she is confined in the Relocation Center under armed guard and held there against her will.

It is conceded by the Department of Justice and by the War Relocation Authority that the appellant is a loyal and law-abiding citizen. They make no claim that she is detained on any charge or that she is even suspected of disloyalty. Moreover, they do not contend that she may be held any longer in the Relocation Center. They concede that it is beyond the power of the War Relocation Authority to detain citizens against whom no charges of disloyalty or subversiveness have been made for a period longer than that necessary to separate the loyal from the disloyal and to provide the necessary guidance for relocation. . . .

It is argued that such a planned and orderly relocation was essential to the success of the evacuation program; that but for such supervision there might have been a dangerously disorderly migration of unwanted people to unprepared communities; that unsupervised evacuation might have resulted in hardship and disorder; that the success of the evacuation program was thought to require the knowledge that the federal government was maintaining control over the evacuated population except as the release of individuals could be effected consistently with their own peace and well-being and that of the nation; that although community hostility toward the evacuees has diminished, it has not disappeared and the continuing control of the Authority over the relocation process is essential to the success of the evacuation program. It is argued that supervised relocation, as the chosen method of terminating the evacuation, is the final step in the entire process and is a consequence of the first step taken. It is conceded that appellant's detention pending compliance with the leave regulations is not directly connected with the prevention of espionage and sabotage at the present time. But it confers power to make regulations necessary and proper for controlling situations created by the exercise of the powers expressly conferred for protection against espionage and sabotage. The leave regulations are said to fall within that category.

First. We are of the view that Mitsuye Endo should be given her liberty. In reaching that conclusion we do not come to the underlying constitutional issues which have been argued. For we conclude that, whatever power the War Relocation Authority may have to detain other classes of citizens, it has no authority to subject citizens who are concededly loyal to its leave procedure. . . .

. . . Executive Order No. 9102 authorizes and directs the War Relocation Authority "to formulate and effectuate a program for the removal" of the persons covered by Executive Order No. 9066 from the prescribed military areas and "for their relocation, maintenance, and supervision." And power is given the Authority to make regulations "necessary or desirable to promote effective execution of such program." Moreover, unlike the case of curfew regulations (Kiyoshi Hirabayashi v. United States, supra), the legislative history of the Act of March 21, 1942, is silent on detention. And that silence may have special significance in view of the fact that detention in Relocation Centers was no part of the original program of evacuation but developed later to meet what seemed to the officials in charge to be mounting hostility to the evacuees on the part of the communities where they sought to go.

We do not mean to imply that detention in connection with no phase of the evacuation program would be lawful. The fact that the Act and the orders are silent on detention does not of course mean that any power to detain is lacking. Some such power might indeed be necessary to the successful operation of the evacuation program. At least we may so assume. Moreover, we may assume for the purposes of this case that initial detention in Relocation Centers was authorized. But we stress the silence of the legislative history and of the Act and the Executive Orders on the power to detain to emphasize that any such authority which exists must be implied. If there is to be the greatest possible accommodation of the liberties of the citizen with this war measure, any such implied power must be narrowly confined to the precise purpose of the evacuation program.

A citizen who is concededly loyal presents no problem of espionage or sabotage. Loyalty is a matter of the heart and mind, not of race, creed, or color. He who is loyal is by definition not a spy or a saboteur. When the power to detain is derived from the power to protect the war effort against espionage and sabotage, detention which has no relationship to the objective is unauthorized.

Nor may the power to detain an admittedly loyal citizen or to grant him a conditional release be implied as a useful or convenient step in the evacuation program, whatever authority might be implied in case of those whose loyalty was not conceded or established. If we assume (as we do) that the original evacuation was justified, its lawful character was derived from the fact that it was an espionage and sabotage measure, not that there was community hostility to this group of American citizens. The evacuation program rested explicitly on the former ground not on the latter as the underlying legislation shows. The authority to detain a citizen or to grant him a conditional release as protection against espionage or sabotage is exhausted at least when his loyalty is conceded. If we held that the authority to detain continued thereafter, we would transform an espionage or sabotage measure into something else. That was not done by Executive Order No. 9066 or by the Act of March 21, 1942, which ratified it. What they did not do we cannot do. Detention which furthered the campaign against espionage and sabotage would be one thing. But detention which has no relationship to that campaign is of a distinct character. Community hostility even to loyal evacuees may have been (and perhaps still is) a serious problem. But if authority for their custody and supervision is to be sought on that ground, the Act of March 21, 1942, Executive Order No. 9066, and Executive Order No. 9102, offer no support. And none other is advanced. To read them that broadly would be to assume that the Congress and the President intended that this discriminatory action should be taken against these people wholly on account of their ancestry even though the government conceded their loyalty to this country. We cannot make such an assumption. As the President has said of these loyal citizens: "Americans of Japanese ancestry, like those of many other ancestries, have shown that they can, and want to, accept our institutions and work loyally with the rest of us, making their own valuable contribution to the national wealth and well-being. In vindication of the very ideals for which we are fighting this war it is important to us to maintain a high standard of fair, considerate, and equal treatment for the people of this minority as of all other minorities." Sen. Doc. No. 96, supra, note 7, p. 2.

Mitsuye Endo is entitled to an unconditional release by the War Relocation Authority.

The court was unanimous, but Mr. Justice Murphy and Mr. Justice Roberts each filed a concurring opinion. Mr. Justice Murphy said in part:

I join in the opinion of the Court, but I am of the view that detention in Relocation Centers of persons of Japanese ancestry regardless of loyalty is not only unauthorized by Congress or the Executive but is another example of the unconstitutional resort to racism inherent in the entire evacuation program. As stated more fully in my dissenting opinion in Fred Toyosaburo Korematsu v. United States, 323 U. S. 214, 65 S. Ct. 193, racial discrimination of this nature bears no reasonable relation to military necessity and is utterly foreign to ideals and traditions of the American people.

While the court ruled in the Endo case that an American citizen of unquestioned loyalty should not be detained, the question of detention of American citizens who had not been given leave clearance was not passed upon by the court. The accompanying judicial comments in the majority opinion and the dissenting opinions had made clear, however, that the court was not likely to approve detention of any citizens after the war dangers were over, except on the basis of normal criminal proceedings.

Mr. Justice Roberts said that he could not agree with the reasons stated in the court's opinion. He added that he believed that the Executive Order did authorize the action that was taken by WRA, but that this action was unconstitutional because an admittedly loyal citizen may not be detained against her will as part of a relocation plan.

Thus, the Supreme Court had decided with relative ease that the curfew orders were valid, being justifiable however, only on the ground of military necessity and not on the ground of racial discrimination. It also decided, after a difficult interval of three long years, that evacuation was constitutional, again on the ground only of military necessity, but obviously with much soul searching and by a divided Court. Detention, however, even though only a limited detention and only as a step in a relocation program, the Supreme Court refused to sanction. It decided, instead, that Executive Order 9102, which established WRA and authorized its relocation program, had not *expressly* authorized detention of citizens as part of the process of relocation. Miss Endo could thus be given her freedom without the need for a direct constitutional decision on the scope of the power to detain citizens under the conditions produced by war.

LEGAL SERVICES AND CONSIDERATIONS

During 1942 the legal work of the Authority was supervised by the solicitor, and the work was performed at three different levels — the Washington headquarters; the regional offices in San Francisco, Denver, and Little Rock; and the relocation centers. After the reorganization in December 1942, when the regional offices were abolished, the work of the project attorneys was directly supervised by the solicitor. In San Francisco Robert Cozzens continued as assistant director, and the evacuee property division was maintained there. This office continued to be served by an assistant solicitor who devoted the major portion of his time to property matters until 1945, when he served the San Francisco area office during the relocation period on the West Coast. Also an area attorney was provided for the Seattle and Los Angeles area offices during 1945 and early 1946.

One of the first questions to arise was the degree to which the administration of the centers should conform to the provisions of the Geneva convention on prisoners of war. Since Japan had not ratified the 1932 convention, the United States government was not bound to observe the terms of the convention. Nevertheless, as the WRA program with its limited detention features developed, it became apparent that standards of treatment at least substantially equivalent to those guaranteed by the convention should be observed, to avoid any pretext for reprisal by the Japanese government in the treatment of American civilians in the hands of the Japanese.

With respect to sanitation, medical care, housing, religious freedom, and recreational opportunities, the convention requirements were met. There were certain deviations from the convention requirements because of the varied nature of the population, but on essential matters there was no variation. The alien evacuees in relocation centers were permitted freely to communicate with the Spanish Embassy representing Japanese interests, and periodic visits of inspection were made by representatives of the Embassy with full WRA cooperation. No significant modifications in policy were recommended by the Embassy as a result of these visits.

There was a question of exclusive federal jurisdiction over lands involved in the relocation centers. After a review of the status of the various locations it was decided not to seek exclusive federal jurisdiction. It became apparent that there were really no advantages to be gained from exclusive jurisdiction, but there were some disadvantages. By utilizing state and local services, normal contacts between the evacuees and the outside world could be multiplied and encouraged, and the center itself could become a part of the local community to a greater extent. Consequently state criminal laws were enforced in the centers. State laws concerning marriage, divorce, and the custody of children were observed and enforced. Contracts were made and their validity was determined by the local law. The validity of wills, distribution of estates of intestates, and the form of probate proceedings were determined by local law.

On the other hand, state occupational licensing laws were not enforced. Consequently evacuee professionals such as doctors, dentists, nurses, and many other professional people were not affected. WRA's claim of governmental immunity in such matters was never seriously questioned. On the whole our relationship with the local authorities and the courts was friendly, and little difficulty was encountered.

After careful consideration the political structure evolved for the government of the centers was predicated upon the administrative power to establish and protect all forms of federal functions, with partial delegation of that power to the evacuees. The federal operation being undertaken by WRA was the maintenance and supervision of 110,000 persons in ten separate communities. A program of such magnitude imposed large responsibilities upon the agency to provide food and housing, to create all necessary forms of communal services, to prescribe and enforce standards of health and sanitation, to effect fire prevention, and to take such other measures as might be necessary to insure the welfare of the inhabitants and to protect the federal property. These responsibilities and the corresponding power to meet them necessarily carried with them the authority to protect the functions involved by the issuance of appropriate police regulations and the enforcement of sanctions for noncompliance.

In addition it was essential that regulations be drafted authorizing the evacuee business enterprises and laying down the general rules covering organization, management practices, accounting procedures, and periodic audits.

Such matters as the drafting of the leave regulations and all other regulations were carried out by the solicitor's office in the first instant or the solicitor's office participated in the drafting or review before issuance. That office was an active participant in all phases of program development.

Problems of recruitment arose regarding the twenty-three attorneys for the Washington and field offices. By the spring of 1945 seven of these recruits had entered the armed services and eleven had transferred to other positions in government or into private practice. Under these conditions training was a more or less continuous process.

The supervision of regional and project attorneys required some time of the Washington office. The project attorneys provided three types of services: (1) legal advice and assistance to the project director and center staff; (2) legal services to such various evacuee organizations as the business enterprises, the community council, the judicial commission and others; and (3) assistance to individual evacuees in connection with their legal problems. In other words the project attorney was a man with three hats. He was government lawyer, city attorney, and private attorney to the evacuee population.

LEGAL AID FOR EVACUEES

As the volume of property and personal problems of evacuees in the centers mounted, it became increasingly apparent that many matters, particularly those involving suits by or against evacuees, would require the services of lawyers in private practice. Most of the evacuees had had no pre-evacuation contact with lawyers. Those who did, could not be sure that their former counsel would agree to represent them. To alleviate this situation the San Francisco office, in collaboration with the State Bar of California, devised an attorney referral system.

California attorneys who had previously expressed a desire to engage in state bar war-work activities were polled to determine how many would handle evacuee business. Some 800 favorable responses were received. The names of these attorneys were placed on referral lists classified on the basis of locality and specialty, if any. Whenever an evacuee wished to make use of the referral system, the project attorney notified the San Francisco office, designating the locality in which the legal services were necessary and the field of law involved. The San Francisco office then furnished the project attorney with the names, in alphabetical sequence, of three attorneys in the designated locality and legal specialty. From these the evacuee made his selection. Further information concerning the qualifications of the attorneys involved was furnished on request.

Upon selection of an attorney, the evacuee executed a client's statement designating the selected attorney, stating the nature of the services required, and requesting the attorney to keep the Authority advised as to progress. This request relieved the attorney from any obligation to keep the affairs of his client confidential so far as the Authority was concerned; it was designed to provide a basis for liaison between the attorney selected and the appropriate WRA field attorney who was assisting the evacuee. It also put WRA in position to evaluate the adequacy of the legal services rendered.

The client's statement was sent to the attorney and, upon acceptance, established the lawyer-client relationship. The San Francisco office then placed the name of the selected attorney at the end of the particular referral list to insure complete rotation. If the designated attorney declined to represent an evacuee, or if his services were terminated, the next three names in sequence on the list were submitted to the evacuee. The San Francisco office was authorized to remove individual attorneys from the list for good cause.

Each attorney on the referral list agreed to represent evacuees on the basis of a schedule of fees covering common types of legal services rendered — foreclosures, probate, divorces, leases, collections, contracts, consultation and preparation, trial work, and appellate work. Each evacuee was apprised of the appropriate fee schedule before he executed the client's statement.

The attorney referral system was extensively used by California evacuees and proved to be generally satisfactory. Attempts to work out similar arrangements in Arizona, Oregon, and Washington were unsuccessful. In these three states, if an evacuee wished assistance, the project attorney submitted to him the names of attorneys taken from standard law lists or from names recommended by the appropriate bar association. In the cases of needy evacuees the referral was made to the legal aid society.

In view of the surge of activity by the states of California and Washington in investigations and escheat proceedings, arrangements were made to assure that evacuees were advised of the institution of escheat suits. Research into the alien land laws of the West Coast states was conducted, and a series of solicitor's opinions were issued. Some 50 escheat cases were still pending in California in June of 1946. Legal research was also essential on the whole gamut of property law resulting from requests of project attorneys. Many other problems also called for research and advice to evacuees.

CHAPTER 21

Resume of Crucial Decisions, Key Frustrations, and Major Victories

ONE OF THE MOST CRUCIAL and important decisions involving WRA was made by President Roosevelt and his staff in March 1942. This was the original decision to establish WRA as an independent civilian agency. It had far-reaching and generally beneficial consequences, even though it was probably based at the time on the unwillingness of the Cabinet officers to be responsible for such an obviously controversial and unpopular operation as the WRA program in fact turned out to be.

The first two years of WRA's existence were the toughest, the hottest, and the most crucial because of the need and importance of policy formation where there were no precedents and no guidelines except the Bill of Rights. It was well that we were an independent agency during this period, because it gave us urgently needed flexibility and enabled us quickly to revise and perfect policies as experience and insight into our problems, human and otherwise, pointed the way.

I have always felt sure that any top political appointee such as a Cabinet officer, who was concerned with many other wartime problems, would not have had the time or the opportunity to become involved in the problem of WRA to the extent necessary to understand the complexities and frustrations that we faced during those first 24 months; consequently he would have been tempted to avoid some of the tough decisions that we felt had to be made. As it was we were able to make our own decisions, and we knew that we had to live with our mistakes. It was not necessary to spend precious time in arguing our case for policy approval, or to put up with delays while decisions were forthcoming.

Fortunately we were able to deal directly with Cabinet officers and other top level officials when the need arose to press for support, to argue against discrimination, or to urge policy revision and removal of restrictions.

Mr. Harold Smith, the director of the budget, had been responsible for selecting both WRA directors and recommending their appointment by the president. During the first two years I visited him regularly to discuss our problems and to keep him informed. During nearly every visit he would remind me that he was not my boss, but it was helpful during troubled and strenuous times to have someone near the president to talk to, even though he was reluctant to advise or interfere.

The decision in February 1944 to place WRA within the Department of the Interior under Secretary Ickes also proved to be an excellent and important decision, though I opposed it at the time. This move came when we were still under fire following the Tule Lake affair, and the backing of a Cabinet officer of Secretary Ickes' caliber and reputation was most helpful. The secretary later stated in one of his columns — which he wrote after he left the Cabinet — that he had examined the policies of WRA and found them sound and that his role was one of support. He put it this way, "I claim no credit for the result that was finally attained except that I stood shoulder to shoulder with Dillon Myer and let my fists fly on occasion."

That he did, and it was most effective and greatly appreciated.

IMPORTANT WRA DECISIONS

Three of the most important decisions that I made as Director of WRA were:

1. The decision to focus our major objective upon relocation outside of centers, which was made in June and July of 1942 and expedited and expanded in October and November 1942;

2. The decision in July 1942 to press for a change in army policy to allow Nisei to join the armed forces;

3. The decision to press for revocation of the Army West Coast ban and to schedule the closing of the relocation centers while the war was still on.

The decision to carry out a positive and aggressive relocation program with the establishment of area and local offices and the collaboration of local resettlement committees in all parts of the United States proved to be highly important both to the evacuees and to WRA. From the standpoint of public relations, it proved to be essential to have the support that such a program engendered at a time when we needed support the most. Particularly after the Dies subcommittee hearings of 1943, the good people who had learned to know relocatees and who had become conversant with the WRA program through participation as members of community resettlement committees really rolled up their sleeves and went to work to put the record straight. And it badly needed straightening after the attempts of the Dies committee and others to twist it out of all recognition.

The change in the War Department policy, which we urged, to allow enlistment of the Nisei and the reinstitution of the selective service process was essential to the cause of the evacuees in that it provided the opportunity to prove their patriotism in a dramatic manner and to refute the campaign of the racists in such a positive manner that many of them, including the California Department of the American Legion, withdrew from the field completely and permanently in the face of the Nisei war record in both the European and Pacific Theater.

The decision to press for revocation of the West Coast exclusion order, and the scheduling of relocation center closings, before the surrender of Japan was a crucial and important one. The problems of jobs and housing were much on our minds. Even more important was the knowledge that institutionalization had affected a large segment of the center population, and it was fast becoming a chronic situation. As indicated earlier, literally thousands of the evacuees had come to enjoy the community life and the ease of center living. Furthermore, many had been isolated so long with little news except the diatribes and threats of the racists that they were fearful that they would be in danger if they returned to their homes and normal community life.

It was just about impossible to explain these problems to many people of goodwill in such a way as to give them a real understanding of the situation. As a consequence, we were faced with opposition both from the population within the centers and from many good and well-intentioned people on the outside. Many of the exclusionists, such as Hood River residents and growers in the big valley of California who had an economic interest in keeping the Japanese population away from the West Coast, opposed our final relocation plans.

In spite of the unpopularity of this decision at the time it was made, we are glad to say the final relocation turned out well for the evacuees in spite of rigorous opposition.

The decision to convene the top staff from the relocation cel·ters along with the key staff from Washington and the regions in San Francisco on August 13, 1942, to participate in writing the policy guides and procedures, was not only essential to good administration but also most useful in providing the bulwark of our defenses during the many months of harassment that followed. We were called upon to defend ourselves before the Senate Military Affairs Committee and the Costello Subcommittee of the House of Representatives, both of which were actuated by the American Legion and other groups who poured out their hatred for the Japanese people by attacking WRA. At times we felt that we were getting some of the abuse that people would have liked to heap upon the military. Attacking the armed forces is of course just about unthinkable in wartime, but were were available as scapegoats and wide open for such attacks.

The policies initiated during the August 1942 conference in San Francisco generally stood the test of time, although revisions and amplifications were made as the need arose. Our major mistake at that time was the exclusion of the Issei from membership on the center community councils — an error which was later rectified. The important policy decisions relating to such matters as evacuee employment and compensation, community government, internal security, agriculture, industry, mess operations, business enterprises, and other phases of center management all required careful thought and in some cases hard decisions.

After the Poston and Manzanar incidents we reconvened the key staff members at San Francisco to review particularly the community government and internal security policies. Three important decisions grew out of this conference. One was the decision to allow Issei to serve as community council members. Another was that we should make only limited revisions in the internal security policy and should ask the FBI to assign an officer to review our policy in this field. The third was to recruit an anthropologically trained community analyst for each center. Establishment of such a staff was recommended by the late John Provinse, who was an anthropologist and head of our community management division. These analysts both at the centers and at national headquarters proved most helpful to the project directors and to key staff members in Washington, keeping them informed regarding the current problems and thinking of the evacuees during the next three years of our existence.

Beginning with the policy conference of August 1942 in San Francisco and continuing throughout all of the months of WRA's existence, the key staff members were brought together time and again to discuss policy or policy revision. After each such conference the job of developing detailed advance plans was assigned to a staff committee or to individual staff members. These plans then were reviewed and commented upon by the total group before final adoption. In some cases involving participation by the relocation centers, either the project directors or some staff members named by them were brought in to assist in the planning or the review or both.

The decision to follow this administrative procedure involving staff participation proved to be highly important, since there were no precedents. We needed to call upon all of the "know how" and experience that was available.

The one occasion where detailed advance planning broke down was after the mass movement of evacuees into and out of Tule Lake in connection with the segregation program. Because of our preoccupation with the immediate problems of segregation, we failed to look ahead in that instance as we should have. If we had had the time and staff and foresight to plan this phase, we might have been able to forestall or at least mitigate the happenings of November 1-4, 1943.

I take great pride in the effective cooperation which the staff gave me in helping to think through our various unprecedented problems, and the job they did on detailed planning of the necessary steps and in the execution of these plans. If ever an agency required a solid base and a solid front with which to face its detractors WRA was it. The process of policy making, scheduling, and staff cooperation in execution was essential to our continued existence and to the completion of our job. I shall forever be grateful for the efficient and dedicated staff work that we had all along the line.

I have already mentioned the importance of the decisions of the War Department in allowing and encouraging Nisei to volunteer for the 442nd Combat Team and in making Nisei eligible again for draft through selective service process. These decisions were essential in gaining public acceptance of the status of the evacuees, and perhaps they were essential to the completion of the WRA program. The help of the officers of the 442nd Regimental Combat Team and of Colonel Moore and General Joseph Stilwell in clearing out the last pockets of resistance in our war against the racists and the greedy was important in assuring acceptance back on the West Coast.

FRUSTRATIONS

The first major frustration or rebuff faced by WRA was the antagonistic and hostile atmosphere engendered by the western governors at the Intermountain Conference on April 7, 1942. Fortunately the effects of this setback were short lived due to the tremendous and insistent demand for agricultural labor in that area and the subsequent decision three months later to proceed with a general relocation program in spite of this first dramatic opposition.

The frustrations and concern resulting from the Poston and Manzanar incidents were real and baffling. However, the blowoffs at these centers helped clear the air, and the resulting policy review with attendant results proved to be constructive.

In early 1943 the lack of opportunity for joint and detailed planning between the War Department's adjutant general's office and WRA in relation to the proposed registration and recruitment that followed the announcement of plans for the 442nd Combat Team was a major frustration. While the whole idea was an important and constructive one, more time and thought should have been given to joint detailed plans. Had this been done, we believe that the results could have been much better than they were.

One of the most frustrating problems was the continuation and intensification of the campaign against the evacuees and the WRA by certain West Coast elements, such as the California Joint Immigration Committee, the Hearst Press, the *Los Angeles Times,* and all of the other fomenters of hate who had played a part in the furore which led up to the evacuation. It was natural to assume that after the evacuation had been ordered, our major public relations problems would lie within that part of the United States outside of the West Coast states. This did not prove to be true. On the contrary, many of our top staff and I had to spend a great deal of time and energy during most of the existence of WRA in carrying the fight into the West Coast areas. The hearings and the investigations of the congressional committees were of course a part of this same pattern.

The Tule Lake problem of November 1-4, 1943, and the aftermath, created real problems including further hearings by the Dies Subcommittee and a California State Legislative Committee — not to mention the low state of our public relations in early 1944.

The relations with the Western Defense Command's Wartime Civil Control Administration (WCCA), which maintained a sizeable staff in San Francisco throughout the war from March 1942 to September 1945, was a long series of frustrations. The points of view of Colonel Karl Bendetsen and General William Wilbur, who headed the WCCA throughout most of the war period, were so completely opposed to those of us in WRA that relations were nearly always difficult and at times downright impossible.

VICTORIES

The relocation of more than 50,000 evacuees throughout the United States, and the tremendous record of the Nisei, plus the revocation of the exclusion orders during the war period, were by all odds the major accomplishments that helped us to complete our job and to close out the WRA program by June 30, 1946.

One of the other major developments growing out of the relocation program and the war record of the Nisei in the armed forces was the almost complete elimination of the effects of the "yellow peril" propaganda that had been effectively disseminated across the United States throughout forty years or more by the Native Sons of the Golden West, the California Joint Immigration Committee, and others. Other important developments resulting from these major developments are covered in Chapter 22.

Results and Afterthoughts

IT WOULD HAVE BEEN CONSIDERED unthinkable if some official of the United States government had recommended to the president in any peacetime year, 1935 for instance, that 70,000 American citizens should be summarily evacuated from a broad area of the country without hearings or trials, and merely on the grounds of their racial ancestry. The response would have been an immediate nationwide repudiation of such a proposal — newspaper editors and columnists throughout the country, organizations dedicated to civil rights, and thousands of ordinary citizens would have been deeply shocked, and we may be quite sure that such a recommendation would have been rejected.

Yet when Lt. Gen. John L. DeWitt made such a recommendation in February of 1942, it went almost unnoticed in many sections of the country, was approved by a number of keen and conscientious observers of public affairs, and was ultimately sanctioned by the president and by the members of his Cabinet who were directly concerned. There probably were a number of reasons for such a paradox. We were at war; high officials were occupied with pressing problems demanding immediate answers; and perhaps the most significant reason is that in a society such as ours, when war strikes, the military tends to be considered sacrosanct and unchallengeable.

The phrase "military necessity" generally silences any argument or protest. People who protest action that the military says is "necessary to the prosecution of the war" are likely to be considered unpatriotic.

General DeWitt, in his final report, in a chapter entitled "Need for Military Control and for Evacuation," made four major points as reasons for the need for evacuation. In essence they were:

1. The West Coast Japanese were "a tightly knit and unassimilated racial group."

2. This group had many organizational and personal ties with the homeland of Japan.

3. The group had shown a pronounced tendency to settle in the vicinity of vital defense installations and facilities.

4. There was evidence of persistent communications between unknown persons on the West Coast and the Japanese forces at sea.

General DeWitt's first point is at least a highly dubious thesis upon which to base an evacuation, in view of the very eagerness of most Nisei to become American and their conspicuous success in doing so.

On the second point, the general seems to have overlooked the fact that the organizations were known to the intelligence agencies and that they were under surveillance; in fact most of the leaders of these organizations had already been interned by the FBI.

In regard to the third point, the general admitted that there was no substantial evidence of subversive motives lying behind this pattern of settlement. He cites two areas as examples, both in Santa Barbara County. In one of these areas the settlement of Japanese was primarily due to the purchase of a farm there in the early years of the century by a prominent and prosperous Japanese farmer who attracted others as workers and associates. In the other area the settlement was due to the fact that Japanese farmers were willing to work comparatively small pockets of land between the oil fields and along the seashore which other farmers were not interested in tackling. Yet the report declares it is "beyond doubt" that these settlements were not the results of coincidence, and thus, by clear implication, part of "some vast conspiracy."

In relation to his fourth point, General DeWitt's report mentions "hundreds of reports nightly of signal lights visible from the coast, and interceptions of unidentified radio transmissions."

In the spring of 1944 Attorney General Biddle asked the Federal Communications Commission for comment on this part of the report, and Chairman Fly replied as follows:

You direct attention particularly to [General DeWitt's] reference to hundreds of reports of such signaling by means of signal lights and unlawful radio transmitters and state that investigation by the Department of Justice of great numbers of rumors concerning signal lights and radio transmitters proved them, without exception, to be baseless. . . .

Throughout this period (from December 1941 to July 1942) on the West Coast . . . the Commission's Radio Intelligence Division was engaged in a comprehensive surveillance of the entire radio spectrum to guard against any unlawful radio activity. . . . In the early months of the war, the Commission's field offices and stations on the West Coast were deluged with calls, particularly from the Army and Navy, reporting suspicious radio signaling and requesting identification of radio signals. . . . There were no radio signals reported to the Commission which could not be identified, or which were unlawful. Like the Department of Justice, the Commission knows of *no evidence of any illicit radio signaling in this area during the period in question.* (Emphasis supplied.)

Thus, all four of the major reasons advanced by General DeWitt for urging mass evacuation are found to be tenuous, highly arguable, or wholly unfounded. From time to time General DeWitt made various statements regarding the importance of racial ties in the case of Japanese, such as one made in April 1943 before the House Committee on Naval Affairs in San Francisco, which illustrates a strong bias. This statement is quoted in part:

[There] is the development of a false sentiment on the part of certain individuals and some organizations to get the Japanese back on the West Coast. I don't want any of them here. They are a dangerous element. There is no way to determine their loyalty. . . . It makes no difference whether he is an American citizen, he is still Japanese. . . . You needn't worry about the Italians at all except in certain cases. Also the same for the Germans except in individual cases. But we must worry about the Japanese all of the time until he is wiped off of the map.

There is a great deal of evidence to suggest that General DeWitt was by no means free of racial feelings regarding the Japanese at the time of ordering the evacuation and later. His reasons given above, when combined with various statements, such as the one above made in April 1943, make out a case of racial bias.

As director of the WRA, I believed, and still believe, that a selective evacuation of people of Japanese descent from the West Coast military area may have been justified and feasible in early 1943, but I do not believe that a mass evacuation was ever justified;

furthermore I believe that there was no valid argument for the continuation of the exclusion orders beyond the spring of 1943, as indicated by our letter to Secretary Stimson in March of 1943.

Quite obviously General DeWitt had the WRA in mind in his reference to "individuals and organizations" in his testimony.

SOME WORTHWHILE RESULTS

In spite of the fact that I have felt that the mass evacuation of all Japanese Americans was unnecessary, it nonetheless yielded some excellent results that were entirely unanticipated by the anti-Japanese exclusionists who supplied many of the pressures responsible for the evacuation.

The most important result of the WRA program was the relocation of more than 50,000 Japanese Americans all across the United States and into the armed forces during the war period. This dispersion of the population led to an understanding and an acceptance on the part of the great American public that would never have been possible otherwise. It also had a tremendous effect upon the understanding, outlook, and perspective of the Nisei in particular, which provided new opportunities and support for them and developed confidence in themselves which would not have happened otherwise. The record of both the civilian relocatees as well as those in uniform was a proud one. As a result, the term Nisei began to connote loyalty and to become generally accepted as a term of respect.

The breaking down of the results of the "Yellow Peril" propaganda, which had been most effective and widely accepted by the American public, was essential to the elimination of the literally hundreds of discriminatory laws and practices that had been adopted over a half century. Relocatees, with the help of hundreds of civic and fair-minded people who served as members of community resettlement committees, and with the dramatic record of the 442nd Combat Team and the Nisei who served so effectively in the Military Intelligence in the Pacific Theater to supplement their efforts, executed the most massive and effective public relations job of the century, Madison Avenue notwithstanding.

DISCRIMINATORY LAWS AND PRACTICES

Almost every type of discriminatory practice dreamed up by the exclusionists and the racists was effectuated by the simple process of passing a law or an ordinance providing that those persons not eligible for American citizenship were barred from participation in activities in free America generally believed to be the right or opportunity of each and every resident.

It is not widely known that our first naturalization law passed by the United States Congress in 1790 provided that any alien "being a free white person . . . may be admitted to become a citizen." In 1870 following the Civil War, Negroes were made eligible for naturalization. In 1940 the privilege of naturalization was extended to the American Indian and other "descendants of races indigenous to the Western Hemisphere." In 1943, as a gesture to our Chinese Allies, resident Chinese became eligible for naturalization. In 1946 resident Filipinos and East Indians were added to those eligible. However, it was not until 1952 that an immigration and nationality bill was enacted into law which eliminated race as a disqualification for naturalization. Thus, 162 years after passage of the first naturalization law, the Japanese people and most other Asiatics of the so-called Asia-Pacific Triangle for the first time became eligible to apply for American citizenship.

The 1790 law "free white" provision was supported by unanimous decision of the Supreme Court in the Ozawa case in 1922.

The passage of the 1952 Immigration and Nationality Act did more than any other action to eliminate legal discriminatory practices, because at one fell swoop it eliminated all the laws on the statute books throughout the country which were based on ineligibility for American citizenship. Further amendments of October 1965 eliminated the discriminatory provisions, including the Pacific Triangle and the National Origins concepts.

The War Relocation Authority Final Report entitled *W.R.A.: A Story of Human Conservation,* in a discussion of the racial restriction in the 1790 Immigration Law, had this to say in part:

There are a great many reasons why this purely racial restriction should be removed from our naturalization laws. But perhaps the most important is that it has been used by racist elements in various Western States as the basis for discriminatory legislation which severely hampers thousands of people from making a living because their ancestors happened to be Japanese or Filipino or Hindu. The so-called "alien land laws," for example, are nearly all phrased so that their provisions apply to "aliens ineligible for naturalization." This formula, sharply delimiting the economic opportunities of Japanese and other Oriental aliens while staying within the allowable limits of the Constitution, was discovered over 30 years ago by U. S. Webb, the then Attorney General of California and his close associate, Francis J. Heney, co-author with Webb of the first alien land law. . . . Thus, in these particular states, the Japanese alien, whose whole background and training may be agricultural, is prevented from engaging in farming except as a paid laborer despite the fact that he may have had sons in the American armed forces who had given up their lives for their country.

WRA believes that this situation is wholly indefensible and recommends the passage of legislation which would extend the privilege of naturalization equally to members of all of the races of the world. In addition, the Authority feels that all discriminatory State laws or local regulations against persons of Japanese descent which still remain in effect and which would not be abrogated by this process of broadening the naturalization laws should be repealed.

It so happened that the alien land laws were technically set aside by the U.S. Supreme Court in 1948 before the passage of the 1952 act, but there were other laws on the statute books of many states requiring citizenship as a basis for licenses to practice. Nearly all states require citizenship as a qualification for attorneys or public accountants. Many states have such a requirement for architects, dentists, physicians, teachers, funeral directors, and barbers.

The Japanese American Citizens League was undoubtedly the most effective advocate in behalf of the 1952 Immigration and Nationality Act, and the organization of course had strong backing from all over the United States as a result of the Nisei military record and the widespread support resulting from relocatees and their friends. Between 1952 and the end of 1964 a total of 46,041 Japanese aliens became naturalized United States citizens. Nearly half of these became citizens within the first five years after the passage of the 1952 act.

One other important piece of legislation spearheaded by the JACL during the latter 1940s was a bill in 1947 which provided that wives of soldiers who had married within 30 days after the passage of this bill would be admissable to the United States. This of course temporarily set aside the 1924 exclusion act for many brides.

Still another important act had to do with the problem of more than 4,000 Issei who had come to the United States under the treaty merchants act over a period of many years. Because of the abrogation of treaty in 1940, all of those who had come as traders under the act were subject to deportation, even though many of them had married American citizens and had raised families of American-born children. Some had sons in the American armed forces. Several hundred individual bills were introduced to set aside deportation proceedings, but finally in 1948 an act was passed which authorized the attorney general to deal with the matter as he would with Europeans.

Two very important Supreme Court cases were tried previous to the passage of the 1952 Immigration and Nationality Act. The Oyama litigation was an alien land law case that had been tried in the local courts and the California Supreme Court. All ruled that there had been a violation of the law in the acquisition of property. The Supreme Court accepted the case for review, and in 1948 determined that the alien land laws could not abrogate the right of American citizens to inherit or receive property. Subsequent to this ruling California did not press other escheatment cases, and both the Oregon and California supreme courts declared the alien land laws unconstitutional.

The other case grew out of legislation passed by the California Legislature during the war to deny commercial fishing licenses to aliens ineligible for American citizenship. The Takahashi case, which challenged the California act, was passed upon by the Supreme Court in 1949. The Court found this act unconstitutional.

On November 5, 1946, an amendment appeared on the ballot in California known as Proposition 15 "Validation of Legislative Amendments to Alien Land Law." This amendment, according to its sponsors (state senators Jack Tenny of Los Angeles County and Hugh M. Burns of Fresno County), provided in part as follows:

This amendment merely validates statutes pursuant to the Alien Land Law heretofore enacted by the legislature and now in full force and affect.

Its enactment by the people will close loopholes in legislative enactments based on constitutional ground.

This legislation would have reconfirmed an interest in having the law maintained.

The Anti-Discrimination Committee of the Japanese American

Citizens League, with the support of a number of civic groups, worked hard to defeat this measure. They were well rewarded, for when the votes were tallied 1,143,780 votes were tabulated against and only 797,067 in favor.

Mike Masaoka, executive secretary of the JACL Anti-Discrimination Committee, was quoted on November 9, 1946, in the *Pacific Citizen* as follows:

> The election results prove that most Californians feel that Japanese Americans and their Issei parents have earned the right to justice and fair treatment. . . . They provided the first real public opinion poll of California citizens on an issue involving the state's residents of Japanese ancestry since 1920. . . . The lesson of the vote on "Proposition 15" is that the war is over and the people of California will not approve discriminatory and prejudiced treatment of persons of Japanese ancestry.

HAWAIIAN STATEHOOD

It is quite clear that the acceptance of Hawaiian statehood by the U.S. Congress was greatly expedited by the general acceptance of evacuee relocatees and the military record of the Nisei.

REACTIONS IN JAPAN

During the war, we in WRA pleaded with the various congressional representatives, and administrative departments and agencies, including the War Department, that our treatment of Japanese Americans in War Relocation Centers and elsewhere would not only dictate reciprocal treatment by the Japanese of American prisoners of war but would also add, or detract, from the propaganda claims of Tojo in Tokyo and others in Berlin and Rome that we in the United States were engaged in a race war, as witness our mistreatment of Japanese Americans.

We think that the record justifies our wartime contentions. But, in the postwar period, we have learned that many leading Japanese officials believe that the conduct of the Japanese and Japanese Americans, as well as their treatment by WRA, contributed much to the postwar goodwill and friendly relations that have developed between once defeated and devastated Japan and the United States.

For instance, Ambassador of Japan Ryuji Takeuchi, addressing the Mountain Plains District Council Convention of the JACL in Omaha, Nebraska, November 27, 1965, stated in part:

No tribute to Japanese Americans would be complete, however, without some mention, however brief, of their outstanding record in World War II when they proved, in spite of being called upon to endure unprecedented suffering and sacrifice, that — in the words of the late President Roosevelt — "Americanism is a matter of the mind and the heart, and not one of race or ancestry."

Even though some 110,000 of the 130,000 Japanese on the continental United States were interned in wartime camps, several thousand volunteered for combat duty and distinguished themselves in both the European and Pacific theaters. And the epic of the 442nd Regimental Combat Team, the most decorated unit in American military history for its size and length of service, is well known in Japan.

Many in high places in Japan share my conviction that the magnificent and dignified conduct of Japanese Americans in World War II contributed much to the remarkable and friendly relations that now exist between the United States and Japan.

The late Prime Minister of Japan, Hayato Ikeda, expressed himself to some Japanese Americans in this country, to the effect that the new Japan owes much to the way that those of Japanese ancestry conducted themselves both in War Relocation Centers and without, as well as in the armed forces, to prove that the Japanese people and nation are entitled to the same hopes and aspirations as are other peoples and nations. He credited Japanese Americans in informal talks in Washington, D.C., Los Angeles, and Hawaii in the late winter of 1961 with having made a significant contribution to the fact that the American government and people have accorded such goodwill and helpful cooperation to Japan in the post-surrender era and after Japan regained her sovereignty in 1952 as a member of the family of nations.

EVACUEE ATTITUDES

Relocation centers were called "concentration camps" by many writers and commentators, but they were very different from the normal concept of what a concentration camp is like.

First of all, the centers were not prison camps. The War Relocation Authority looked upon the centers as way stations at which the people who had been evacuated could be provided with quarters, food, and other basic necessities temporarily until they could be resettled in normal communities either throughout the United States outside of the evacuated area or back on the West Coast whenever the exclusion order could be lifted.

A large number of the evacuees looked upon the centers as havens of rest and security. This was especially true of many of the elderly Issei, particularly during the months after the turmoil of the evacuation and the period of adjustment to community living had been pretty well accepted.

It must be remembered that here was a minority group who over the years had become inured to discrimination and race-baiting. In spite of this, many had done well economically, but many others had worked hard to secure a mere minimum subsistence.

We should not forget that approximately 40,000 of the 111,000 people had never been eligible to apply for American citizenship; consequently their only citizenship ties were to Japan. Throughout many years they had accepted the American way of life, but they always had to remember that they could not turn their backs on the country of their birth. Once the war with Japan was declared, many were fearful of what would happen to them as aliens of a country with which their adopted country was at war. They had no interest in taking sides in the war on either side. Some were fearful that they might be sent back to Japan, and they felt that they must avoid any kind of war effort in behalf of the United States for fear of reprisals if they were forced to return to Japan. Furthermore, many had relatives in Japan who might suffer because of their activity. So they were caught on the horns of a real dilemma — between the loyalty that most felt toward the United States and the ties of citizenship which they had with the country of their birth. There, of course, was fear of possible bodily harm to themselves or their property due to wartime hysteria.

As the months of 1942 and 1943 passed, several thousand of the more aggressive Nisei who were firmly bent on an American way of life resettled in communities outside of relocation centers and away from the West Coast. Also in 1943, the more aggressive among the dissidents, many of whom wished to avoid the draft, and those oriented toward Japan, were separated and sent to the Tule Lake Center. As a result, the remaining centers were more and more dominated by the Issei who were wanting rest and security, and by some who wanted to be undisturbed while awaiting the opportunity to return to California or other West Coast states.

Of the 70,000 people left in centers in 1944, probably at least half had never had it so good.

As a result of (1) being torn between ties to two countries at war, (2) fear of discrimination and perhaps bodily harm, (3) enjoyment of association with their own kind and people in the same boat, and (4) the economic security and a chance to rest, there were several thousand people who were loath to face the world on the outside again. During a period of a few months they had become habituated to a type of community living that had many pleasant features.

It should be remembered that all the Issei, except a few treaty merchants, had lived in the United States for at least 18 years and most had been here for anywhere from 20 to 40 years. (The so-called exclusion law was enacted in 1924.) They had raised their families here, and for the most part they had come to accept the American ways and standards. The Nisei attended the public schools, and — except for the Kibei, who returned to Japan for their education — they grew up as well-indoctrinated American youngsters who helped to indoctrinate their parents. Most parents in turn came to realize over the years that the interests and loyalties of the Nisei were with the United States. These parents — in spite of the fact that they themselves could not secure American citizenship — had accepted the American birthplace of their children and also the American way for themselves.

Those of us who were closely associated with the evacuees soon learned about the complex pattern and the wide diversity of interests represented. We soon became convinced that few, if any, of these people were dangerous to the intersts of the United States. However, because the general public was not as convinced of this as we were, it became necessary to establish a rather elaborate leave procedure. Furthermore, this policy was essential for the protection of evacuees, because they had all been tarred with the same brush by the evacuation and establishment of centers.

Most people did not know, or tended to forget, that the Department of Justice, almost immediately after Pearl Harbor, had placed in internment camps about 3,000 aliens who had maintained contact with Japan or who were under suspicion for other reasons.

Nearly all employees of WRA in positions of responsibility concluded early in the program that the relocation camps were bad for the evacuated people — in spite of the fact that many evacuees learned to enjoy center life — and bad for the future health of American democracy.

We were unhappy with the fact of detention, even though it was extremely limited. We also were much aware of the group stigma attached to the centers, but perhaps the fact of government control over all really essential operations and its effects upon the lives of the people was one of the most worrisome problems to some of us. The factor of government control was not peculiar to the WRA centers. Whenever any government agency sets up camps or reservations for displaced people and receives appropriated funds for their maintenance and operation, it is bound to find, as we did, that it has to exercise a rather large measure of supervision, or at least veto power, over the community operations. This creates an institutionalized environment, which in turn produces frustration, demoralization, and a feeling of dependency among the residents. We believe that, even without the factors of detention and group stigma, centers such as ours would be undesirable places in which to live and that the idea of putting displaced people in camps is invariably a bad one. The institutionalizing effects of camp life are subtle, difficult to combat, and self perpetuating.

After my WRA experience, I served for nearly three years as commissioner of the Bureau of Indian Affairs. There, on the reservations, I found an almost incurable institutionalization process. If anyone doubts the thesis set forth in regard to camps and the effect of government controls, all he will need to do is to make a study of our most classic examples, the Indian reservations.

While we had regrets about the use of a certain amount of compulsion which seemed necessary to the closing of the centers, we have no regrets about having completed the closing in reasonable time and that we may have avoided the maintenance of something akin to our Indian reservations.

PROBLEMS STILL TO BE FACED

While the major discriminatory acts and procedures have been eliminated, some areas require continued attention. Occasional cases of discrimination regarding the right to purchase homes in certain neighborhoods still come to light, but not as many as formerly. Some old and useless laws still on the statute books should be eliminated — for example, the Alien Land Law in the state of Washington.

PROGRESS AMONG THE NISEI

The Nisei, who were mostly youngsters under 25 at the time of evacuation, have matured. Because of their interest in education, many of them not only have come a long way but are making a tremendous contribution to their country in a wide category of the professions as well as in the arts and sciences, and in business.

I am proud to list some examples of outstanding representatives in various areas of their choice.

Two outstanding architects come quickly to mind. Minoru Yamasaki, of Detroit, has become known throughout the world for his work. Gyo Obata, son of the famous Issei artist Chiura Obata, became the architect for the new Space Museum Building in Washington, D.C.

Mike Masaoka, who for years was executive officer of the Japanese American Citizens League, has become one of the best known and respected persons among the hundreds of people in Washington who are representatives of organizations and firms in the nation's capital.

In the field of politics our Nisei congressional representatives from Hawaii stand out. Senator Dan Inouye and Representative Spark Matsunaga were both officers in the 442nd Combat Team. Representative Patsy Mink is another respected Nisei member of Hawaii's congressional delegation. James Kanno was the first Nisei to be elected mayor of a California city — Fountain City, Orange County, in 1957. More recently, Tom Kitayama was elected mayor of Union City, California; and Kazuo Hikida was elected mayor of Teton City, Idaho. Ken Nakaoka was elected as a city councilman in Gardena, California; and Frank Ogawa became city councilman of Oakland, California.

In the diplomatic field, Henry Gosho, better known as Hank, was placed in charge of the Far East area for the United States Information Agency. He was promoted to Foreign Service Officer Class II, following several months of special service in Vietnam.

In the newspaper field two names come to mind quickly. William Hosokawa, who edited the Heart Mountain relocation center newspaper for many months in 1942 and 1943, became associate editor of the *Denver Post*.

Dr. Kiyoshi George Togasaki, a native San Francisco Nisei,

became publisher of the *Japan Times,* the largest English language newspaper in Japan. He also was elected vice president of Rotary International. The Japanese government decorated him with their highest civilian award. He is also a co-founder of the International Christian University.

Among the scientists is Tets Iwasaki of Pasadena, California, who was graduated from California Institute of Technology and Massachusetts Institute of Technology before the evacuation. He became a space scientist with NASA (National Aeronautics and Space Agency), working on the moon project. Another scientist, Dr. Henry Tsuchiya of Seattle, during 1966 received a three-month assignment at the University of Tokyo under the United States-Japan Cooperative Science Program sponsored by the U. S. National Science Foundation and the Japan Society for the Promotion of Science.

Among the many Japanese Americans in the educational field is an outstanding Nisei, Ben Sanematsu, who lost his eyesight while an evacuee at Poston relocation center. Following his return to California he withdrew from the world for a time, but he emerged again to become a "white cane" man, took graduate work, married, and began to teach mathematics to the blind students in a San Jose, California, high school. He has also served as a consultant on this highly specialized type of teaching to many schools throughout the country.

Another educator of note is Dr. Baron Goto, one-time Agricultural Extension Director for Hawaii, who later became vice chancellor of the East West Center in Honolulu.

Judge John Aiso was appointed as a superior court judge by Governor Earl Warren.

Judge Stephan Tamura became a member of the California District Court of Appeals by appointment by Governor Pat Brown.

Harry Takagi, one of many U. S. civil servants, became a member of the Board of Veterans Appeals in the Veterans Administration in Washington, D. C.

K. Patrick Okura of Omaha, Nebraska, served as sociologist at Boys Town for ten years. A past president of the Japanese American Citizens League, he assumed the task of acting in charge of the Mental Health Program for Nebraska.

Yori Wada of San Francisco was appointed as a member of the California Youth Commission by Governor Pat Brown.

Minoru Yasui, a prominent lawyer in Denver, Colorado, became chairman of the Mayor's Commission on Human Relations.

Paul Watanabe from Seattle became president of the Los Angeles, California, Human Relations Commission. He also became president and founder of a number of banks and savings associations.

Dr. Thomas Omori, Azusa, California, was chosen vice president of the Aerojet Corporation.

Ray Sato, Hood River, Oregon, was one of the early returnees to Hood River in early 1945 when it was not too comfortable there. During early 1966 Ray was named Orchard Man of the Year for Hood River Valley, an honor bestowed by a professional panel which considered production, management, horticultural practices, and overall farm appearance of nominees from all over the valley. Ray became operator of an orchard of 100 acres of apples and pears.

Tom Takamine of Denver, Colorado, became the largest potato distributor in the Rocky Mountain area. Tom Imaizumi, a grower from San Diego, California, invented many farm-labor-saving machines and other items of equipment.

The Reverend Dai Kitagawa, a good friend who served as my interpreter at a four-hour meeting at Tule Lake in 1943, moved to Geneva, Switzerland, to work with World Church Service.

In the entertainment world, Pat Suzuki, a former evacuee from Cressey, California, became well known to television fans. Yuriko Amemiya of New York, a dancer with the Martha Graham troupe, has appeared in the movies.

Hideo Sasaki of Lexington, Massachusetts, professor and chairman of the Department of Landscape Architecture, Graduate School of Design, Harvard University, was appointed by President Kennedy to membership in the United States Commission on Fine Arts.

Isamu Noguchi of New York is known as a world-famed sculptor. Harry Osaki of Pasadena, California, has won many prizes as a silversmith. George Nakashima of Bucks County, Pennsylvania, became a world famous furniture designer.

Among the military, Capt. Shokichi Takita of Seattle and Lt. Edwin M. Fujenaga of Hilo, Hawaii, accepted service in a Ballistic Missile Launch Center near Cheyenne, Wyoming, with responsibility for ten Minuteman missiles — a far cry from 1942.

Lt. Comdr. Takeshi Yoshihara of Seattle, Washington, was the first Nisei to graduate from the United States Naval Academy at Annapolis, Maryland. George Shibata, the first Nisei to graduate from the United States Military Academy, West Point, served as a jet pilot in the Korean War, and later became an assistant city attorney in California.

Tommy Kono of Sacramento, California, was twice Olympic Champion weightlifter, representing the United States.

These persons are only a few of the many who might well be included in this list.

AFTERTHOUGHTS

As I look back on my four years' experience as Director of the War Relocation Authority, I realize that I learned many things. We all learned from first-hand experience how low some of the worst of the avaricious and race-baiting segments of our population could stoop. On the other hand, we had the support of the best persons and organizations in the land. The people of good will appear to be slower in getting into action than do the mean elements of society, but once they do act, they move intelligently, effectively, and persistently.

We learned that the difference between success and failure is often knife-blade thin and that persistence is important.

We also learned that when the people of the United States have the opportunity to understand the problems of the underdog and those discriminated against, they really do believe in the Bill of Rights and are ready to do something about it. We came to the realization that it is a sad fact that most people do not understand that the emotions of fear and hate are so closely associated. If we could eliminate fear from the human population, we undoubtedly would eliminate most of the hatred that exists.

A provision in Title II of the Internal Security Act of 1950 reads as follows:

The President is authorized to make public proclamation of an Internal Security Emergency . . . and is authorized to apprehend and . . . detain . . . each person as to whom there is reasonable ground to believe . . . probably will conspire with others to engage in acts . . . of sabotage . . . Persons apprehended shall be confined in places of detention . . .[1]

---

[1]Public Law 831, 81st Congress; Internal Security Act of 1950 [frequently referred to as the Emergency Detention Act; also the McCarran Act], Title II, Sections 102-104.

The United States Senate, in late 1969, voted to revoke Title II of the 1950 Internal Security Act. Hopefully the House of Representatives will follow the Senate's good example. The very fact that Title II was enacted in the first instance is a warning to the good people of the United States that we must be forever watchful if we are to avoid the use of internment camps based solely upon suspicion.

In view of the above provisions it is well that we recall Mr. Justice Jackson's words of dissent in the Koromatsu case in which he said,

A military order however unconstitutional, is not apt to last longer than the military emergency. Even during that period a succeeding commander may revoke it all. But once a Judicial opinion rationalizes such an order to show that it conforms to the Constitution, or rather rationalizes the Constitution to show that the Constitution sanctions such an order, the court for all time has validated the principle of racial discrimination in criminal procedure and of transplanting American citizens. The principle then lies about like a loaded weapon ready for the hand of any authority that can bring forward a plausible claim of an urgent need. Every repetition imbeds that principle more deeply in our law and thinking and expands it to new purposes.[2]

---

[2]*Korematsu* v. *U.S.* [323 U.S. 214].

Appendixes

Final Recommendations of the Commanding General,
Western Defense Command and Fourth Army,
Submitted to the Secretary of War

HEADQUARTERS WESTERN DEFENSE COMMAND AND FOURTH ARMY

Presidio of San Francisco, California
Office of the Commanding General

February 14, 1942

014.31 (DCS)
Memorandum for: The Secretary of War,
(Thru: The Commanding General,
Field Forces, Washington, D.C.)
Subject: Evacuation of Japanese and other Subversive Persons from the Pacific Coast.

1. In presenting a recommendation for the evacuation of Japanese and other subversive persons from the Pacific Coast, the following facts have been considered:

a. Mission of the Western Defense Command and Fourth Army.

(1) Defense of the Pacific Coast of the Western Defense Command, as extended, against attacks by sea, land or air;

(2) Local protection of establishment and communications vital to the National Defense for which adequate defense cannot be provided by local civilian authorities.

b. Brief Estimate of the Situation.

(1) Any estimate of the situation indicates that the following are possible and probable enemy activities:

   (a) Naval attack on shipping in coastal waters;
   (b) Naval attack on coastal cities and vital installations;
   (c) Air raids on vital installations, particularly within two hundred miles of the coast;
   (d) Sabotage of vital installations throughout the Western Defense Command.

Hostile Naval and air raids will be assisted by enemy agents signaling from the coastline and the vicinity thereof; and by supplying and otherwise assisting enemy vessels and by sabotage.

Sabotage, (for example, of airplane factories), may be effected not only by destruction within plants and establishments, but by destroying power, light, water, sewer and other utility and other facilities in the immediate vicinity thereof or at a distance. Serious damage or destruction in congested areas may readily be caused by incendiarism.

(2) The area lying to the west of the Cascade and Sierra Nevada Mountains in Washington, Oregon and California, is highly critical not only because the lines of communication and supply to the Pacific theater pass through it, but also because of the vital industrial production therein, particularly aircraft. In the war in which we are now engaged racial affinities are not severed by migration. The Japanese race is an enemy race and while many second and third generation Japanese born on United States soil, possessed of United States citizenship, have become "Americanized," the racial strains are undiluted. To conclude otherwise is to expect that children born of white parents on Japanese soil sever all racial affinity and become loyal Japanese subjects, ready to fight and, if necessary, to die for Japan in a war against the nation of their parents. That Japan is allied with Germany and Italy in this struggle is no ground for assuming that any Japanese, barred from assimilation by convention as he is, though born and raised in the United States, will not turn against this nation when the final test of loyalty comes. It, therefore, follows that along the vital Pacific Coast over 112,000 potential enemies, of Japanese extraction, are at large today. There are indications that these are organized and ready for concerted action at a favorable opportunity. The very fact that no sabotage has taken place to date is a disturbing and confirming indication that such action will be taken.

c. Disposition of the Japanese.

(1) Washington. As the term is used herein, the word "Japanese" includes alien Japanese and American citizens of Japanese ancestry. In the State of Washington the Japanese population, aggregating over 14,500, is disposed largely in the area lying west of the Cascade Mountains and south of an east-west line passing through Bellingham, Washington, about 70 miles north of Seattle and some 15 miles south

of the Canadian border. The largest concentration of Japanese is in the area, the axis of which is along the line Seattle, Tacoma, Olympia, Willapa Bay and the mouth of the Columbia River, with the heaviest concentration in the agricultural valleys between Seattle and Tacoma, viz., the Green River and the Puyallup Valleys. The Boeing Aircraft factory is in the Green River Valley. The lines of communication and supply including power and water which feed this vital industrial installation, radiate from this plant for many miles through areas heavily populated by Japanese. Large numbers of Japanese also operate vegetable markets along the Seattle and Tacoma water fronts, in Bremerton, near the Bremerton Navy Yard, and inhabit islands in Puget Sound opposite vital naval ship building installations. Still others are engaged in fishing along the southwest Washington Pacific Coast and along the Columbia River. Many of these Japanese are within easy reach of the forests of Washington State, the stock piles of seasoning lumber and the many sawmills of southwest Washington. During the dry season these forests, mills and stock piles are easily fired. (See inclosed map.)

(2) Oregon. There are approximately 4,000 Japanese in the State of Oregon, of which the substantial majority reside in the area in the vicinity of Portland along the south bank of the Columbia River, following the general line Bonneville, Oregon City, Astoria, Tillamook. Many of these are in the northern reaches of the Willamette Valley and are engaged in agricultural and fishing pursuits. Others operate vegetable markets in the Portland metropolitan area and still others reside along the northern Oregon sea coast. Their disposition is in intimate relationship with the northwest Oregon sawmills and lumber industry, near and around the vital electric power development at Bonneville and the pulp and paper installations at Camas (on the Washington State side of the Columbia River) and Oregon City (directly south of Portland). (See inclosed map.)

(3) California. The Japanese population in California aggregates approximately 93,500 people. Its disposition is so widespread and so well known that little would be gained by setting it forth in detail here. They live in great numbers along the coastal strip, in and around San Francisco and the Bay Area, the Salinas Valley, Los Angeles and San Diego. Their truck farms are contiguous to the vital aircraft industry concentration in and around Los Angeles. They live in large numbers in and about San Francisco, now a vast staging area for the war in the Pacific, a point at which the nation's lines of communication and supply converge. Inland they are disposed in the Sacramento, San Joaquin and Imperial Valleys. They are engaged in the production of approximately 38% of the vegetable produce of California. Many of them are engaged in the distribution of such produce in and along the water fronts at San Francisco and Los Angeles. Of the 93,500 in California, about 25,000 reside inland in the mentioned valleys where they are largely engaged in vegetable production cited above, and 54,600 reside along the coastal strip, that is to say, a strip of coast line varying from eight miles in the north to

twenty miles in width in and around the San Francisco bay area, including San Francisco, in Los Angeles and its environs, and in San Diego. Approximately 13,900 are dispersed throughout the remaining portion of the state. In Los Angeles City the disposition of vital aircraft industrial plants covers the entire city. Large numbers of Japanese live and operate markets and truck farms adjacent to or near these installations. (See inclosed map.)

          d. Disposition of Other Subversive Persons.

      Disposed within the vital coastal strip already mentioned are large numbers of Italians and Germans, foreign and native born, among whom are many individuals who constitute an actual or potential menace to the safety of the nation.

      2. Action recommended.

          a. Recommendations for the designation of prohibited areas, described as "Category A" areas in California, Oregon and Washington, from which are to be excluded by order of the Attorney General all alien enemies, have gone forward from this headquarters to the Attorney General through the Provost Marshal General and the Secretary of War. These recommendations were made in order to aid the Attorney General in the implementation of the Presidential Proclamations of December 7 and 8, 1941, imposing responsibility on him for the control of alien enemies as such. These recommendations were for the exclusion of all alien enemies from Category "A." The Attorney General has adopted these recommendations in part, and has the balance under consideration. Similarly, recommendations were made by this headquarters, and adopted by the Attorney General, for the designation of certain areas as Category "B" areas, within which alien enemies may be permitted on pass or permit.

          b. I now recommend the following:

          (1) That the Secretary of War procure from the President direction and authority to designate military areas in the combat zone of the Western Theater of Operations, (if necessary to include the entire combat zone), from which, in his discretion, he may exclude all Japanese, all alien enemies, and all other persons suspected for any reason by the administering military authorities of being actual or potential saboteurs, espionage agents, or fifth columnists. Such executive order should empower the Secretary of War to requisition the services of any and all other agencies of the Federal Government, with express direction to such agencies to respond to such requisition, and further empowering the Secretary of War to use any and all federal facilities and equipment, including Civilian Conservation Corps Camps, and to accept the use of State facilities for the purpose of providing shelter and equipment for evacuees. Such executive order to provide further for the administration of military areas for the purposes of this plan by appropriate military authorities acting with the requisitioned assistance of the other federal agencies and the cooperation of State and local agencies. The executive order should further provide that by reason of military necessity the right of all persons,

whether citizens or aliens, to reside, enter, cross or be within any military areas shall be subject to revocation and shall exist on a pass and permit basis at the discretion of the Secretary of War and implemented by the necessary legislation imposing penalties for violation.

(2) That, pursuant to such executive order, there be designated as military areas all areas in Washington, Oregon and California, recommended by me to date for designation by the Attorney General as Category "A" areas and such additional areas as it may be found necessary to designate hereafter.

(3) That the Secretary of War provide for the exclusion from such military areas, in his discretion, of the following classes of persons, viz:

(a) Japanese aliens.
(b) Japanese-American citizens.
(c) Alien enemies other than Japanese aliens.
(d) Any and all other persons who are suspected for any reason by the administering military authorities to be actual or potential saboteurs, espionage agents, fifth columnists, or subversive persons.

(4) That the evacuation of classes (a), (b), and (c) from such military areas be initiated on a designated evacuation day and carried to completion as rapidly as practicable.

That prior to evacuation day all plans be complete for the establishment of initial concentration points, reception centers, registration, rationing, guarding, transportation to internment points, and the selection and establishment of internment facilities in the Sixth, Seventh, and Eighth Corps Areas.

That persons in class (a) and (c) above be evacuated and interned at such selected places of internment, under guard.

That persons in class (b) above, at the time of evacuation, be offered an opportunity to accept voluntary internment, under guard, at the place of internment above mentioned.

That persons in class (b) who decline to accept voluntary internment, be excluded from all military areas, and left to their own resources, or, in the alternative, be encouraged to accept resettlement outside of such military areas with such assistance as the State governments concerned or the Federal Security Agency may be by that time prepared to offer.

That the evacuation of persons in class (d) be progressive and continuing, and that upon their evacuation persons in class (d) be excluded from all military areas and left in their own resources outside of such military areas, or, in the alternative, be offered voluntary internment or encouraged to accept voluntary resettlement as above outlined, unless the facts in a particular case shall warrant other action.

(5) The Commanding General, Western Defense Command and Fourth Army, to be responsible for the evacuation, administration, supply and guard, to the place of internment; the Commanding Generals

of the Corps Areas concerned to be responsible for guard, supply and administration at the places of internment.

(6) That direct communication between the Commanding General, Western Defense Command and Fourth Army and the Corps Area Commanders concerned for the purpose of making necessary arrangements be authorized.

(7) That the Provost Marshal General coordinate all phases of the plan between the Commanding General, Western Defense Command and Fourth Army, on the one hand, and the Corps Area Commanders on the other hand.

(8) That all arrangements be accomplished with the utmost secrecy.

(9) That adult males (above the age of 14 years) be interned separately from all women and children until the establishment of family units can be accomplished.

(10) No change is contemplated in Category "B" areas.

3. Although so far as the Army is concerned, such action is not an essential feature of the plan, but merely incident thereto, I, nevertheless, recommend that mass internment be considered as largely a temporary expedient pending selective resettlement, to be accomplished by the various Security Agencies of the Federal and State Governments.

4. The number of persons involved in the recommended evacuation will be approximately 133,000. (This total represents all enemy aliens and Japanese-American citizens in Category "A" areas recommended to date.)

5. If these recommendations are approved detailed plans will be made by this headquarters for the proposed evacuation. The number evacuated to be apportioned by the Provost Marshal General among the Corps Area Commanders concerned as the basis for formulating their respective plans. It is possible that the State of California, and perhaps the State of Washington, will be able to offer resettlement facilities for a given number of evacuees who may be willing to accept resettlement.

6. Pending further and detailed study of the problem, it is further recommended: (1) That the Commanding General, Western Defense Command and Fourth Army, coordinate with the local and State authorities, in order to facilitate the temporary physical protection by them of the property of evacuees not taken with them; (2) That the Commanding General, Western Defense Command and Fourth Army, determine the quantity and character of property which the adult males, referred to in paragraph 2b (9), may be permitted to take with them; and (3) That the Treasury Department or other proper Federal agency be responsible for the conservation, liquidation, and proper disposition of the property of evacuees if it cannot be cared for through the usual and normal channels.

J. L. DeWitt
Lieutenant General, U. S. Army,
Commanding.

Authorizing the Secretary of War to Prescribe Military Areas

Executive Order No. 9066

Whereas, The successful prosecution of the war requires every possible protection against espionage and against sabotage to national-defense material, national-defense premises and national-defense utilities as defined in Section 4, Act of April 20, 1918, 40 Stat. 533, as amended by the Act of November 30, 1940, 54 Stat. 1220, and the Act of August 21, 1941, 55 Stat. 655 (U.S.C., Title 50, Sec. 104):

Now therefore, by virtue of the authority vested in me as President of the United States, and Commander in Chief of the Army and Navy, I hereby authorize and direct the Secretary of War, and the Military Commanders whom he may from time to time designate, whenever he or any designated Commander deems such action necessary or desirable, to prescribe military areas in such places and of such extent as he or the appropriate Military Commander may determine, from which any or all persons may be excluded, and with respect to which, the right of any person to enter, remain in, or leave shall be subject to whatever restriction the Secretary of War or the appropriate Military Commander may impose in his discretion. The Secretary of War is hereby authorized to provide for residents of any such area who are excluded therefrom, such transportation, food, shelter, and other accommodations as may be necessary, in the judgment of the Secretary of War or the said Military Commander, and until other arrangements are made, to accomplish the purpose of this order. The designation of military areas in any region or locality shall supersede designations of prohibited and restricted areas by the Attorney General under the Proclamation of December 7 and 8, 1941, and shall supersede the responsibility and authority of the Attorney General under the said Proclamations in respect of such prohibited and restricted areas.

I hereby further authorize and direct the Secretary of War and the said Military Commanders to take such other steps as he or the appropriate Military Commander may deem advisable to enforce compliance with the restrictions applicable to each Military area hereinabove authorized to be designated, including the use of Federal troops and other Federal Agencies, with authority to accept assistance of state and local agencies.

I hereby further authorize and direct all Executive Departments, independent establishments and other Federal Agencies, to assist the Secretary of War or the said Military Commanders in carrying out this Executive Order, including the furnishing of medical aid, hospitalization, food, clothing, transportation, use of land, shelter, and other supplies, equipment, utilities, facilities, and services.

This order shall not be construed as modifying or limiting in any way the authority heretofore granted under Executive Order No. 8972, dated December 12, 1941, nor shall it be construed as limiting or modifying the duty and responsibility of the Federal Bureau of Investigation, with respect to the investigations of alleged acts of sabotage or the duty and responsibility of the Attorney General and the Department of Justice under the Proclamations of December 7 and 8, 1941, prescribing regulations for the conduct and control of alien enemies, except as such duty and responsibility is superseded by the designation of military areas hereunder.

Franklin D. Roosevelt

The White House, February 19, 1942.

Establishing the War Relocation Authority in the Executive Office of the President and Defining its Functions and Duties

Executive Order No. 9102
Dated March 18, 1942
7 F. R. 2165

By virtue of the authority vested in me by the Constitution and statutes of the United States, as President of the United States and Commander in Chief of the Army and Navy, and in order to provide for the removal from designated areas of persons whose removal is necessary in the interests of national security, it is ordered as follows:

1. There is established in the Office for Emergency Management of the Executive Office of the President the War Relocation Authority, at the head of which shall be a Director appointed by and responsible to the President.

2. The Director of the War Relocation Authority is authorized and directed to formulate and effectuate a program for the removal, from areas designated from time to time by the Secretary of War or appropriate military commander under the authority of Executive Order No. 9066 of February 19, 1942, of the persons or classes of persons designated under such Executive Order, and for their relocation, maintenance, and supervision.

3. In effectuating such program the Director shall have authority to:

(a) Accomplish all necessary evacuation not undertaken by the Secretary of War or appropriate military commander, provide for the relocation of such persons in appropriate places, provide for their needs in such manner as may be appropriate, and supervise their activities.

(b) Provide, insofar as feasible and desirable, for the employment of such persons at useful work in industry, commerce, agriculture, or public projects, prescribe the terms and conditions of such public employment, and safeguard the public interest in the private employment of such persons.

(c) Secure the cooperation, assistance, or services of any governmental agency.

(d) Prescribe regulations necessary or desirable to promote effective execution of such program, and, as a means of coordinating evacuation and relocation activities, consult with the Secretary of War with respect to regulations issued and measures taken by him.

(e) Make such delegations of authority as he may deem necessary.

(f) Employ necessary personnel, and make such expenditures, including the making of loans and grants and the purchase of real property, as may be necessary, within the limits of such funds as may be made available to the Authority.

4. The Director shall consult with the United States Employment Service and other agencies on employment and other problems incident to activities under this order.

5. The Director shall cooperate with the Alien Property Custodian appointed pursuant to Executive Order No. 9095 of March 11, 1942, in formulating policies to govern the custody, management, and disposal by the Alien Property Custodian of property belonging to foreign nationals removed under this order or under Executive Order No. 9066 of February 19, 1942; and may assist all other persons removed under either of such Executive Orders in the management and disposal of their property.

6. Departments and agencies of the United States are directed to cooperate with and assist the Director in his activities hereunder. The Departments of War and Justice, under the direction of the Secretary of War and the Attorney General, respectively, shall insofar as consistent with the national interest provide such protective, police and investigational services as the Director shall find necessary in connection with activities under this order.

7. There is established within the War Relocation Authority the War Relocation Work Corps. The Director shall provide, by general regulations, for the enlistment in such Corps, for the duration of the present war, of persons removed under this order or under Executive Order No. 9066 of February 19, 1942, and shall prescribe the terms and conditions of the work to be performed by such Corps, and the compensation to be paid.

8. There is established within the War Relocation Authority a Liaison Committee on War Relocation which shall consist of the Secretary of War, the Secretary of the Treasury, the Attorney General, the Secretary of Agriculture, the Secretary of Labor, the Federal Security Administrator, the Director of Civilian Defense, and the Alien Property Custodian, or their deputies, and such other persons or agencies as the Director may designate. The Liaison Committee shall meet at the call of the Director and shall assist him in his duties.

9. The Director shall keep the President informed with regard to the progress made in carrying out this order, and perform such related duties as the President may from time to time assign to him.

10. In order to avoid duplication of evacuation activities under this order and Executive Order No. 9066 of February 19, 1942, the Director shall not undertake any evacuation activities within military areas designated under said Executive Order No. 9066, without the prior approval of the Secretary of War or the appropriate military commander.

11. This order does not limit the authority granted in Executive Order No. 8972 of December 12, 1941; Executive Order No. 9066 of February 19, 1942; Executive Order No. 9095 of March 11, 1942; Executive Proclamation No. 2525 of December 7, 1941; Executive Proclamation No. 2526 of December 8, 1941; Executive Proclamation No. 2527 of December 8, 1941; Executive Proclamation No. 2533 of December 29, 1941; or Executive Proclamation No. 2537 of January 14, 1942; nor does it limit the functions of the Federal Bureau of Investigation.

Public Law No. 503 (77th Congress)

Dated March 21, 1942

To provide a penalty for violation of restrictions or orders with respect to persons entering, remaining in, leaving, or committing any act in military areas or zones.

Be it enacted by the Senate and House of Representatives of the United States of America in Congress assembled, That whoever shall enter, remain in, leave, or commit any act in any military area or military zone prescribed, under the authority of an Executive order of the President, by the Secretary of War, contrary to the restrictions applicable to any such area or zone or contrary to the order of the Secretary of War or any such military commander, shall, if it appears that he knew or should have known of the existence and extent of the restrictions or order and that his act was in violation thereof, be guilty of misdemeanor and upon conviction shall be liable to a fine of not to exceed $5,000 or to imprisonment for not more than one year, or both, for each offense.

President Roosevelt's Letter of Approval Regarding the Proposed Japanese American Combat Team

THE WHITE HOUSE

February 1, 1943

My dear Mr. Secretary:

The proposal of the War Department to organize a combat team consisting of loyal American citizens of Japanese descent has my full approval. The new combat team will add to the nearly 5,000 loyal Americans of Japanese ancestry who are already serving in the armed forces of our country.

This is a natural and logical step toward the reinstitution of the selective service procedures which were temporarily disrupted by the evacuation from the West Coast.

No loyal citizen of the United States should be denied the democratic right to exercise the responsibilities of his citizenship, regardless of ancestry. The principle on which this country was founded and by which it has always been governed is that Americanism is a matter of the mind and heart; Americanism is not, and never was, a matter of race or ancestry. A good American is one who is loyal to this country and to our creed of liberty and democracy. Every loyal American citizen should be given an opportunity to serve this country wherever his skills will make the greatest contribution — whether it be in the ranks of our armed forces, war production, agriculture, government service, or other work essential to the war effort.

I am glad to observe that the War Department, the Navy Department, the War Manpower Commission, the Department of Justice, and the War Relocation Authority are collaborating in a program which will assure the opportunity for all loyal Americans, including Americans of Japanese ancestory, to serve their country at a time when the fullest and wisest use of our manpower is all important to the war effort.

Very sincerely yours,
/s/ Franklin D. Roosevelt

Peak Populations of Relocation Centers
Reached January 1,1943

CENTER	POPULATION
Central Utah (Topaz)	8,232
Colorado River (Poston)	18,039
Gila River	13,420
Granada	7,656
Heart Mountain	11,062
Jerome	7,932*
Manzanar	10,121
Minidoka	9,861
Rohwer	8,548
Tule Lake	15,369†
Total	110,310

*The Jerome center reached its peak population on March 1, 1943, with 8,587.
†Tule Lake reached its peak after segregation on January 1, 1945, with 18,734. By this date the total population of all centers was down to 80,878.

Office of War Information, War Relocation Authority
The Tule Lake Incident

November 14, 1943

Dillon S. Myer, Director of the War Relocation Authority, today issued the following statement regarding the events that occurred between November 1 and November 4 at the Tule Lake Center in northern California:

1. Tule Lake is the only center maintained by the War Relocation Authority for segregation purposes. It was established originally in 1942 as one of 10 relocation centers for persons of Japanese ancestry who were evacuated from the West Coast military area. In September of this year, however, it was made the focal point in a segregation program carried out by the War Relocation Authority and since that time has occupied a peculiar status among WRA centers.

During February and March of this year, a registration program was conducted at all relocation centers for the purpose of accumulating information on the background and attitudes of all adult residents. As part of this program, citizen evacuees at the centers were questioned concerning their allegiance to the United States, and alien evacuees were questioned about their willingness to abide by the Nation's laws. After the results of registration were compiled and analyzed, WRA began a program to separate from the bulk of the population at relocation cen-

[316]

ters, those evacuees who have indicated by word or action that their loyalties lie with Japan.

Four major groups were designated for segregation:

(1) Those who requested repatriation or expatriation to Japan;

(2) Citizens who refused during registration to state unqualified allegiance to the United States and aliens who refused to agree to abide by the laws of the United States;

(3) Those with intelligence records or other records indicating that they might endanger the national security or interfere with the war effort;

(4) Close relatives of persons in the above three groups who expressed a preference to remain with the segregants rather than disrupt family ties.

The major movement of segregants into Tule Lake from other WRA centers and of non-segregants from Tule Lake to other WRA centers was started in early September and completed about the middle of October. The process, which was carried out jointly by WRA and the Army, entirely without incident, involved the movement of approximately 9,000 evacuees from other centers into Tule Lake and the removal from Tule Lake to other centers of approximately the same number. Slightly more than 6,000 residents of Tule Lake who had been designated for segregation or who wished to remain with segregated relatives were retained there. At the present time, there are at the Manzanar Relocation Center in California approximately 1,900 evacuees who are awaiting transfer to Tule Lake. They will be transferred as soon as necessary housing can be completed, probably in the early part of 1944.

2. The Army has the responsibility of providing full protection of the area surrounding the Tule Lake Center. A man-proof fence surrounds the external boundaries of the center; troops patrol that fence; other necessary facilities are at all times in readiness. In September, when Tule Lake was transformed into a segregation center, the Army substantially increased the number of troops assigned to guard duty at the center and built the present manproof fence around the external boundary outside the ordinary wire fence which was erected at the time of the center's establishment. At this time also additional military equipment was provided.

During the recent disturbance at the Tule Lake Center, the War Relocation Authority and the Army have been in constant contact regarding necessary safety measures. Special arrangements were made for prompt communication between the WRA staff and the officer commanding the troops at Tule Lake.

Like all WRA centers, Tule Lake has been operated, ever since the time of its establishment in 1942, under the terms of an agreement between WRA and the War Department. WRA is responsible for all phases of internal administration of the center. The Army, from the beginning, has been responsible for guarding the external boundaries of the center, and for controlling the entry and departure of all persons of Japanese descent.

WRA maintains order within the center through civilian guards assisted by a staff of evacuees. The understanding with the Army provides that when a show of greater force is necessary to maintain order within the center, WRA will call upon the Army to move inside the center and take full control.

3. Immediately following the segregation movement, some of the evacuees at the Tule Lake Center began to create difficulties. All available evidence indicates that a small, well-organized group—composed chiefly of persons transferred to Tule Lake from the other centers — was attempting to gain control of the community and disrupt the orderly process of administration. Against this background, a serious accident occurred at the center on October 15. A truck, carrying 29 evacuee workers and driven by an evacuee, was over-turned while attempting to pass another truck on the road from the center to the WRA farm. All occupants of the truck were injured and one of them subsequently died. On the day following the accident, no evacuee workers reported for duty at the farm.

For a period of approximately 10 days thereafter, work on the harvesting of crops stopped, but no formal representations were made to WRA by evacuee workers. Then on October 25, a group of evacuees who claimed to represent the community met with Project Director Ray Best and submitted a series of questions and demands. Among other things, this committee asked whether the residents of Tule were regarded by the United States government as prisoners of war and stated that the residents would not engage in the harvesting of crops for use at other WRA centers. Project Director Best told the committee: (1) that the residents of Tule Lake were regarded as segregants and not as prisoners of war, (2) that WRA does not operate on the basis of demands, and (3) that if the residents of Tule Lake were unwilling to harvest the crops, some other method of harvesting them would be found.

Faced with the onset of winter and the possibility of losing approximately $500,000 worth of vegetables, WRA immediately began recruiting loyal evacuees from other centers to carry out the harvesting work at Tule Lake. A crew of 234 was recruited and is still engaged in harvesting work on the Tule Lake farm. These evacuees are quartered outside the boundaries of the center, wholly apart from the population of the center.

4. On the morning of Monday, November 1, D. S. Myer, National Director of the War Relocation Authority, and Robert B. Cozzens, Assistant Director of the Authority in San Francisco, arrived at the Tule Lake center for an inspection and consultation with key WRA staff members and with evacuee representatives. The original arrangement called for Mr. Myer and Mr. Cozzens to meet with evacuee representa-

tives on the day following their arrival. However, during the lunch hour, a report was received by Project Director Best that certain evacuees were making unauthorized announcements in the evacuee messhalls. Residents were being told, according to this report, that Mr. Myer was to make a speech from the main administration building shortly after lunch. On receiving this report, Mr. Myer and Mr. Best immediately made a quick automobile inspection trip through the evacuee section of the center. They observed that large numbers of men, women and children were proceeding in an orderly manner from the evacuee barracks in the direction of the administration building.

By 1:30 p.m., Mr. Myer and Mr. Best had returned to the administration building and a crowd estimated between 3,500 and 4,000 had congregated immediately outside. One young man from the evacuee group then entered the administration building and asked whether a committee of 17 evacuees might have a conference with Mr. Myer. This request was granted and Mr. Myer, Mr. Cozzens, Mr. Best and other staff members met with the committee. The committee presented a series of demands including the resignation of project director Best and several other WRA staff members at the center.

While the discussion was going on, word was received that a group of about a dozen evacuees had entered the center hospital and beaten the Chief Medical Officer, Dr. Reece M. Pedicord. The conference was interrupted while one WRA staff member left the administration building, passed through the crowd, and went to the hospital for a check-up on the situation there. After this man had returned — wholly unmolested — with the report that Dr. Pedicord had been badly battered but was receiving adequate medical attention and that order prevailed in the hospital, the conference was resumed. Meanwhile, a small group of evacuees had gone into the administration building and installed a public address system with WRA permission.

At the conclusion of the conference, Director Myer was asked to address the crowd briefly over the address system and agreed to do so. Mr. Myer told the crowd substantially what he had told the committee: (1) that WRA would consider requests made by the evacuee population provided they were in the framework of national policy; (2) that WRA would not accede to demands; (3) that WRA was under the impression that the majority of residents at Tule Lake wanted to live in a peaceful and orderly atmosphere; (4) that if the residents of the center could not deal peacefully with WRA they would have to deal with someone else; and (5) that once the segregation process was wholly completed with the movement from Manzanar, the community at Tule Lake should attempt to select a committee — more directly representative of its wishes than the current one — to deal with the War Relocation Authority. After Mr. Myer had concluded his remarks, two members of the evacuee committee addressed the crowd briefly in Japanese. Immediately following the completion of these speeches, at about 4:30 p.m., the crowd broke up quickly and peacefully and returned to family living quarters. During the entire conference and the time when committee members were addressing the crowd, a member of the War Relocation Authority staff who is fully competent in the Japanese language was present and was able to indicate to Mr. Myer and Mr. Best the nature of all remarks made in Japanese.

5. While the meeting was in progress in the administration building a number of automobiles at the center were slightly damaged. Some of these automobiles belonged to visitors and some to WRA personnel. One visitor reported that a window of his car was broken and a sun visor removed. (This statement has not been verified by other evidence.) A door handle was broken off one car. Radio aerials were removed from two cars and windshield wipers from about twelve cars. Air was released from tires of several cars. The paint on two cars was scratched.

In the struggle during which Dr. Pedicord was beaten, a wooden railing in the hospital office was knocked down. A careful investigation has revealed no reliable evidence of any property damage during this incident other than that listed here.

Several WRA employees and visitors to the center who were in the area outside the administration building at the time the crowd was forming were approached by some of the evacuees directing the movements of the crowd and told to go inside the building. Aside from Dr. Pedicord, however, no WRA employees or visitors were beaten or injured during this incident. The evacuee employees in the administration office left their work. A few individuals reported they saw knives and clubs in the hands of some of the evacuees. The great majority of WRA personnel reported following the meeting that they had seen no weapons of any kind.

6. After dispersal of the crowd on Monday afternoon, a calm marked by some evidence of sub-surface tension prevailed in the evacuee community for approximately three days. Orders were sent out following the Monday meeting forbidding any meetings or assembly of evacuees in the administrative area. The internal security force was strengthened and authority was given for any member of the internal security staff, under certain specified conditions, to summon the Army directly without consultation with the Project Director or any other superior officer.

On Thursday afternoon, November 4, work was started on a fence separating the evacuee community from the section of the center where the administrative buildings are located and WRA staff members are housed. That evening a crowd of about 400 evacuees, mainly young men — many of them armed with clubs — entered the administration area. Most of the crowd entered the warehouse area. A few entered the motor pool area and some surrounded the Project Director's residence. The advance of this crowd was resisted by several WRA internal security officers, one of whom tripped, struck his head on a stone, and was then struck by evacuees with clubs. No other persons were injured. As the crowd closed in around Mr. Best's home, he telephoned Lt. Col. Verne Austin, commanding officer of the military unit outside the center, and asked the Army to assume full control of the project area. Troops entered the center at once.

7. During and immediately following the evacuee meeting on Monday, a number of the WRA staff became apprehensive concerning their personal safety. Most of them remained calm but a few became almost hysterical. All were offered the opportunity to leave the center until they felt secure in returning there, and a number of them did so. Since the incident on Monday, twelve people have resigned voluntarily, and two have resigned or were separated at the request of the Authority.

8. A large number of the evacuees at Tule Lake are citizens of the United States, with the constitutional rights of citizens. Many of them are children under 17, and they, together with a very large number of the adults, have no responsible part in the recent events.

In presenting this factual statement, the War Relocation Authority wants to emphasize that reports of the events at Tule Lake are being watched in Tokyo. Already some of the recent newspaper accounts have been used by the Japanese Government for propaganda purposes. There is every possibility that they may be used as a pretext for retaliatory action against American civilians and prisoners of war under Japanese control. Under these circumstances, it is imperative that the situation at Tule Lake be handled with a scrupulous regard for accuracy.

9. In view of the serious international implications in the situation at Tule Lake, the War Relocation Authority has been particularly careful in preparing the information contained in this statement. There have been so many exaggerated, even hysterical, reports that the staff at Tule Lake, confronted with an otherwise complicated and difficult situation, has been able to verify conclusively only the information presented in this statement. As this is written, further investigation is being made to check the accuracy of many of the allegations that have appeared in the press and to complete this story in all its pertinent details. The major events, however, have now been fully documented and can for the first time be presented to the public in an official statement.

Memorandum to Secretary Harold Ickes Following WRA Transfer to the Department of the Interior

Subject: Major Problems of the War Relocation Authority — Present, and Future

Dear Mr. Ickes:

This memorandum is an attempt to outline for you some of the problems of the War Relocation Authority, a summary of the present status, and a brief outline of problems ahead as we now see them.

In general the problems with which we have had to deal in the past have been divided into six major groups:

1. Recruitment, training, and maintenance of a staff for ten relocation centers, other field offices, and the Washington office.

It was a major task to locate personnel during the spring and summer of 1942 to administer ten cities ranging in size from 7,000 to 17,500. Each of these cities had most of the problems of any normal city of similar size with some additional ones which a normal city does not have. It was necessary to provide at each center a school system, sanitary facilities, fire department, police department, and other services. In addition it was necessary to supply medical service and hospitals for the total population, provide transportation, supplies, and facilities for feeding the total population in mess halls, which included problems with which the Army never had to deal because they handle only men whereas we had men, women, and children. Special provisions had to be worked out for the organization of community enterprises such as stores, barber shops, shoe shops, etc.,

[322]

because of the unusual situation existing in each center. A wholly new type of governmental structure was required, including provisions for courts, community representation in administration, and special arrangements for community activities, all of which had to be considered in the recruitment, selection, and training of personnel. This basic job was only well under way when it became necessary to establish property offices up and down the West Coast in order to render service to the evacuees in relation to both personal and real property, and immediately following that it became necessary to establish field offices at approximately fifty points throughout the country in order to facilitate the relocation program.

Living conditions in relocation centers have been primitive and highly undesirable, particularly during the early months of center existence. Because of the emotions involved it was necessary to select with care all the individuals employed, not only with respect to their professional competence but also their feelings about racial minorities and, particularly, any prejudices which might affect their ability to get along with evacuees.

2. The formulation of policies and procedures relating to the operation of the centers, and attendant problems.

Certain decisions had to be made very early in the program in order to present a budget to the Congress and to effect the framework of an organization. Because the job to be done was without precedent, many of the policies and procedures could not be established until a certain amount of experience had been gained by the Authority. Consequently, the major policies relating to administration were not drafted in detail until late August, 1942. It became essential then to take time out to draft policies needed to give guidance to the various centers. A major portion of these basic policies were put into effect during late August and early September of 1942. They have been continually revised and augmented since that time. They had to be drafted with care so that they would be acceptable to the public and the Congress and at the same time be acceptable to the evacuees so that orderly administration could be established within the relocation centers. Every step had to be reasoned through from the standpoint of both the general public and the evacuees, and reasons why each of the policies was established had to be sound and clear-cut.

3. The formulation and execution of relocation and segregation policies and procedures.

The formulation of policies relating to relocation outside the centers and the consideration of the segregation problem started almost immediately after the inception of the Authority. Seasonal leave policies were worked out with the War Department during May, 1942. The first indefinite leave regulation was issued on July 20, 1942. Leave procedures were reconsidered in August and September and were revised effective October 1, 1942. Here again it was necessary to keep in mind the problem of securing public and evacuee acceptance and to lay the ground work for more detailed procedures to be developed over a period of time providing for leave clearance or ultimate segregation of evacuees to a segregation center. These policies have had to be revised from time to time to meet new problems which have developed as relocation proceeded. Only recently we have revised the seasonal leave program in order to meet the present day problems.

The problem of securing information regarding each individual and family which would provide the background necessary for proper placement outside of relocation centers and employment within the centers, and provide basic information which would assist in the segregation process, was one of the most difficult ones we have had to handle. With the announcement by the Secretary of War of plans to organize a Japanese American combat team in January of 1943, procedures were worked out jointly by representatives of the Army, Navy, and the War Relocation Authority to register everyone in the centers 17 years of age and over, both citizens and aliens, using a questionnaire developed with the Office of Naval Intelligence and other agencies, and including the now famous questions 27 and 28 relating to willingness to serve in the United States Army and allegiance to the United States. Following the completion of the registration program steps were taken immediately in collaboration with the Japanese American Joint Board to complete the leave clearance procedures and determine which evacuees should be denied leave clearance. The information secured on these registration forms was supplemented by any information available in the files of the Federal Bureau of Investigation, Naval Intelligence, Military Intelligence, and from any other source. On the basis of knowledge gained from all of these sources the actual segregation process got under way late in July of 1943 at which time the WRA center at Tule Lake was designated as the segregation center. The major movement was completed during September and October of 1943 and the bulk of the Manzanar group was moved during the third week of February, 1944. There will be approximately 1500 or 2000 people to be moved to Tule Lake during the next two or three months. This whole process has been complex, time consuming, and it is one of those jobs that may never be completely finished, since new developments may necessitate further denials of leave clearance.

4. The formulation and execution of policies which provide for services to evacuees in relation to their property problems, both personal and real property located within the evacuated area.

This problem has received little public attention but is nevertheless important. The Federal Reserve Bank and the Farm Security Administration in the beginning handled services to evacuees in connection with their property. The Federal Reserve Bank rendered service in the warehousing of personal property and aided in problems connected with urban property, while the Farm Security Administration handled problems connected with rural property. WRA took over the responsibility for these services in August, 1942. A property office was established in San Francisco and sub-offices have been set up in Los Angeles, Sacramento, Portland, and Seattle. Evacuees either owned or operated approximately $200,000,000 worth of property. Much of this is being looked after by agents selected by the evacuees themselves. However, WRA has made provision for warehousing all personal property left on the Coast for those evacuees who wish to have such service. We also help in the sale and leasing of real property if such service is requested by the evacuees and if they provide power of attorney. The job of transporting household goods from local points to key warehouses and from those warehouses to other parts of the country as evacuees continue to relocate is a tremendous one.

5. Relations with other government agencies.

Our major contacts with other government agencies have been with the War and Justice Departments. Throughout the spring, summer, and fall of 1942 a close liaison with the War Department was necessary because of the movement of about 110,000 people from Army assembly centers to relocation centers. During this period Army engineers were responsible for the construction of the ten centers. An agreement has been in effect throughout the existence of the Authority whereby the War Department is responsible for the external guard at relocation centers and for having troops available should a show of force be needed within a center. The Army Quartermaster Corps has done most of the procurement of food, other than that which is produced on the projects themselves, and has also provided procurement service for medical equipment and supplies. Many other matters involve liaison with the Army, including continuous contact with the Western Defense Command relating to evacuee travel in and out of centers located within the evacuated area.

We have had continuous relationships with the Alien Enemy Control Unit, the Immigration and Naturalization Service, and the Federal Bureau of Investigation in the Department of Justice. We have maintained liaison with the State Department in relation to the international aspect of the program, particularly the problem involving exchange of nationals with Japan, and contacts with the Spanish Consul who represents the protecting power for the Japanese government. Other contacts with government agencies involve relationship with the Office of War Information, Treasury Department, particularly the Alien Property Custodian, War Manpower Commission, Federal Security Agency, Civil Service Commission, National Youth Administration, Office of Education, Navy Department, Coast Guard, and others.

Policies controlled by some of these agencies have had a very important effect upon the program of the War Relocation Authority. The War Department, for example, has controlled the policy relating to the evacuated area, including movement of people in and out of that area, and the policy regarding Selective Service as it relates to Japanese Americans. These two matters are of tremendous importance to our program and have required continuous contact throughout. Many policies established by the War Department and other agencies have had a direct or indirect effect upon the morale of both the staff and the evacuees. We have made announcements of procedures that have been agreed upon and then have seen them changed from time to time by certain agencies following the attacks of the Dies Committee or for some other reason. This has had a serious effect on our relationships with evacuees as well as the public at large. While many of these actions did not directly affect a large number of evacuees, they serve to prove to a great majority of them that the government intended to continue to discriminate against American citizens of Japanese ancestry. Specific examples are the revision by the War Department of Selective Service procedures in March, 1942, whereby Japanese Americans were reclassified into 4-F and later into 4-C, which procedures were not changed so as to permit their induction under Selective Service until January, 1944; a change in rules by the Civil Service Commission, after we had worked out definite procedures for examinations and entrance into government service, which set the evacuees apart from other American citizens; initiation of procedures which interfered with merchant ship service by sailors of Japanese ancestry on the East Coast, after we thought we had worked out provisions with the Coast Guard and intelligence agencies; and a reversal of policy by NYA, after we had entered into a training agreement which was running smoothly. This reversal came as a result of the Dies Committee campaign in May and June of 1943.

6. The general problem of public relations.

The problem of acceptance by communities outside the West Coast area of evacuees interested in relocating has been a much simpler one than we had anticipated in the early part of the program. Generally speaking our public relations throughout the Midwest, South and East have been excellent. This is probably due to the fact that we concentrated on these areas, established offices, and developed a staff whose chief job was to secure understanding and acceptance by the public. After the evacuees were moved from the West Coast we assumed our major public relations problem would be in other portions of the country and did not make the provision on the West Coast that we perhaps should have in view of the campaign which has been carried on by the Hearst press, the Native Sons of the Golden West, the California Department of the American Legion, and certain labor groups along the Coast, particularly Dave Beck of the Teamsters Union. This campaign started almost immediately after WRA was established, with demands that the whole program be turned over to the War Department, that all people of Japanese ancestry be excluded from the West Coast for the duration and from the country after the war, that they be interned for the duration and not allowed to relocate in other parts of the country.

These organizations instigated an investigation by the Senate Military Affairs Committee under the leadership of Senator Chandler of Kentucky which began in January, 1943, and continued intermittently throughout the spring, summer, and fall. The results of that investigation did not satisfy certain West Coast interests; consequently, the Dies Committee was brought into the picture in early May, 1943, and has continued since then. Their most intensive drive was made during May, June, and July of 1943 but the investigation continued following the Tule Lake incident in

November and I am sure they plan to continue to harass the Authority whenever an opportunity is presented. Our relationship with the West Coast Congressional Delegation has been very good for the most part when considered on an individual basis. A few individuals are quite antagonistic to our program and have carried the torch for the West Coast organizations mentioned above. The outstanding ones in this group are John Costello, Clair Engle, John Phillips, Norris Poulson, Alfred Elliott, and more recently Harry Sheppard. Senator Wallgren was quite antagonistic during 1942, but in recent months has been very quiet and reasonably friendly. Other members of Congress who have supplemented the campaign of West Coast critics are Congressman Rankin of Mississippi, Senator Stewart of Tennessee, and upon occasion Senator Chandler of Kentucky, Senator Reynolds of North Carolina, and Congressman J. Parnell Thomas of New Jersey, a member of the Dies Committee. I may have overlooked a few, but outside of this small group our general relationship with the Congress has been excellent.

We have had the support throughout the United States of hundreds of people of good will who have rendered real service in the relocation aspect of our program in particular, and in doing so have been very helpful in handling the public relations problems. The outstanding organizations that have supported the program are: Federal Council of Churches, Home Missions Council of North America, American Friends Service Committee, Committee on American Principles and Fair Play (which operates in California, Washington, and Oregon), the YMCA, YWCA, Japanese American Student Relocation Council, Committee on Resettlement of Japanese Americans, Protestant Church Committee for Japanese Service, Common Council for American Unity, Denver Council of Churches, Citizens Committee for Resettlement for Work with Japanese Evacuees, Japanese American Citizens League, American Civil Liberties Union, and others.

Among the members of Congress who have been friendly and helpful are Congressman Eberharter of Pennsylvania, a member of the Dies Committee, Congressman Judd of Minnesota, Senator Murdock and Senator Thomas of Utah, Senator O'Mahoney of Wyoming, Senator Hayden of Arizona, Congressman Chenowith of Colorado, Congressmen Outland, Holifield, Tolan, Will Rogers, Ford, Voorhis, all of California, Congressman Coffee of Washington, and many others who have been sympathetic but not particularly active.

SUMMARY OF PRESENT STATUS AND PROBLEMS AHEAD

At the present time we have nine relocation centers and one segregation center. The Jerome Relocation Center, Denson, Arkansas will be closed in June, leaving eight relocation centers at the beginning of the next fiscal year. Approximately 92,000 people live in relocation centers and the segregation center. When segregation is completed there will be between 18,000 and 19,000 people at Tule Lake and approximately

70,000 in the other eight or nine centers. Over 18,000 are out on indefinite leave at the present time and about 2,000 on seasonal leave. Our major problems at the present time are the completion of leave clearance hearings and the segregation process, realigning and expediting our relocation program in order to secure family relocation, and public relations — a problem which is continually stirred up by the organizations mentioned in 6.

As relocation proceeds the character of the population within the centers changes and will continue to do so, leaving a residue of older Issei and young children as compared with the mixed population we had in the beginning. This creates a real problem affecting the relocation program and the administration of the centers. It becomes harder to maintain the American institutions and avoid further Japanization of youngsters. This is a natural development resulting from the draining off of the American citizens in the age group from 18 to 35 or 40, who are most easily relocated. It will become more and more difficult to get families made up largely of very young and older people to relocate in normal communities for several reasons. There will be a smaller number of able-bodied workers, the older people will have some language difficulties, the housing problem is more acute, and they are not sure they can find security in outside communities. We anticipate a continued campaign by West Coast organizations which have funds and personnel to devote to a campaign for the exclusion of people of Japanese ancestry from the West Coast or at least for the prevention of their return during the war.

As the war proceeds and it becomes less essential from a military standpoint to maintain the evacuated area, we have the problem of working out a plan with the Army for an orderly reopening of the evacuated area step by step which will facilitate relocation, avoid violence, and at the same time get the job reasonably well done before the war is finally over, so that evacuees will not have to reestablish themselves during a period when there will be competition with a large number returning from the war.

Property problems on the Coast will continue to exist and will become more troublesome. As time goes on we will need to consider conducting our program in such a way as to have needed information in case post-war claims are presented, and at the same time render adequate service to evacuees who cannot return to the Coast in the meantime. There is, of course, the whole question of post-war relocation in case we don't get the job done during the war period, and that problem has not yet been seriously considered.

> Sincerely,
> /s/ D. S. Myer
> Director

cc: Mr. Fortas
DSMyer:ih
2/29/44

Amendment to the National Act of 1940, Public Law No. 405, 78th Congress

(i) Making in the United States a formal written renunciation of nationality in such form as may be prescribed by and before such officer as may be designated by, the Attorney General, whenever the United States shall be in a state of war and the Attorney General shall approve such renunciation as not contrary to the interests of national defense.

Signed by the President on July 1, 1944
as Public Law 405 (78th Congress)

Note: According to the *Pacific Citizen,* July 8, 1944: "Attorney General Biddle testified that there were between '300 and 1000' persons of Japanese ancestry at the Tule Lake segregation center who had expressed a desire to renounce their citizenship and have asked expatriation. . . .

"It was stressed that the measure signed by President Roosevelt was designed to deal specifically with the group of between '300 and 1000' citizens of Japanese ancestry at the Tule Lake segregation center."

Confidential Letter to All Project Directors

DEPARTMENT OF THE INTERIOR
WAR RELOCATION AUTHORITY
Washington

Dec. 8, 1944

CONFIDENTIAL

TO: All Project Directors

Attached is a copy of a general statement covering certain policy decisions that have now been made in connection with the lifting of the West Coast exclusion orders. A supply of additional copies is being forwarded to you for general distribution both to the staff and to the evacuees. This material, however, should be held in strict confidence until you get word from this office.

You will note that we have scheduled the closing of all relocation centers within one year. Our job now is to see that this is done and that all of the eligible people now residing in the centers are located either in the former evacuated zone or elsewhere in the United States. I cannot impress too strongly on you that this is our job and that we must accomplish it.

It is tremendously important to everyone concerned that the final program of liquidating the relocation centers be completed while there is a good demand for workers throughout the country in war plants, in civilian goods production, service occupations and in food production. As we approach the end of the war, these opportunities will not be so plentiful and if liquidation of the program should be postponed until that time, our task would be immeasurably harder. It will be almost impossible if evacuees have to compete with returning soldiers and with other people who may be seeking adjustment during the reconversion project.

The announcement of the reopening of the Coast area will be received by many of the evacuees as welcome news. The closing of the relocation centers, however, will be interpreted by some as the loss of sanctuary and security. You should see that all of the evacuees understand the basic policies of the War Relocation Authority with regard to the closing of the centers. All questions should be answered firmly and positively but in a courteous manner and without the use of threats of any kind. Much will depend on the diplomacy and sound judgment which you and members of your staff show in this regard.

In discussing relocation to the West Coast with evacuees, Project Directors and their staffs should proceed at all times on the basic assumption that the movement will be an orderly one and that returning evacuees will be readily accepted by their friends and neighbors. Any tendency to discuss possible dangers or potentialities of violence should be discouraged.

There will be questions as to why the centers are to be closed before the end of the war. The answer is obvious, that with the lifting of the restrictions on the Coast, the great majority of the people of Japanese ancestry are now free to go anywhere and the reason for which the relocation centers were established no longer exists. They are being kept in operation during the final period of the program so that center residents will have ample time and opportunity for the development of sound relocation plans. The opportunity for resettlement now is far better than it would be at the end of the war. Resettlement now is for the benefit of the evacuees.

Some will ask what the War Relocation Authority will do if certain individuals or groups do not relocate.

The answer should be simply that we don't think anyone will actually refuse. Ample provision is being made so that each individual may make a satisfactory transition back to private life.

There will be some who will want to know whether the War Relocation Authority will make loans for farm or business financing. The answer should be that the War Relocation Authority is not a lending agency and has no intention of becoming one. There are other Federal agencies equipped with authority and funds to take care of such needs.

There will be evacuees who will want to regain possession of their land or other property in the Coast area immediately. Some may wish to break leases or institute legal proceedings for the ejection of tenants. Such action should be discouraged wherever possible, because it will certainly result in adverse publicity and make the job of orderly resettlement more difficult, not only for the individual concerned but for other evacuees.

You will, of course, realize that there are some detailed points of policy which have been determined but which have not been covered in the general statement for distribution to the evacuees. We are supplying some of this information to you below, and we will furnish more as additional policy decisions are made, so that you can make it available to key members of your staff.

There may be citizen evacuees who will want to know whether renunciation of citizenship under the recent law passed by Congress will mean that they would remain in or be sent to Tule Lake until the end of hostilities with Japan. The War Relocation Authority will not make any further determinations under leave clearance procedures. The Army authorities now designate those [whose movements will be restrained or] who will not be eligible to return to the West Coast area. Doubtless a renunciation of citizenship, if accepted by the Attorney General of the United States, would result in some action by the military — possibly a recommendation for internment, but it is not the responsibility of the War Relocation Authority.

The lifting of the West Coast ban means that any individual (except those who may be designated by the War Department for further investigation) may leave the relocation center at any time. Assistance, however, will be given only to those who have an approved plan of relocation. We believe it is desirable to give this assistance and to supervise the movement of the people for their own interest but there is no reason why an eligible individual or family may not leave of his own choice without regard to any plan or assistance which the War Relocation Authority may offer. Likewise, they are free to remain residents of the relocation centers while the centers are operated, provided they conduct themselves in such a manner as not to disrupt the center operations or interfere with the relocation program. We have no obligation to provide center residence for those who are now free to return to their former homes unless they are willing to abide by project regulations and help in maintaining a peaceful community.

There may be questions about purchase of Government property now in use at the projects. This will all be sold through regular surplus property procedure as indicated in our policy statement.

You may have individuals who will want to make brief trips to the evacuated area for the purpose of scouting or for the disposal of property. It may be distinctly understood that any such travel will be at the evacuee's own expense and that he must secure short term leave for this purpose. Otherwise he will not be readmitted to the center. Reinductions to the center should be kept to a minimum, involving students at the end of the school year or others who are entitled to such readmission. Likewise, visits to centers should be permitted only where the visiting evacuee has secured the approval of the appropriate relocation office or (in the case of visiting between centers) of the Project Director at the center where the visiting evacuee resides.

Unless this policy is rigidly enforced and strongly impressed on the minds of the evacuees, there may be a widespread tendency for relocated evacuees to leave their jobs without proper War Manpower Commission clearance, and there may also be serious transportation congestion in the vicinity of the centers. Consequently we are authorizing you as Project Director to deny admission to all evacuees who attempt to visit your center without securing proper clearance in advance.

Applications for repatriation or expatriation are no longer factors to be considered in relocation planning. Also the WRA "stop list" will no longer be taken into consideration in connection with departures from the relocation centers. The Army now has full responsibility for designating those persons whose freedom of movement is to be restrained. A new stop list will be provided by the War Department. There will be family members in the centers where the breadwinner is in internment and this will be given as a reason why the family cannot successfully relocate. These people should be encouraged to make application to live in a family internment camp, or to relocate despite the absence of the breadwinner. We should at all times recognize, as we have in the past, the right of the older and more mature children to make their own decisions, in situations involving family residence in an internment camp or the right to resume normal lives in American communities.

/s/ D. S. Myer
Director

cc: Mr. Cozzens
Director's copy
AMarkley:mh
12/7/44

Population in Relocation Centers on January 1, 1943 and January 1, 1945 by Age Groups

Age Groups	January 1, 1943	January 1, 1945	Decrease or Increase
< 5	8,110	7,422	—688
5-9	7,161	6,183	—978
10-14	9,537	7,231	—2,306
15-19	15,484	8,707	—6,777
20-24	15,656	7,411	—8,245
25-29	9,642	5,737	—3,905
30-34	4,766	3,713	—1,053
35-39	4,974	2,951	—2,023
40-44	6,764	5,030	—1,734
45-49	5,889	5,527	—362
50-54	6,249	4,527	—1,722
55-59	6,459	5,922	—537
60-64	5,367	5,178	—189
65-69	2,888	3,690	+802
70-74	944	1,206	+262
≧ 75	350	443	+93
Total	110,240	80,878	—29,362

Note: On January 1, 1943, Nisei under 25 years of age were preponderant. The majority of the residents during the two years were under 30 years of age. More than one-third of the under-30 age-group relocated during this period, nearly 4,000 of these being children under 15 years of age.

The following material shows the widespread news interest about Japanese Americans in 1945.

Department of the Interior
WAR RELOCATION AUTHORITY

Washington, D.C., — DAILY NEWS DIGEST — Wed., March 28, 1945

San Francisco *Examiner,* March 28
OREGON JAP LAND BAN BECOMES LAW
(Salem, Oregon, INS) — Governor Earl Snell signs Oregon's anti-Japanese Alien Land Bill which prevents Japanese aliens from living on or using land purchased in the name of a citizen relative. (P. 3, 1 in.) A1710

San Francisco *Chronicle,* March 28
THE ARMY HAS INDUCTED 17,600 NISEI TO DATE (WRA Release) (P. 5, 3 in.)

N. Y. *Herald Tribune,* March 28
17,600 JAPANESE IN U. S. ARMY (AP, p. 8, 1 in.)

N. Y. *Times,* March 28
17,600 NISEI INDUCTED INTO ARMY (AP, p. 8, 1 in.)
Inductions of Japanese-Americans into the U. S. Army since Nov. 1, 1940, total 17,600, Dillon S. Myer "reported" yesterday. "Half of these came from continental U. S. and half from Hawaii," papers state.
(Ed. note: There are no official figures available indicating how many of this number are from the mainland or Hawaii. From information at hand the best estimate would indicate that they are about equally divided.)
A1711

San Francisco *News,* March 27
KEY TO MINORITY PROBLEM IS CONSIDERATION OF ALL
HUMAN BEINGS, SAYS YWCA LEADER
Interview with Miss Esther Briesemeister, veteran of two years' work
in relocation centers elicits statement that "Just plain ordinary kindness is
the answer to the problem of returning Nisei in California. I find that most
people, regardless of private prejudices, are resolved to accept their fellow
Americans of Japanese ancestry. In San Francisco, the Chinese Christian
youth groups are taking the lead in planning to welcome the Nisei as part
of the world fellowship gathering." (P. 5, 12 in., with cut)   A1712

Oregon *Journal,* March 23
MARKET SNUBS NISEI GARDENERS THIRD TIME
(Maryhill, Wash.) — Japanese truck gardener and son left Portland
East Side Farmers Market with a substantial amount of produce still on
truck for third time. (P. 3, 2 in.)   A1713

San Francisco *Examiner,* March 28
JAPS (Letter)
Reader, signed "Know a Little", advocates sending all Japanese back
to Japan, giving an opportunity to those who lived here to be "the makers
of the new Japan." (Editorial page, 5 in.)   A1714

Seattle *Times,* March 26
FOES OF NISEI NURSE RAPPED
American soldier in France, Pfc. Yozo Miyako, criticizes Harborview
Hospital nurses for opposition to Masako Takayoshi. (P. 4, 5 in.)   A1715

Salem, Ore. *Journal,* March 7
NISEI MADE GOOD IN BATTLE (Editorial)
Notes that, despite Hood River Legion post's reversal of policy on
Nisei names on honor roll, "There is no repentance shown and no apology
for this exhibition of hysterical prejudice," since the post commander said
the post is still opposed to return of Japanese Americans to Hood River
valley, which is a "defiance of the constitutional rights" of both citizens
and veterans.
Points out that Nisei soldiers fight in both European and Pacific areas,
and mentions the 14 Nisei with Merrill's Marauders. (6 in. dbl. col.)
                                                                      A1716

San Francisco *Call Bulletin,* March 22
BACKERS TO WAGE FLOOR FIGHT FOR ANTI-BIAS BILL
(Sacramento, March 22) — At this time sponsors of anti-discrimination employment bill announced they would carry their fight to the Assembly floor after failing to get a committee recommendation for its
passage. One of the bill's opponents, Gilford G. Rowland, representing
the Calif. Employers' Council, said the bill would mean veterans of the
Pacific could be sent to jail if they refused to hire Japanese for work.
(11 in.)   A1717

San Francisco *Chronicle,* March 27
NISEI BECOMES WRA SECRETARY
(Los Angeles, AP) — Elva Shinozaki is now employed in the Los Angeles WRA office as a secretary, after two years with WRA office in Cincinnati. (P. 1, 2 in.)   A1718

Bainbridge, Wash., *Review,* March 23
J. NAKATA SELECTS MOSES LAKE AS NEW HOME SITE
Johnny Nakata, Winslow, former owner of Eagle Harbor Market, will probably settle in Moses Lake, Wash., as he feels the atmosphere there is "less tense." (P. 2, 5 in.)   A1719

Portland, Ore., *Journal,* March 23
ANTI-JAP MEET HELD
Oregon Property Owners Protective League, Inc., holds a mass meeting and forms a local chapter. (P. 5, 3 in.)   A1720

The Olympus, (High School Paper) Feb. 14
"Bring the Japanese back" is gist of Olympia (Wash.) High School "Sentiment" interviews with Caucasian students on the return of evacuees. (P. 1½ p.)   A1721

Chicago, Ill., *Defender,* March 10 (Negro Paper)
S. I. HAYAKAWA (Column, "Second Thoughts")
Test of "racism" in Univ. of Ill. class conducted two years ago, showed half of the pupils to be "racists," and half to be fair toward Japanese Americans.
Columnist was impressed by the fact that the racists had never met a Japanese or Japanese American, but had their notions of them from caricatures of the enemy and "inflammatory accounts of Japanese atrocities in war-bond oratory," while the non-racists had known at least one Japanese or Japanese American. (16 in., thumbnail cut.)   A1722

California Monthly, March (Magazine)
RETURN OF THE NISEI
University of California publication reports that "California's student body and faculty have turned their attention to problems of relocating American Japanese on the Pacific Coast." Mentions three alumni who have been helping to forward the program: Victor Furth, of the San Fran. WRA office, and Dave Tatsuno, returnee from Utah, both of whom spoke at a campus forum: Monroe E. Deutsch, Vice-President of U. C., who was on the Executive Committee of San Francisco Fair Play conference. (3 in.)   M

Chicago *Daily News,* March 22
BEAT ME, PROFESSOR, EIGHT TO THE BAR, by Emery Hutchison
Writer of "Words and Music" column does story about Dr. S. I. Hayakawa, professor of English at Illinois Institute of Technology, who has become a historian of jazz and an amateur boogie woogie player (Photo and 14 in. text.)   A1723

Norfolk, Va., *Virginian-Pilot,* March 15
HOOD RIVER LEGIONNAIRES ADMIT A MISTAKE (Editorial)
Points out that Hood River post shows by its decision to restore the Nisei names it is "growing up to a real sense of its responsibilities," just as Hollywood post 591, which admitted a Nisei to membership, is suffering from "growing pains." These evidences of growth are a result of a "blood transfusion" from new members, veterans of World War II, with their "new vigor and new appreciation of American principles." (8 in.)
A1724

Hartford, Conn., *Times,* March 12
RELOCATING THE NISEI (Editorial)
"New Englanders cannot afford to indulge themselves in the belief that all the prejudice [against returnees] is confined to the Pacific Coast," says Hartford editorial, since barriers against them have appeared in New England too. Blames New England prejudice on fear of workers that Nisei would take their jobs. However, only 310 have come to New England — "hardly enough . . . to cause consternation."
"Zones of tolerance" seem to be Chicago, Cleveland and Cincinnati, with Illinois the most receptive state. Americans are going to have to solve Japanese-American problem fairly if they are to face international problems with a clear conscience. (11 in.)
A1725

War Relocation Authority Appropriations, Expenditures, and Savings (in Dollars)

Year	Original Appropriation	Transfer by Warrant	Recessions	Savings	Net Amount of Appropriation Expended
1942	8,000,000		1,700,000	-0-	6,300,000
1943	70,000,000			15,272,147	54,727,853
1944	48,170,000			5,577,142	42,592,858
1945	39,000,000	+ 225,000 Soc. Sec.	1,500,000	2,563,296	34,711,704
1946	25,000,000	†1,400,000 Soc. Sec.	2,500,000	1,020,385	20,079,615
Total	190,170,000	1,625,000	5,700,000	24,432,970	158,412,030

†Transfer funds expended by Social Security Board for welfare needs 1,625,000

Net Total Expenditures by WRA 160,037,030*

* Does not include funds expended by the War Department covering evacuation costs and costs of construction of WRA centers.

Editorial From the *Washington Post* by Alan Barth, March 28, 1946

JOB WELL DONE

The most distasteful of all war jobs, the detention upon mere suspicion and without trial of approximately 120,000 persons of Japanese ancestry, two-thirds of them citizens of the United States, has now been liquidated. It was a job made necessary through the decision early in 1942 of Gen. John L. DeWitt to exclude all Japanese-Americans from the Western Defense Command, of which he was at that time the commander. His exclusion order has since been validated by the Supreme Court on grounds of military necessity. For our part, however, we hold still to the opinion we have expressed on a number of occasions that the exclusion was altogether unnecessary, that it was prompted much more by blind racial prejudice than by military considerations and that the Supreme Court's validation of it amounted, as Mr. Justice Murphy charged in a dissenting opinion, to a "legalization of racism." The treatment accorded this helpless minority remains a smudge upon our national honor and a threat to elementary principles of freedom.

Once the exclusion error was committed, guardianship of the uprooted Japanese-Americans became a Federal responsibility. They had to be kept in detention centers until they could be relocated in parts of the country other than the West Coast. The burden of discharging this unhappy obligation was given to an emergency agency, the War Relocation

Authority, headed at first by Milton Eisenhower, later and through most of its existence by Dillon S. Myer. It performed its task with humanity, with efficiency and with a conscientious sense of trusteeship toward the evacuees which made some amends for the terrible hardship inflicted upon them. All the men associated in this undertaking, and in particular Mr. Myer, who fought valiantly and pertinaciously against prejudice for the rights of these unfortunates in his charge, can take pride in a difficult job exceedingly well done.

When at last the Army rescinded its exclusion order about 57,500 evacuees moved back to their former homes in the West Coast States. But about 51,800 settled eastward in new homes. Perhaps the dispersal will have some benefits in better integration of the Japanese-Americans into the American society. The loyalty of those left here has been meticulously scrutinized. Out of the whole number in the relocation centers, some 3000, including quite innocent family members, were transferred to internment camps administered by the Department of Justice; and about 4700 persons were voluntarily repatriated to Japan — many of them, no doubt, because the treatment they received here convinced them they had no hope of leading free lives in America. It seems to us that we owe those who remain generous help in getting reestablished and restitution for their property losses.

CM-3863

Citation Presented to Dillon S. Myer, by the Japanese American
Citizens League, on May 22, 1946

TO DILLON S. MYER

American and champion of human rights and common decency
Whose courageous and inspired leadership as
National Director of the War Relocation Authority
Against war hysteria, race prejudice, and misguided
      hate, as well as economic greed draped in patriotic
      colors,
Contributed mightily in convincing the American Government
      and public at large
That Americans of Japanese ancestry and their resident
      alien parents
Were, and are, loyal and sincere Americans worthy of every
      right and privilege of the American heritage,
And aided materially in restoring faith and conviction in
      the American way
To these same Americans of Japanese ancestry and their
      resident alien parents
Who were evacuated without trial or hearing by military fiat
      from their homes and associations on the West Coast in
      the spring of 1942,
Relocated in government centers in the wastelands of the west,
And then resettled throughout the United States as proven
      Americans.

TO DILLON S. MYER

Who so capably and ably administered the War Relocation Authority under the most difficult of circumstances and against the most vicious of opposition in a manner which commended him to the American people and the evacuee population at large, this testimonial scroll is gratefully presented by the Japanese-American Citizens League and their friends at this banquet in his honor at the Roosevelt Hotel, New York City, May 22, 1946.

Column by Harold L. Ickes, in the *Washington Evening Star,*
September 23, 1946

Harold L. Ickes
MAN TO MAN

WARTIME ABUSE OF AMERICAN JAPANESE
SHOULD NOW BE CORRECTED BY U.S.

I hope that those who are disposed to be indifferent about our treatment of alien strains will read "Citizen 13660", written by Mine Okubo and published by the Columbia University Press. Both the illustrations and the short text tell, without the rancor that would be understandable, of the treatment of the Japanese who were living in this "land of the brave and home of the free" at the time of the attack on Pearl Harbor.

As a member of President Roosevelt's administration, I saw the United States Army give way to mass hysteria over the Japanese. The investigation of Pearl Harbor disclosed that the Army in Hawaii was more intent upon acts of anticipated sabotage that never occurred than in being alert against a possible surprise attack by the Japanese.

On the mainland, the Army had taken no precautionary measures. Then suddenly it lost its self-control and, egged on by public clamor, some of it from greedy Americans who sought an opportunity to possess themselves of Japanese rights and property, it began to round up indiscriminately the Japanese who had been born in Japan, as well as those born here.

Crowded into cars like cattle, these hapless people were hurried away to hastily constructed and thoroughly inadequate concentration camps, with soldiers with nervous muskets on guard, in the great American desert. We gave the fancy name of "relocation centers" to these dust bowls, but they were concentration camps nonetheless, although not as bad as Dachau or Buchenwald.

Hate Kept at Fever Heat

War-excited imaginations, raw race-prejudice and crass greed kept hateful public opinion along the Pacific Coast at fever heat. Fortunately, the President had put at the head of the War Relocation Authority a strong and able man who was not afraid to fight back. Later the President transferred the agency to the Department of the Interior. I claim no credit for the result that was finally attained except that I stood shoulder to shoulder with Dillon Myer and let my own fists fly on occasion. Mr. Myer fully deserved the Medal for Merit which he was later awarded.

It was to be expected that some native-born Japanese would have to be watched closely. Some wanted to go back to Japan and help has been given them. But, generally speaking, the Japanese, particularly those who had been born in this country and were therefore American citizens, have settled back into American communities and there is no reason to believe that they will not continue to be loyal Americans.

If we Americans, with the Army in the lead, made fools of ourselves for which we ought properly to be ashamed, it must be said that the American Japanese, with very few exceptions, gave an example of human dignity by which all of us might profit. However, they have not had returned to them the property that was rifled from them, or its equivalent.

Property Should Be Restored

A bill was introduced in the recent session of Congress setting up a commission to pass upon the claims of these dispossessed American Japanese for property of which they were despoiled. This bill ought to pass and no time should be lost in making restitution for property that was lost or misappropriated.

If the Japanese had been permitted to continue their normal lives they would have occasioned slight concern. They did not in Hawaii where the proportion of Japanese is much larger than in any State on the mainland and where the temptation to favor Japan was necessarily much greater.

No soldiers wearing the American uniform gave a better account of themselves than did the American-born Japanese. Japanese troops, both from Hawaii and the mainland, as the Army records will show, were outstanding for bravery, intelligence, endurance and daring. Their loyalty was not only unimpeachable, but remarkable, considering the affronts and injustices that had been put upon them and their people.

This whole episode was one in which we can take no pride. To understand just what we did to many thousands of our fellow Americans, we should read "Citizen 13660."

WRA Project Directors

PROJECT DIRECTOR	CENTER	DATES OF SERVICE
Roy Nash	Manzanar, Calif.	June 1942-Sept. 1942
Ralph Merritt		1942-46
Wade Head	Colorado River, Ariz.	1942-43
Duncan Mills		1944-45
Eastburn Smith	Gila River, Ariz.	1942
Roy Bennett		1943-45
Douglas Todd		1945
Elmer Shirrell	Tule Lake, Calif.	1942
Harvey Coverly		1943
Ray Best		1943-46
Harry Stafford	Minidoka, Idaho	1942-45
Christford Rachford	Heart Mountain,	1942
Guy Robertson	Wyoming	1943-45
James G. Lindley	Granada, Colorado	1942-46
Charles Ernst	Central Utah, Utah	1942-44
Louis Hoffman		1945
Raymond Johnson	Rohwer, Arkansas	1942-45
Paul Taylor	Jerome, Arkansas	1942-43
W. O. "Doc" Melton		1943-44
Joseph Smart	Refugee Shelter,	July 1944-May 1945
Clyde Powers	N.Y.	July 1945-Feb. 1946

Key Staff Members

KEY STAFF MEMBERS	TITLE	DATES OF SERVICE
Elmer Rowalt	Deputy Dir.	1942-43*
Philip Glick	Solicitor	1942-43
	Assistant Dir.	1945-46
Edwin Ferguson	Solicitor	1944-46
Leland Barrows	Ass't. Dir. Adm. Mgt.	1942-43
Malcom Pitts	Ass't. Dir. Adm. Mgt.	1944-46
John Baker	Chief, Reports Div.	1942-43
Morrill M. Tozier	Chief, Reports Div.	1944-46
John Provinse	Chief, Community Mgt. Div.	
Ervin J. Utz	Chief, Operations Div.	
Ralph Stauber	Chief, Statistical Div.	
	Chief, Employment Div.	1942-43
Edwin Arnold	Chief, Relocation Div.	1943-44
H. Rex Lee	Chief, Relocation Div.	1945-46
Col. Erle Kress	Army Liaison Representative	1942
Col. Earl Wilson	Army Liaison Representative	1943-46
C. R. Fryer	Regional Dir., San Francisco	1942
Joseph Smart	Regional Dir., Denver	1942
E. H. Whitaker	Regional Dir., Little Rock, Ark.	1942
	Regional Representative	1943-46
Robert Cozzens	Ass't. Regional Dir. and	1942
	Ass't. Dir., San Francisco	1943-46

Relocation Supervisors†

Harold Fistere	New York Cleveland Seattle
Robert Dolins	New York
Robert Cullum	Cleveland Great Lakes
Harold Mann Prudence Ross	Chicago and Mid-West
H. Rex Lee Otis Peterson	Salt Lake City
Charles Miller	Denver San Francisco

*Died in service.
† Listing here is incomplete.

Disposal of the Ten Relocation Centers and the Refugee Shelter

CENTER	AGENCY DESIGNATED FOR DISPOSAL	DATE OF RELEASE BY WRA
Jerome	War Department	10-1-44
Granada	Department of Agriculture, Farm Credit Administration	1-26-46
Central Utah	Department of Agriculture, Farm Credit Administration	2-9-46
Minidoka	Department of Interior, General Land Office*	10-1-44
Heart Mountain	Department of Interior, General Land Office*	2-23-46
Gila River	Department of Interior, General Land Office	2-23-46
Colorado River	Department of Interior, General Land Office†	3-9-46
Manzanar	Department of Interior, General Land Office	3-9-46
Rohwer	Department of Interior, General Land Office	3-9-46
Tule Lake	Department of Interior, General Land Office*	5-4-46
Emergency Refugee Shelter	War Department	2-28-46

*Bureau of Reclamation assumed custody.

† U. S. Indian Service assumed custody.

Bibliography

Books

Adams, Ansel E. *Born Free and Equal: Photographs of the Loyal Japanese Americans at Manzanar Relocation Center.* New York: U.S. Camera, 1944.

Eaton, Allen H. *Beauty Behind Barbed Wire: The Arts of the Japanese in Our War Relocation Camps.* New York: Harper, 1952.

Grodzins, Morton. *Americans Betrayed: Politics and the Japanese Evacuation.* Chicago: Univ. of Chicago Press, 1949.

Hosokawa, Bill. *Nisei: The Quiet Americans.* New York: Morrow, 1969.

La Violette, Forrest E. *Americans of Japanese Ancestry: A Study of Assimilation in the American Community.* Canadian Institute of International Affairs, 1945.

Leighton, Alexander H. *The Governing of Men: General Principles and Recommendations Based on Experience at a Japanese Relocation Camp.* Princeton, N.J.: Princeton Univ. Press, 1945.

Martin, Ralph G. *Boy From Nebraska: The Story of Ben Kuroki.* New York: Harper, 1946. [Tells the story of a Japanese American war hero.]

McWilliams, Carey. *Prejudice: Japanese Americans; Symbol of Racial Intolerance.* Boston: Little, Brown & Co., 1944. [Contains excellent source material, particularly historical background information.]

[349]

O'Brien, Robert W. *The College Nisei: Story of the National Japanese American Student Relocation Council.* Palo Alto: Pacific Books, 1949.

Okubo, Miné. *Citizen 13660.* New York: Columbia University Press, 1946. [Gives sketches of camp life, with comments.]

Smith, Bradford. *Americans From Japan.* The Peoples of America Series. Philadelphia: Lippincott, 1948.

Spicer, E. H., and others. *Impounded People: Japanese-Americans in the Relocation Centers.* Tucson: Univ. of Arizona Press, 1969.

TenBroek, J.; Barnhart, E. N.; and Matson, F. W. *Prejudice, War, and the Constitution: Causes and Consequences of the Evacuation of the Japanese Americans in World War II.* Japanese American Evacuation and Resettlement Series. Berkeley: Univ. of California Press, 1954.

Thomas, Dorothy S. *The Spoilage.* Japanese American Evacuation and Resettlement Series. Berkeley: Univ. of California Press, 1946.

Thomas, Dorothy S. *The Salvage.* Japanese American Evacuation and Resettlement Series. Berkeley: Univ. of California Press, 1952.

Reports of The War Relocation Authority
U.S. Department of Interior
1946

Administrative Highlights of the WRA Program [prepared by Malcolm E. Pitts]

Community Government in the War Relocation Centers

Impounded People: Japanese Americans in the Relocation Centers [prepared by E. H. Spicer]

Legal and Constitutional Phases of the WRA Program [prepared by Glick & Ferguson]

The Evacuated People: A Quantitative Description [prepared by Stauber & French]

The Relocation Program [prepared by H. Rex Lee]

Token Shipment: The Story of the War Refugee Shelter [prepared by Edward B. Marks, Jr.]

Wartime Exile: The Exclusion of Japanese Americans from the West Coast [prepared by Ruth McKee]

Wartime Handling of Evacuee Property

WRA: The Story of Human Conservation [prepared by Morrill Tozier]

State Documents

State of California, Division of Fair Employment Practices. *Californians of Japanese, Chinese [and] Filipino Ancestry: Population, Education, Employment [and] Income.* [By Division of Labor Statistics and Research]. San Francisco, 1965.

United States Executive Documents

Census Bureau, Department of Commerce. "Japanese Population," in *United States Censuses of Population and Housing, 1960:* Nonwhite Population by Race. 1961.
Department of the Army. "Japanese Evacuation From the West Coast," Chapter 5 in *The United States Army in World War II: The Western Hemisphere* [vol. 2]; *Guarding the United States and Its Outposts.* 1964.
Department of War. *Japanese Evacuation From the West Coast, 1942.* [Gen. John L. DeWitt's final report]. 1943.
Selective Service System. Special Groups [with bibliography] [by Campbell C. Johnson]. Special Monograph 10, vol. 1; Appendices A-G, vol. 2. 1953. [Includes reports on the Japanese Americans and selective service.]
War Agency Liquidation Unit, Division of Budget and Administrative Management, Department of the Interior. *People in Motion: The Postwar Adjustment of Evacuated People.* [Prepared by Robert Cullum]. 1947.

United States Congressional Hearings and Reports

House, Select Committee [Tolan] Investigating National Defense Migration. *National Defense Migration,* Preliminary Report and Recommendations on Problem of Evacuation of Citizens and Aliens From Military Areas. Report persuant to H. Res. 113. 77th Cong., 2nd sess. March 10, 1942.
Senate, Military Affairs Committee, Subcommittee on Japanese War Relocation Centers. *Japanese War Relocation Centers;* Report on S. 444, and S. Res. 101 & 111. 78th Cong., 1st sess. May 7, 1943.
House, Special Committee [Costello] on Un-American Activities. *Military Views on Japanese War Relocation Centers,* Report and minority views. [The minority views are those of Mr. Eberharter.] H. rp. 717, 78th Cong., 1st sess. Sept. 30, 1943.
House, Special Committee on Un-American Activities. *Investigations of Un-American Propaganda Activities in the United States,* Hearings on H. Res. 282 [77th Cong.]. 78th Cong., 1st sess. Appendix, pt. 8., Report on Axis front movement in U.S. 2nd sec. Japanese Activities, Nov. 1, 1943.
Senate, Military Affairs Committee. *War Relocation Centers:* Hearings before subcommittee, on S. 444; 78th Cong., 1st sess.; Nov. 24, 1943. 1944. [These hearings relate to events at Tule Lake center, Nov. 1-4, 1943.]
Senate, Military Affairs Committee. *War Relocation Centers;* Hearings [January] before [Chandler] subcommittee on S. 444. 78th Cong., 2nd sess. March 6, 1943.

House, Judiciary Committee. *Equality in Immigration and Naturalization;* Hearings on Immigration and Naturalization. 80th Cong. 1948.

House, Judiciary Committee. *Equality in Immigration and Naturalization;* Joint Hearings before the subcommittees. 82nd Cong. 1951.

House, Judiciary Subcommittee on Immigration and Naturalization. *Immigration Discrimination,* Hearings, Part 3, 1964.

House, Judiciary Subcommittee on Immigration and Naturalization. *Immigration Discrimination,* Hearings, Serial no. 7, 1965.

Senate, Judiciary Subcommittee on Immigration and Naturalization. *Immigration and Naturalization,* Hearings, Part 2, 1965.

Index